The Buddhist Writings
of
Lafcadio Hearn

Frontispiece: Amida rescending from the western paradise. (From the Eugene Fuller Memorial Collection, Seattle Art Museum. Reprinted with permission.)

The Buddhist Writings of Lafcadio Hearn

with an Introduction by Kenneth Rexroth

Ross-Erikson, Inc., Publishers
Santa Barbara

Introduction copyright © 1977 by Kenneth Rexroth.
All rights reserved. Printed in the United States of America.

Library of Congress Number: 77-2496

ISBN: 915520-05-2

Selections from *The Writings of Lafcadio Hearn* are reprinted here courtesy of Houghton Mifflin Company.

Ross-Erikson, Inc., Publishers
223 Via Sevilla
Santa Barbara, California 93109

Table of Contents

Introduction by Kenneth Rexroth	vii
The Stone Buddha	1
Dust	21
Buddhist Allusions in Japanese Folksong	31
Nirvana	50
Within the Circle	92
A Question in the Zen Texts	64
The Literature of the Dead	103
Of Moon Desire	148
Footprints of the Buddha	157
Japanese Buddhist Proverbs	168
A Legend of Fugen-Bosatsu	187
The Sympathy of Benten	191
Buddhist Names of Plants and Animals	202

Beside the Sea	**214**
Otokichi's Daruma	**224**
A Drop of Dew	**236**
Gaki	**240**
The Introduction of Buddhism	**255**
The Higher Buddhism	**277**
Bibliography	**299**

Introduction

> In attempting a book upon a country so well trodden as Japan, I could not hope—nor would I consider it prudent attempting—to discover totally new things, but only to consider things in a totally new way. . . . The studied aim would be to create, in the minds of the readers, a vivid impression of *living* in Japan—not simply as an observer but as one taking part in the daily existence of the common people, and *thinking with their thoughts.*

So Lafcadio Hearn wrote to *Harper's Magazine* in 1889 just prior to leaving for Japan. He kept this promise so well that by his death in 1904 (as Yakumo Koizumi, a Japanese citizen) he was acclaimed as one of America's greatest prose stylists and the most influential authority of his generation on Japanese culture. That reputation has dimmed somewhat since then. Changing tastes in literary styles have made Hearn's work seem old-fashioned, and Japan's astonishing absorption of Western industrial methods and industrial values have made him for a time irrelevant.

Now interest in ancient Japanese culture and religion is again on the rise, and Hearn's work, devoted as it is to what he perceived as lasting and essential in Japanese life, is experiencing a revival. This volume is a definitive collection of Hearn's Buddhist writings, from his exploratory days as a New Orleans journalist to his last years in Tokyo. From these essays and stories emerges a sensitive and durable vision of how Buddhism was and still is lived in Japan—the ancient Buddhist traditions, rituals, myths, and stories that are still

Introduction

preserved, and their effects upon the beliefs and daily life of ordinary Japanese people.

Lafcadio Hearn was born on the Ionian island of Santa Maura in either June or August 1850 and died in Ōkubo, Japan in 1904. His father was an Irish surgeon major stationed in Greece and his mother a Greek woman, famous for her beauty. It was she who named him Lafcadio, after Leudakia, the ancient name of Santa Maura, one of the islands connected with the legend of Sappho. In a relatively short lifespan of fifty-four years he managed to live several different literary lives.

From Greece, at two years of age, he went to Ireland, where his father soon obtained a dissolution of marriage from his mother. She was sent back to Greece. His father quickly re-married and went off to India. That is the last Hearn saw of either of them.

His formal education consisted of one year at a Catholic school in France (he just missed Guy de Maupassant, who entered the school a year later and who later became one of his literary idols), and four years at St. Cuthbert's in England, where he lost one eye in a playing field accident. The disfigurement (the blinded eye was whitened, the good eye protruded from overuse) helped to make Hearn a painfully sensitive and shy person for the rest of his life. At seventeen, as a result of financial and personal misfortunes in the family, he was withdrawn from school. A year later, his uncle gave him passage money to America and advised him to look up a distant relative in Cincinnati. From then on Hearn had to make his own way in the world.

After a year of homelessness and near-starvation in Cincinnati, Hearn got a job as an editor for a trade journal and then as a reporter for the daily *Enquirer*. His assignment

Introduction

was the night watch, his specialty sensational crimes and gory murders. He had good contacts in the coroner's office, and his small, shy figure and one-eyed face did not arouse suspicion among the street people. His stories, with their ghastly descriptions, were frequent features that titillated the *Enquirer*'s readers. The editor reluctantly fired Hearn when rumors began to circulate that he was living with a mulatto woman whom he insisted he had married. (He had, but Ohio law refused to recognize mixed marriages.)

Another daily newspaper, the Cincinnati *Commercial*, hired him immediately. Here Hearn was allowed to contribute brief scholarly essays, local color stories, and prose poems, as well as the sensational stories that had got him his reputation. But he was restless with this kind of newspaper work, and sick of Cincinnati. In 1877 he quit the *Commercial* and left for New Orleans.

There he found work as a reporter for the struggling *Item*, though what he reported was anything he fancied, most often sketches of Creole and Cajun life. His *Item* essays were eccentric, flamboyant, and often self-indulgent, but they caught the eye of New Orleans' literary establishment. When the city's two largest newspapers merged to form the *Times-Democrat*, Hearn was invited to be its literary editor. He translated and adapted French stories (principally Gautier, Maupassant, Flaubert, and Loti—none of whom yet had a reputation in America); he wrote original stories in the lavish prose style he was perfecting at that time; and he collected local legends and factual narratives. His subjects ranged from Buddhism to Russian literature, from popularizations of science to European anti-Semitism. Altogether he offered the people of New Orleans such unpredictable and exotic fare that his reputation soon spread throughout the South. By this

Introduction

time he had become a disciple of his contemporary, Robert Louis Stevenson (or perhaps vice-versa: they developed similarly mellifluous prose styles and shared a fondness for fantastic and exotic subject matter). Hearn was enormously popular. From these years in New Orleans date *Stray Leaves From Strange Literatures*, 1884, *Some Chinese Ghosts*, 1887, and a novel, *Chita*, 1889.

In 1887 Hearn went to the West Indies for *Harper's Magazine* and produced *Two Years in the French West Indies*, 1890, and his last novel, *Youma*, 1890, an unprecedented story about a slave rebellion.

In 1890 he went to Japan for *Harper's* but soon became a school teacher in Izumo, in a northern region then little influenced by Westernization. There he married Koizume Setsuko, the daughter of a Samurai. In 1891 he moved to Kumamoto Government College.

Hearn was by now well known in American as an impressionistic prose painter of odd peoples and places. For this he was at first celebrated and later deprecated. Yet much of his Japanese work is of an entirely different quality and intention. He wrote to his friend Chamberlin in 1893, "After for years studying poetical prose, I am forced now to study simplicity. After attempting my utmost at ornamentation, I am converted by my own mistakes. The great point is to touch with simple words." *The Atlantic Monthly* printed his articles on Japan and syndicated them to a number of newspapers. They were enormously popular when they appeared and became even more so when they were published in two volumes as *Glimpses of Unfamiliar Japan*, 1894.

In 1895 Hearn became a Japanese citizen and took the name of Koizumi Yakumo. In 1896 he became professor of literature at Tokyo Imperial University, a most prestigious academic position in the most prestigious school in Japan.

Introduction

From then until his death he produced his finest books: *Exotics and Retrospectives*, 1898, *In Ghostly Japan*, 1899, *Shadowings*, 1900, *A Japanese Miscellany*, 1901, *Kwaidan*, 1904, *Japan, An Attempt at Interpretation*, 1904. These were translated into Japanese and became at least as popular in Japan as they did in America.

During the last two years of his life, failing health forced Hearn to give up his position at Tokyo Imperial University. On September 26, 1904, he died of heart failure. He had instructed his eldest son to put his ashes in an ordinary jar and to bury it on a forested hillside. Instead, he was given a Buddhist funeral with full ceremony, and his grave is to this day a place of pilgrimage perpetually decorated with flowers.

At the turn of the century, Hearn was considered one of the finest, if not the finest, of American prose stylists. He was certainly one of the masters of the Stevensonian style. As literary tastes changed, he was thought of more as a writer of pretty but dated essays about Japanese tame crickets and of sentimental ghost stories. After his death, his literary reputation was further damaged by the publication of several collections of his florid earlier work. His all-but-final reputation was as a lush, frothy stylist whose essays and stories were about as important as the pressed flowers likely to be found between their pages.

In fact, Hearn's Japanese writings demonstrate economy, concentration, and great control of language, with little stylistic exhibitionism. Their attitude of uncritical appreciation for the exotic and the mysterious is as unmistakably nineteenth century as the fine prose idiom with which it is consistent.

In spite of the incredible changes that have taken place in Japan since Hearn's death in 1904, as an informant of Japanese life, literature, and religion he is still amazingly reliable,

Introduction

because beneath the effects of industrialization, war, population explosion, and prosperity much of Japanese life remains unchanged. For Hearn the old Japan—the art, traditions, and myths that had persisted for centuries—was the only Japan worth paying attention to. Two world wars and Japan's astonishing emergence as a modern nation temporarily extinguished the credibility of Hearn's vision of traditional Japanese culture. But both in the West and in Japan interest in the old forms of Japanese culture is increasing. In Tokyo there are still thousands of people living the old life by the traditional values alongside the most extreme effects of Westernization. Pet crickets, for example, still command high prices, and more people apply their new prosperity to learning tea ceremony, calligraphy, flower arrangement and *sumi-e* painting than ever before. Ghost stories like those told by Hearn are popular on television; three of his own were recently combined to make a successful movie that preserves his title, *Kwaidan*.

One of the foreigners' (and Westernized, secularized Japanese intellectuals') myths of Japan is that the Japanese are a fundamentally secular, irreligious people. Nothing could be less true. The great temples swarm with pilgrims and are packed during their major festivals. Buddhism is more popular than ever, and Shintō and of Shingon and Tendai Buddhism perpetuate rites that began long before the dawn of Japanese history.

Although it is no longer true, if it ever was, that Japan is totally "Westernized," it is certainly the most Post-Modern of all the major nations today. With an economy which has ceased to be based on the mechanical, industrial methods of the nineteenth century (really because the old industrial capital structure was destroyed and everything dates from 1946),

Introduction

Japan has moved into the electronic age more completely than any other nation. Yet any Japanese who wishes can still make immediate contact with the Stone Age.

Hearn foresaw the industrialization of Japan and her development of imperialist ambitions. As much as possible he avoided the atmosphere of modernization, spending his summers away from Tokyo at Yaizu, a small fishing village where today there is a Hearn monument. His happiest period in Japan were the early years he spent as a country school teacher in Matsue on the southwest coast. His house and garden there are still preserved, and a Hearn museum is located next door. The essay "In a Japanese Garden" in his book *Glimpses of Unfamiliar Japan* describes his home and Matsue.

Beginning with Charles Eliot's *Japanese Buddhism*, there has grown up an immense bibliography of Buddhological works in Western languages. Since World War II, there is an ever greater store in the United States of books on Zen, which has become a popular form of Existentialism. There is no interpreter of Japanese Buddhism quite like Hearn, but he is not a Buddhologist. Far from it. Hearn was not a scholar, nor was he in the Western sense a religious believer. What distinguishes him is an emotional identification with the Buddhist way of life and with Buddhist cults. Hearn is as good as anyone at providing an elementary grounding in Buddhist doctrine. But what he does incomparably is to give his reader a feeling for how Buddhism is *lived* in Japan, its persistent influence upon folklore, burial customs, children's riddles, toys for sale in the marketplace, and even upon the farmer's ruminations in the field. For Hearn, Buddhism is a way of life, and he is interested in the effects of its doctrine upon the daily actions and common beliefs of ordinary people. Like the

Introduction

Japanese themselves, he thinks of religion as something one does, not merely as something one believes, unlike the orthodox Christian whose Athanasian Creed declares: "Whosoever would be saved, it is necessary before all things that he believe . . ."

One of the things Hearn admires about Buddhism is its adaptability to the spiritual and historic needs of a people. If they need a pantheon of gods, Buddhism makes room for them. If they need to fix upon a savior, Buddhism provides one. But the Buddhist elite, the more learned monks, never lose sight of the true doctrine. I will never forget a symposium in which I once took part along with a number of Buddhist clergy. A Westerner asked the leading Shinshu abbot, "Do you really believe in the existence of supernatural beings like Amida and Kannon, and in a life after death in the True Land Paradise of Amida?" The abbot answered very quietly, "These are conceptual entities." In fact the Diamond and Womb Mandalas with their hundreds of figures (sometimes represented by quasi-Sanskrit letters) are tools for mediation. The monk moves from the guardian gods at the outer edge, in to the central Buddha—the Vairocana—and at last beyond him to the Adi Buddha—the Pure, unqualified Void.

Yet, popular rather than "higher" Buddhism is Hearn's main subject, and he always is careful to distinguish between the metaphysically complex Buddhism of the educated monks and the simpler, more colorful Buddhism of the ordinary people.

The only peculiarity in Hearn's Buddhism is his habit of equating it with the philosophy of Herbert Spencer, now so out of date. However, this presents few difficulties for the modern reader, as his Spencerianism can be said to resemble Buddhism more than his Buddhism resembles Herbert Spen-

Introduction

cer. Also, it is not Spencer's Darwinism, "red in tooth and claw," but Spencer's metaphysical and spiritual speculations that have influenced Hearn's interpretation of Buddhism. We must not forget that Teilhard de Chardin, who certainly is not out of date, is, in the philosophical sense, only Herbert Spencer sprinkled with holy water. Philosophies and theologies come and go, but the group experience of transcendence is embedded in human nature, and when it is abandoned, theology, philosophy, and eventually culture, perish.

It is difficult to think of a better guide to Japanese Buddhism for the completely uninformed than Hearn, though there are others who may be his equals. Certainly the popularizers of Zen are not. Zen, after all, is a very special sect, in many ways more Vedantist or Taoist than Buddhist. And of course as the religion of the Japanese officer caste and of the great rich it plays in Japan a decidedly reactionary role. Hearn's Buddhism is far less specialized than Zen. It is the Buddhism of the ordinary Japanese Buddhist of whatever sect.

The first distinction to be made in any consideration of Buddhism itself is that Christianity is the only major religion whose adherents live lives and hold beliefs diametrically opposed to those of its founder. Nothing could be less like the life of Jesus than that of the typical Christian, clerical or lay. Imagine thirteen men with long beards, matted hair, and probably lice, in ragged clothes and dusty bare feet, taking over the high altar at St. Peter's in Rome or the pulpit of a fashionable Fifth Avenue sanctuary. The Apostolic life survives in only odd branches of Christianity: the Hutterites, some Quakers, even Jehovah's Witnesses, but not, as everyone knows, in official and orthodox denominations. Catholicism carefully quarantines such people in monasteries and

Introduction

nunneries where a life patterned on that of the historic Jesus is not wholly impossible to achieve. The opposite is true of Buddhism. No matter how far the sect—Lamaism, Zen, or Shingon—may have moved from the Buddhologically postulated original Buddhist Order, all sects of Buddhism are pervaded by the personality of the historic Siddhartha Guatama.

The historicity of almost all the details of what are generally considered to be the earliest Buddhist documents is subject to dispute and in many instances is improbable. The earliest surviving Life of Buddha was written hundreds of years after his death. The prevailing form of Buddhism in Japan, Mahayana, seems to Westerners more like a group of competing, highly speculative philosophies than a religion. The complete collection of Hinanya, Mahayana and Tantric Buddhist texts makes up a very large library. In addition, there are many thousands of pages of noncanonical commentary and speculation. Yet out of it all emerges, with extraordinary clarity, a man, a personality, a way of life and a basic moral code.

Buddha was born in Kapilavastu, now Rummimdei, Nepal, sometime around 563 B.C. and died about 483 B.C. in Kusimara, now Kasia, India. His personal name was Siddhartha Guatama. Buddha, The Enlightened One, is a title, not a name, as is Sakumuni, the saint of the Saka clan. In Japan, the historic Buddha is commonly known as Shakya. He was a member of the Kshatriya warrior caste, the son of the ruler of a small principality.

For six years Buddha lived with five other ascetics in a grove at Uruvela practicing the most extreme forms of self-mortification and the most advanced techniques of Hatha Yoga, until he almost died of starvation. He gave up ascetic

Introduction

life, left his companions, and traveled on. At Bodh Gaya he seated himself under a Bo tree *(ficus religiosa)* and resolved not to get up until he had achieved true enlightenment. Maya, the personification of the world's illusion, with his daughters and all the attendant incarnate sins and illusions, attacked him without success. Guatama Siddhartha achieved final illumination, entered Nirvana and arose a Buddha: an Enlightened One. He returned to his five companions at Uruvela and preached to them the Middle Way between self-indulgence and extreme asceticism. They were shocked and repudiated him, but after he had preached to them the Noble Eight-Fold Way and the Four Truths, they became the first Buddhist monks.

The first Truth is the Truth of suffering: birth is pain, old age is pain, sickness is pain, death is pain, the endless round of rebirths is pain, the five aggregates of grasping are pain. The second Truth is the cause of pain: the craving that holds the human being to endless rebirth, the craving of the passions, the craving for continued existence, the craving for non-existence. The third Noble Truth is the ending of pain: the extirpation of craving. The fourth Noble Truth is the means of arriving at the cessation of pain: the Noble Eight-Fold Path, which is right views, right intentions, right speech, right action, right livelihood, right effort, right mindfulness, right concentration (or contemplation). This doctrine is the essence of Buddhism, common to all of its otherwise divergent sects. It is always there, underlying the most extreme forms of Tantrism or Amidism. It produces in the personality of the devout Buddhist what the Japanese would call the *iro*, the essential color of the Buddha-life.

As Hinduism was taking form in the Upanishads, it began to teach the doctrine of the identity of the individual

Introduction

self, the Atman, and of the universal self, Brahman as Atman. Buddha attacked the Atman doctrine head-on, denying the existence of the individual or absolute self. He taught that the self is simply a bundle of *skandas*, the five aggregates of grasping: body, feeling, perception, mental elements, and consciousness. The *skandas* that comprise the self are momentary and illusory in the flux of Being—but they do cause and accumulate *karma*, the moral residue of their acts in this life and in past lives. It is *karma* which holds the aggregates embedded in the bonds of craving and consequence until the *skandas* disintegrate in the face of Ultimate Enlightenment. In the most philosophical teaching of Buddhism, it is the *karma* and the *skandas* which reincarnate. The individual consciousness or soul, as we think of it, disappears. But the universal belief in the reincarnation of the individual person has always overridden this notion. The ordinary Buddhist in fact believes in the rebirth of the self, the *atman*.

It is these doctrines which distinguish Buddhism. Many ideas which we think of as especially Buddhist are actually shared by Hinduism, by Jainism, and in fact by many completely secular modern Indians—transmigration, Yogic practices (some modern Buddhologists have held that Buddhism is only a special form of Yoga, anticipating its final synthesis in the Yoga Sutras of Patanjali). Vedic gods appear at all the crucial moments in Buddha's life, from his conception to his entry into final Nirvana. Some time after its inception, Buddhism developed the practice of *bhakti*, personal devotion to a Savior, parallel to that of Hinduism. But always what distinguishes Buddhism is the Buddha Way, the Buddha-life, the all-pervasive personality of its founder, as the personality of Krishna in the *Bhagavad Gita* does not.

The fifty years after his illumination Buddha spent traveling and preaching, usually with a large entourage of monks.

Introduction

In his eightieth year he stopped at the home of Cunda the smith, where he and his followers were given a meal of something to do with pigs. The language is obscure—pork, pigs' food, or something that had been trampled by pigs. Buddha became ill and later stopped in the gardens of Ambhapala, where he announced to his monks that he was about to enter Paranirvana, the final bliss. He lay down under the flowering trees and died, mourned by all creation, monks, laymen, gods, and the lowest animals. His last words were, "The combinations of the world are unstable by nature. Monks, strive without ceasing."

This is the account preserved by the Pali texts, the sacred books of the Theravada Buddhists, of the religion of Ceylon, Burma, and the countries of the Indo-Chinese peninsula. Pali is a dialect of a small principality in Northern India, now forgotten in its homeland. The Pali texts are earlier than all but fragments of Buddhist Sanskrit documents, but this does not necessarily mean that the Hinayana ("The Lesser Vehicle") Buddhism which they embody is the most primitive form of the religion. Theirs is simply the religion of the Theravada, "The religion of the Elders," one of the early sects. However, up until the reign of Ashoka, the saintly Buddhist emperor who ruled more of the Indian sub-continent than anyone before him, Buddhism seems to have been a more or less unified religion resembling the later Hinayana. From the reign of Ashoka to the beginning of the Christian era two currents in Buddhism began to draw more and more apart until Mahayana, "The Greater Vehicle," became dominant in the North and in Java. All the forms of Japanese Buddhism with which Hearn came into contact are rooted in the Mahayana tradition.

The many Mahayana texts are differentiated from the postulated Buddha Word as it appears in Pali by several

Introduction

radically different, indeed contradictory, beliefs and practices. In Hinayana man achieves Nirvana, or advances towards it in a future life, solely by his own efforts to overcome the accumulated evil *karma* of thousands of incarnations. There is devotion to the Founder as the Leader of the Way, but no worship, because there is nothing to worship. The difference is the same as that which the Roman Catholic Church calls *dulia*, adoration of the saints, and *latria*, adoration of God. Mahayana introduced the idea of saviors, *Bodhisattvas*, who have achieved Buddhahood but who have taken a vow not to enter Nirvana until they can take all sentient creatures with them. As saviors they are worshipped with a kind of *hyper-dulia*, as is the Blessed Virgin in Roman Catholicism. Buddhism was influenced by the great wave of personal worship that swept through India, *bhakti*, the adoration of Krishna, the incarnation of Vishnu, or of Kali, the female embodiment of the power of Shiva. At least theoretically above the Boddhisattvas arose a pantheon of Buddhas of whom Vairocana was primary. Later, an Adi-Buddha was added above him. It is disputable if either properly can be called the Absolute. If there is any absolute in Buddhism, it is Nirvana, which in fact means the religious experience itself. From Vairocana emanate the four Dhyana Buddhas, the Buddhas of Contemplation, of whom Amida is the best known, and of whom the historic Shakyamuni is only one of four, although in his most transcendental form he can be equated with Vairocana or the Adi Buddha.

The story of the development of Mahayana as it spread from what is now Afghanistan and Russian Turkestan to Mongolia and Indonesia to Tibet, China and Japan, while it died out in India, would take many thousands of words to tell. There are traces of Buddhism in China two hundred years or

Introduction

more before the Christian era. Its official introduction is supposed to have occurred in the first century A.D.. From then until the Muslim conquest of India, Chinese pilgrims visited India and brought back caravan loads of statuaries and *sutras* (sacred texts) which were translated into Chinese.

Indian missionaries emigrated to China and taught and translated. Buddhism was introduced into Korea in the fourth century and had thoroughly established itself in the three countries of the peninsula by the seventh. From there it passed to Japan in the sixth century.

The first missionaries converted the Soga Clan, which was then the power behind the Japanese throne. For the greater part of a century Buddhism was almost exclusively the religion of a faction of the nobility, and its fortune varied with the factional struggles of the court. in 593 A.D. Prince Shōtoku became the effective head of state. His knowledge of Buddhism and of the more profound meanings of Mahayana was extraordinary. He not only saved Buddhism from rapidly becoming a cult of magic and superstition, but like Ashoka in India before him, he went far to make it a religion of the people. He copied *sutras* in characters of gold on purple paper. He preached the doctrines of Mahayana to the common people as well as to the court. He established hundreds of monasteries, nunneries and temples. Not least, he promulgated a kind of charter which modern Japanese called The Seventeen Article Constitution, in which Buddhist ethics and, to a lesser degree, Confucianism were established as the moral foundations of Japan. To this day he is regarded by many as an avatar of Avalokitesvara, *Kuan Yin* in Chinese and *Kannon* or *Kwannon* in Japanese—the so-called Goddess of Mercy and the most popular of all Bodhisattvas.

By the eighth century Buddhism had become Japan's

Introduction

official state religion, a feat Hearn credits to Buddhism's absorption and expansion of the older Shintō worship of many gods, ghosts, and goblins (the gods, Buddhas or Bodhisattvas, the ghosts beings in transit from one incarnation to another, and the goblins, *gakis*, beings suffering in a lower state of existence). By the thirteenth century most of the major forms of Japanese Buddhism—a religion quite distinct from Buddhism elsewhere in the world—had been established, though minor sects continued to proliferate.

Ten large sects dominate Japanese Buddhism. The oldest of these are Tendai and Shingon. First was Tendai, established by the monk Saichō in 804 on Mt. Hiei northeast of Kyoto *(Heian kyo)*, facing the most inauspicious direction. Not long afterwards the monk Kukai returned from China and introduced Shingon, which became the Japanese form of Tantric Buddhism. In China, Tendai attempted a synthesis of the various schools and cults in the great complex of monasteries on Mt. T'ien Tai. The similar monastic city on Mt. Hiei sheltered a wide variety of cults, doctrines, and philosophies. Basically, however, Japanese Tendai modified what in India was known as "right-handed" Tantrism, which we see today in the Yellow Hat sect of Tibetan Lamaism in exile. All the great Buddhist *sutras* were studied, the doctrine of the Void, the doctrine of Mind Only, the vision of reality as the interpenetration of compound infinitives of Buddha natures of the Avatamsaka Sutra, and the complex panpsychism of the Lankavatara Sutra. Most popular, however, was the Lotus Sutra *(Hokkekyo* in Japanese), the Saddharma Pundarika Sutra, the only major Buddhist document a Japanese lay person is at all likely to have read. Tendai is a ceremonial religion, and only in recent years has it done much for the laity except to permit them to participate in pilgrimages and to watch public ceremonies.

Introduction

Shingon is even more esoteric than Tendai and is in fact Japanese Lamaism. Its doctrines are occult, its mysteries are not divulged to the people, and many of its rites are kept secret. The worship of Buddhas and Bodhisattvas as sexual dualities or as terrifying wrathful figures is not as common in Japan as in Tibet, though in both cultures the emphasis on magic formulas, gestures, spells and special methods of inducing trance remains essential. It is not known how many Tantric *shastras* (scriptures secondary to *sutras*) survive and are studied in Shingon monasteries, but recent discoveries and paintings of this literature are read by the more learned Japanese monks. "Lefthanded" Tantrism, with its cult of erotic mysticism, survives underground in Tachigawa Shingon.

The worship of Amida which began in India around the advent of the Christian era, almost certainly under the influence of Persian religion, effected a complete revolution in Japanese Buddhism when it was introduced in the ninth century. Originally sheltered within the Tendai sect, Amidism grew to be the most popular form of Buddhism in Japan—and the one with which Hearn was most familiar. Amida is the Buddha of Endless Light whose paradise, The Pure Land, is in the west. He has promised that any who believe in him and call on his name will be saved and at death will be reborn in his Pure Land. Buddha, of course, insisted that by oneself one is saved and thus achieves, not paradise, but Nirvana, which far transcends any imaginable paradise. Hearn, however, observed that few Japanese even knew of the concept of Nirvana. For them Amida's Pure Land was the highest heaven imaginable. Buddha also forbade worship of himself or others and considered the gods inferior to human beings because they could not escape the round of rebirths and enter Nirvana. Amidism, as a gesture to orthodoxy, teaches that the older Buddhism is too hard for this corrupt age and that

Introduction

the Pure Land, unlike other paradises, provides a direct stepping stone to Nirvana. As the Amidist sects developed in Japan, the doctrine of salvation by faith became more and more extreme. At first, it was necessary to invoke the name of Amida many times a day and especially with one's last words, but finally one had only to invoke it once in a lifetime. This was enough to erase the *karma*, the consequences, of a life of ignorance and sin.

The Japanese monk Nichiren, who played a role not unlike that of the Hebrew Prophets, taught that salvation could be won by reciting the words *"Namu Myōhōrengekyō,"* "Hail to the Lotus Sutra!" The Lotus Sutra is a sort of compendium of Mahayana Buddhism, lavishly embroidered with miraculous visions, with thousands upon thousands of Buddhas, Bodhisattvas, gods, demigods and lesser supernatural beings. But its important chapter is the Kannon (*Avalokitshivara*), which raises the Bodhisattva to a position similar to that of Amida, The Savior of the World, "He Who Hears The World's Cry." The earliest Kannon statues and paintings seem to have reached Japan from the oasis cities of Central Asia. Their peculiar sexlessness led the Japanese, as it did the Chinese, to think of the Bodhisattva as a woman. Not just Westerners, but most Japanese, refer to him as the Goddess of Mercy, and cheap modern statues which depict him holding a baby bear a striking resemblance to popular representations of the Virgin Mary.

The secret of the tremendous success of Amidism and Nichirenism is that they are congregational religions. The largest of all Buddhist sects, the Amidist Jodo-Shinshu, is in this sense much like a modern Christian denomination. But, in other respects, and despite its tremendous pilgrimages, Buddhism seems inaccessible to the common Japanese. Very few

Introduction

people know anything about the profound and complex metaphysics of Mahayana speculation. A surprising number do know the life of Buddha as it is told in Hinayana, which scarcely exists in Japan, and do try to model their lives on the Buddha-life—with remarkable success. But for most secular Japanese, a Buddhist monk is just a kind of undertaker, to be called upon only when somebody dies.

Zen Buddhism cultivated a special sensibility that many Japanese people think of as Japanese. The tea ceremony, *sumi-e* ink painting, the martial arts (archery, sword play, *jiujitsu judo*, *aikido*, wrestling), flower arrangement, pottery, and *haiku* survive as creative expressions of the Zen sensibility in pursuit of perfection. But this sensibility has weakened in most modern Japanese.

Zen is often translated as Enlightenment *(Ch'an* or Dhyana), but it means something like illumination, specifically illumination achieved by systematic religious meditation of the kind we identify as yoga. It is supposed to have been introduced to China by a missionary Indian monk, Bodhidharma, probably in the sixth century. It spread to Japan in the thirteenth as the long civil wars were beginning, became popular with the military castes and the great rich, and for a long time dominated the intellectual and artistic life of the country. Zen owed its powerful influence to the fact that it began as a revolt against the Buddhist cults of its time and reverted to what the nineteenth century was to call "Primitive" Buddhism. It rejected the salvation by faith and the devotional worship of Amidism, the cults of Kannon and the Lotus Sutra ("By yourself alone shall you be saved," says Gautama). It reinstated yogic meditation with a view to final enlightenment as the central and essential practice of the Buddhist religious life. Finally, it reinstated Shakyamuni himself, Shaka, as he is

Introduction

known in Japanese: its special interpretation of the Buddha-life is modeled on his.

Since World War II, Zen Buddhism has become enormously popular in the West, and largely in response to its reception here it has seen an intellectual revival in Japan. Although Hearn was familiar with Zen theories and practices, and had Zen Buddhist friends, he wrote little about the sect that was to become the most influential in the West. Neither Zen as a manifestation of aristocratic traditions nor Zen as a popular fad interested him. Instead, he kept his eye on what had persisted in Japanese Buddhism through the centuries among the farmers, fishermen, and other poor folk. Many of their beliefs inform their stories, and many of their customs in turn have stories behind them. It was the survival of Buddhism in such forms that above all else engaged Hearn.

Hearn's role in the spread of Buddhism to the West was a preparatory one. He was the first important American writer to live in Japan and to commit his imagination and considerable literary powers to what he found there. Like the "popular" expressions of Buddhist faith that were his favorite subject, Hearn popularized the Buddhist way of life for his Western readers. And he was widely read, both in his articles for *Harper's Magazine* and the *Atlantic Monthly*, and in his numerous books on Japan. Hearn's essays, with their rich descriptions and queer details, almost never generalizing but staying with a particular subject, always backed by the likeable and enthusiastic personality of Hearn himself, and always factually reliable, satisfied the vague and growing curiosity of his American readers about the mysterious East.

At St. Cuthbert's school, at age fifteen, Hearn had discovered that he was a pantheist. That is not unusual for a fifteen-year-old, and the fact that pantheism is unaccepted in

Introduction

Christian doctrine or in Western philosophical thought normally suffices to extinguish the common adolescent philosophy or to transmute it to something less vulnerable. But the idea stuck with Hearn, and when finally, at forty, he arrived in Japan, he was delighted to find that he could now exercise and explore his intuition of God-in-All. If Hearn entered Japanese culture and achieved understanding of Japanese Buddhist (and Shintō) thought with unprecedented rapidity for a Westerner, it is because his own spirit had always longed for an atmosphere in which his belief in the sentience and blessedness of all Nature could flourish.

Hearn never became a Buddhist, and he remained skeptical about certain of Buddhism's key doctrines—such as the relationship of *karma* and rebirth—but he passionately believed that Buddhism promoted a far better attitude toward daily life than did Christianity. It would be up to more scholarly and less imaginative writers to begin to translate and preach specific Buddhist doctrines, but Hearn has done much to translate the spirit of Japanese Buddhism and to prepare Western society for it.

KENNETH REXROTH

The Stone Buddha

I

On the ridge of the hill behind the Government College — above a succession of tiny farm fields ascending the slope by terraces — there is an ancient village cemetery. It is no longer used: the people of Kurogamimura now bury their dead in a more secluded spot; and I think their fields are beginning already to encroach upon the limits of the old graveyard.

Having an idle hour to pass between two classes, I resolve to pay the ridge a visit. Harmless thin black snakes wiggle across the way as I climb; and immense grasshoppers, exactly the color of parched leaves, whirr away from my shadow. The little field path vanishes altogether under coarse grass before reaching the broken steps at the cemetery gate; and in the cemetery itself there is no path at all — only weeds and stones. But there is a fine view from the ridge: the vast green Plain of Higo, and beyond it bright blue hills in a half-ring against the horizon light, and even beyond them the cone of Aso smoking forever.

Below me, as in a bird's-eye view, appears the college, like a miniature modern town, with its long ranges of many windowed buildings, all of the year 1887 They represent the purely utilitarian architecture of the nineteenth century: they might be situated equally well in Kent or in Auckland or in New Hampshire without appearing in the least out of tone with the age. But the terraced fields above and the figures toiling in them might be of the fifth century. The language cut upon the haka whereon I lean is transliterated Sanscrit. And there is a Buddha beside me, sitting upon his lotus of stone just as he sat in the days of Kato Kiyomasa. His meditative gaze slants down between his half-closed eyelids upon the Government College and its tumultuous life; and he smiles the smile of one who has received an injury not to be resented. This is not the expression wrought by the sculptor: moss and scurf have distorted it. I also observe that his hands are broken. I am sorry, and try to scrape the moss away from the little symbolic protuberance on his forehead, remembering the ancient text of the "Lotus of the Good Law":

> There issued a ray of light from the circle of hair between the brows of the Lord. It extended over eighteen hundred thousand Buddha fields, so that all those Buddha fields appeared wholly illuminated by its radiance, down to the great hell Aviki, and up to the limit of existence. And all the beings in each of the Six States of existence became visible — all without exception. Even the Lord Buddhas in those Buddha fields who had reached final Nirvana, all became visible.

The Stone Buddha

II

THE sun is high behind me; the landscape before me as in an old Japanese picture-book. In old Japanese color-prints there are, as a rule, no shadows. And the Plain of Higo, all shadowless, broadens greenly to the horizon, where the blue spectres of the peaks seem to float in the enormous glow. But the vast level presents no uniform hue: it is banded and seamed by all tones of green, intercrossed as if laid on by long strokes of a brush. In this again the vision resembles some scene from a Japanese picture-book.

Open such a book for the first time, and you receive a peculiarly startling impression, a sensation of surprise, which causes you to think: "How strangely, how curiously, these people feel and see Nature!" The wonder of it grows upon you, and you ask: "Can it be possible their senses are so utterly different from ours?" Yes, it is quite possible; but look a little more. You do so, and there defines a third and ultimate idea, confirming the previous two. You feel the picture is more true to Nature than any Western painting of the same scene would be — that it produces sensations of Nature no Western picture could give. And indeed there are contained within it whole ranges of discoveries for you to make. Before making them, however, you will ask yourself another riddle, somewhat thus: "All this is magically vivid; the inexplicable color is Nature's own. *But why does the thing seem so ghostly?"*

Well, chiefly because of the absence of shadows. What prevents you from missing them at once is the astounding skill in the recognition and use of color-values. The scene, however, is not depicted as if illumined from one side, but as if throughout suffused with light. Now there are really moments when landscapes do wear this aspect; but our artists rarely study them.

Be it nevertheless observed that the old Japanese loved shadows made by the moon, and painted the same, because these were weird and did not interfere with color. But they had no admiration for shadows that blacken and break the charm of the world under the sun. When their noon-day landscapes are flecked by shadows at all, 't is by very thin ones only — mere deepenings of tone, like those fugitive half-glooms which run before a summer cloud. And the inner as well as the outer world was luminous for them. Psychologically also they saw life without shadows.

Then the West burst into their Buddhist peace, and saw their art, and bought it up till an Imperial law was issued to preserve the best of what was left. And when there was nothing more to be bought, and it seemed possible that fresh creation might reduce the market price of what had been bought already, then the West said: "Oh, come, now! you must n't go on drawing and seeing things that way,

The Stone Buddha

you know! It isn't Art! You must really learn to see shadows, you know — and pay me to teach you."

So Japan paid to learn how to see shadows in Nature, in life, and in thought. And the West taught her that the sole business of the divine sun was the making of the cheaper kind of shadows. And the West taught her that the higher-priced shadows were the sole product of Western civilization, and bade her admire and adopt. Then Japan wondered at the shadows of machinery and chimneys and telegraph-poles; and at the shadows of mines and of factories, and the shadows in the hearts of those who worked there; and at the shadows of houses twenty stories high, and of hunger begging under them; and shadows of enormous charities that multiplied poverty; and shadows of social reforms that multiplied vice; and shadows of shams and hypocrisies and swallow-tail coats; and the shadow of a foreign God, said to have created mankind for the purpose of an auto-da-fé. Whereat Japan became rather serious, and refused to study any more silhouettes. Fortunately for the world, she returned to her first matchless art; and, fortunately for herself, returned to her own beautiful faith. But some of the shadows still clung to her life; and she cannot possibly get rid of them. Never again can the world seem to her quite so beautiful as it did before.

III

JUST beyond the cemetery, in a tiny patch of hedged-in land, a farmer and his ox are ploughing the black soil with a plough of the Period of the Gods; and the wife helps the work with a hoe more ancient than even the Empire of Japan. All the three are toiling with a strange earnestness, as though goaded without mercy by the knowledge that labor is the price of life.

That man I have often seen before in the colored prints of another century. I have seen him in kakemono of much more ancient date. I have seen him on painted screens of still greater antiquity. Exactly the same! Other fashions beyond counting have passed: the peasant's straw hat, straw coat, and sandals of straw remain. He himself is older, incomparably older, than his attire. The earth he tills has indeed swallowed him up a thousand times a thousand times; but each time it has given back to him his life with force renewed. And with this perpetual renewal he is content: he asks no more. The mountains change their shapes; the rivers shift their courses; the stars change their places in the sky: he changes never. Yet, though unchanging, is he a maker of change. Out of the sum of his toil are wrought the ships of iron, the roads of steel, the palaces of stone; his are the hands that pay for the universities and the new learning, for the telegraphs and the electric lights and the repeating-rifles, for the machinery of science and the machinery of commerce and the machinery of war. He is the giver of all; he is given in return — the right to labor forever. Wherefore he ploughs the centuries under, to plant new lives of men. And he will thus toil on till the work of the world shall have been done — till the time of the end of man.

And what will be that end? Will it be ill or well? Or must it for all of us remain a mystery insolvable?

Out of the wisdom of the West is answer given: "Man's evolution is a progress into perfection and beatitude. The goal of evolution is Equilibration. Evils will vanish, one by one, till only that which is good survive. Then shall knowledge obtain its uttermost expansion; then shall mind put forth its most wondrous blossoms; then shall cease all struggle and all bitterness of soul, and all the wrongs and all the follies of life. Men shall become as gods, in all save immortality; and each existence shall be prolonged through centuries; and all the joys of life shall be made common in many a paradise terrestrial, fairer than poet's dream. And there shall be neither rulers nor ruled, neither governments nor laws; for the order of all things shall be resolved by love."

But thereafter?

"Thereafter? Oh, thereafter by reason of the persistence of Force and other cosmic laws, dissolution must come: all integration must yield to disintegration. This is the testimony of science."

Then all that may have been won, must be lost;

all that shall have been wrought, utterly undone. Then all that shall have been overcome, must overcome; all that may have been suffered for good, must be suffered again for no purpose interpretable. Even as out of the Unknown was born the immeasurable pain of the Past, so into the Unknown must expire the immeasurable pain of the Future. What, therefore, the worth of our evolution? what, therefore, the meaning of life — of this phantom-flash between darknesses? Is your evolution only a passing out of absolute mystery into universal death? In the hour when that man in the hat of straw shall have crumbled back, for the last mundane time, into the clay he tills, of what avail shall have been all the labor of a million years?

"Nay!" answers the West. "There is not any universal death in such a sense. Death signifies only change. Thereafter will appear another universal life. All that assures us of dissolution, not less certainly assures us of renewal. The Cosmos, resolved into a nebula, must recondense to form another swarm of worlds. And then, perhaps, your peasant may reappear with his patient ox, to till some soil illumined by purple or violet suns." Yes, but after that resurrection? "Why, then another evolution, another equilibration, another dissolution. This is the teaching of science. This is the infinite law."

But then that resurrected life, can it be ever new?

The Stone Buddha

Will it not rather be infinitely old? For so surely as that which is must eternally be, so must that which will be have eternally been. As there can be no end, so there can have been no beginning; and even Time is an illusion, and there is nothing new beneath a hundred million suns. Death is not death, not a rest, not an end of pain, but the most appalling of mockeries. And out of this infinite whirl of pain you can tell us no way of escape. Have you then made us any wiser than that straw-sandaled peasant is? He knows all this. He learned, while yet a child, from the priests who taught him to write in the Buddhist temple school, something of his own innumerable births, and of the apparition and disparition of universes, and of the unity of life. That which you have mathematically discovered was known to the East long before the coming of the Buddha. How known, who may say? Perhaps there have been memories that survived the wrecks of universes. But be that as it may, your annunciation is enormously old: your methods only are new, and serve merely to confirm ancient theories of the Cosmos, and to recomplicate the complications of the everlasting Riddle.

Unto which the West makes answer: "Not so! I have discerned the rhythm of that eternal action whereby worlds are shapen or dissipated; I have divined the Laws of Pain evolving all sentient existence, the Laws of Pain evolving thought; I have discovered and proclaimed the means by which sorrow may be lessened; I have taught the necessity of effort, and the highest duty of life. And surely the knowledge of the duty of life is the knowledge of largest worth to man."

Perhaps. But the knowledge of the necessity and of the duty, as you have proclaimed them, is a knowledge very, very much older than you. Probably that peasant knew it fifty thousand years ago, on this planet. Possibly also upon other long-vanished planets, in cycles forgotten by the gods. If this be the Omega of Western wisdom, then is he of the straw sandals our equal in knowledge, even though he be classed by the Buddha among the ignorant ones only — they who "people the cemeteries again and again."

"He cannot know," makes answer Science; "at the very most he only believes, or thinks that he believes. Not even his wisest priests can prove. I alone have proven; I alone have given proof absolute. And I have proved for ethical renovation, though accused of proving for destruction. I have defined the uttermost impassable limit of human knowledge; but I have also established for all time the immovable foundations of that highest doubt which is wholesome, since it is the substance of hope. I have shown that even the least of human thoughts, of human acts, may have perpetual record — making self-registration through tremulosities invisible that pass to the eternities. And I have

The Stone Buddha

fixed the basis of a new morality upon everlasting truth, even though I may have left of ancient creeds only their empty shell."

Creeds of the West — yes! But not of the creed of this older East. Not yet have you even measured it. What matter that this peasant cannot prove, since thus much of his belief is that which you have proved for all of us? And he holds still another belief that reaches beyond yours. He too has been taught that acts and thoughts outlive the lives of men. But he has been taught more than this. He has been taught that the thoughts and acts of each being, projected beyond the individual existence, shape other lives unborn; he has been taught to control his most secret wishes, because of their immeasurable inherent potentialities. And he has been taught all this in words as plain and thoughts as simply woven as the straw of his rain-coat. What if he cannot prove his premises? you have proved them, for him and for the world. He has only a theory of the future, indeed; but you have furnished irrefutable evidence that it is not founded upon dreams. And since all your past labors have only served to confirm a few of the beliefs stored up in his simple mind, is it any folly to presume that your future labors also may serve to prove the truth of other beliefs of his, which you have not yet taken the trouble to examine?

"For instance, that earthquakes are caused by a big fish?"

The Buddhist Writings of Lafcadio Hearn

Do not sneer! Our Western notions about such things were just as crude only a few generations back. No! I mean the ancient teaching that acts and thoughts are not merely the incidents of life, but its creators. Even as it has been written, "All that we are is the result of what we have thought: it is founded on our thoughts; it is made up of our thoughts."

IV

AND there comes to me the memory of a queer story.

The common faith of the common people, that the misfortunes of the present are results of the follies committed in a former state of existence, and that the errors of this life will influence the future birth, is curiously reinforced by various superstitions probably much older than Buddhism, but not at variance with its faultless doctrine of conduct. Among these, perhaps the most remarkable is the belief that even our most secret thoughts of evil may have ghostly consequences upon *other people's lives*.

The house now occupied by one of my friends used to be haunted. You could never imagine it to have been haunted, because it is unusually luminous, extremely pretty, and comparatively new. It has no dark nooks or corners. It is surrounded with a large bright garden — a Kyūshū landscape

The Stone Buddha

garden without any big trees for ghosts to hide behind. Yet haunted it was, and in broad day.

First you must learn that in this Orient there are two sorts of haunters: the Shi-ryō and the Iki-ryō. The Shi-ryō are merely the ghosts of the dead; and here, as in most lands, they follow their ancient habit of coming at night only. But the Iki-ryō, which are the ghosts of the living, may come at all hours; and they are much more to be feared, because they have power to kill.

Now the house of which I speak was haunted by an Iki-ryō.

The man who built it was an official, wealthy and esteemed. He designed it as a home for his old age; and when it was finished he filled it with beautiful things, and hung tinkling wind bells along its eaves. Artists of skill painted the naked precious wood of its panels with blossoming sprays of cherry and plum tree, and figures of gold-eyed falcons poised on crests of pine, and slim fawns feeding under maple shadows, and wild ducks in snow, and herons flying, and iris flowers blooming, and long-armed monkeys clutching at the face of the moon in water: all the symbols of the seasons and of good fortune.

Fortunate the owner was; yet he knew one sorrow — he had no heir. Therefore, with his wife's consent, and according to antique custom, he took a strange woman into his home that she might give him a child — a young woman from the country, to whom large promises were made. When she had borne him a son, she was sent away; and a nurse was hired for the boy, that he might not regret his real mother. All this had been agreed to beforehand; and there were ancient usages to justify it. But all the promises made to the mother of the boy had not been fulfilled when she was sent away.

And after a little time the rich man fell sick; and he grew worse thereafter day by day; and his people said there was an Iki-ryō in the house. Skilled physicians did all they could for him; but he only became weaker and weaker; and the physicians at last confessed they had no more hope. And the wife made offerings at the Ujigami, and prayed to the Gods; but the Gods gave answer: "He must die unless he obtain forgiveness from one whom he wronged, and undo the wrong by making just amend. For there is an Iki-ryō in your house."

Then the sick man remembered, and was conscience-smitten, and sent out servants to bring the woman back to his home. But she was gone — somewhere lost among the forty millions of the Empire. And the sickness ever grew worse; and search was made in vain; and the weeks passed. At last there came to the gate a peasant who said that he knew the place to which the woman had gone, and that he would journey to find her if supplied with means of travel. But the sick man, hearing, cried out: "No! she would never forgive me in

The Stone Buddha

her heart, because she could not. It is too late!"
And he died.

After which the widow and the relatives and the little boy abandoned the new house; and strangers entered thereinto.

Curiously enough, the people spoke harshly concerning the mother of the boy — holding her to blame for the haunting.

I thought it very strange at first, not because I had formed any positive judgment as to the rights and wrongs of the case. Indeed I could not form such a judgment; for I could not learn the full details of the story. I thought the criticism of the people very strange, notwithstanding.

Why? Simply because there is nothing voluntary about the sending of an Iki-ryō. It is not witchcraft at all. The Iki-ryō goes forth without the knowledge of the person whose emanation it is. (There *is* a kind of witchcraft which is believed to send Things — but not Iki-ryō.) You will now understand why I thought the condemnation of the young woman very strange.

But you could scarcely guess the solution of the problem. It is a religious one, involving conceptions totally unknown to the West. She from whom the Iki-ryō proceeded was never blamed by the people as a witch. They never suggested that it might have been created with her knowledge. They even sympathized with what they deemed to be her just plaint. They blamed her only for having been too angry — for not sufficiently controlling her unspoken resentment — because she should have known *that anger, secretly indulged, can have ghostly consequences.*

I ask nobody to take for granted the possibility of the Iki-ryō, except as a strong form of conscience. But as an influence upon conduct, the belief certainly has value. Besides, it is suggestive. Who is really able to assure us that secret evil desires, pent-up resentments, masked hates, do not exert any force outside of the will that conceives and nurses them? May there not be a deeper meaning than Western ethics recognize in those words of the Buddha — "Hatred ceases not by hatred at any time; hatred ceases by love: this is an old rule"? It was very old then, even in his day. In ours it has been said, "Whensoever a wrong is done you, and you do not resent it, then so much evil dies in the world." But does it? Are we quite sure that not to resent it is enough? Can the motive tendency set loose in the mind by the sense of a wrong be nullified simply by non-action on the part of the wronged? Can any force die? The forces we know may be transformed only. So much also may be true of the forces we do not know; and of these are Life, Sensation, Will — all that makes up the infinite mystery called "I."

The Stone Buddha

V

"The duty of Science," answers Science, "is to systematize human experience, not to theorize about ghosts. And the judgment of the time, even in Japan, sustains this position taken by Science. What is now being taught below there — my doctrines, or the doctrines of the Man in the Straw Sandals?"

Then the Stone Buddha and I look down upon the college together; and as we gaze, the smile of the Buddha — perhaps because of a change in the light — seems to me to have changed its expression, to have become an ironical smile. Nevertheless he is contemplating the fortress of a more than formidable enemy. In all that teaching of four hundred youths by thirty-three teachers, there is no teaching of faith, but only teaching of fact — only teaching of the definite results of the systematization of human experience. And I am absolutely certain that if I were to question, concerning the things of the Buddha, any of those thirty-three instructors (saving one dear old man of seventy, the Professor of Chinese), I should receive no reply. For they belong unto the new generation, holding that such topics are fit for the consideration of Men-in-Straw-Rain-coats only, and that in this twenty-sixth year of Meiji, the scholar should occupy himself only with the results of the systematization of human experience. Yet the systematization of human experience in no wise enlightens us as to the Whence, the Whither, or, worst of all! — the Why.

The Laws of Existence which proceed from a cause — the cause of these hath the Buddha explained, as also the destruction of the same. Even of such truths is the great Sramana the teacher.

And I ask myself, Must the teaching of Science in this land efface at last the memory of the teaching of the Buddha?

"As for that," makes answer Science, "the test of the right of a faith to live must be sought in its power to accept and to utilize my revelations. Science neither affirms what it cannot prove, nor denies that which it cannot rationally disprove. Theorizing about the Unknowable, it recognizes and pities as a necessity of the human mind. You and the Man-in-the-Straw-Rain-coat may harmlessly continue to theorize for such time as your theories advance in lines parallel with my facts, but no longer."

And seeking inspiration from the deep irony of Buddha's smile, I theorize in parallel lines.

VI

THE whole tendency of modern knowledge, the whole tendency of scientific teaching, is toward the ultimate conviction that the Unknowable, even as the Brahma of ancient Indian thought, is inaccessible to prayer. Not a few of us can feel that

The Stone Buddha

Western Faith must finally pass away forever, leaving us to our own resources when our mental manhood shall have been attained, even as the fondest of mothers must leave her children at last. In that far day her work will all have been done; she will have fully developed our recognition of certain eternal spiritual laws; she will have fully ripened our profounder human sympathies; she will have fully prepared us by her parables and fairy tales, by her gentler falsehoods, for the terrible truth of existence; prepared us for the knowledge that there is no divine love save the love of man for man; that we have no All-Father, no Saviour, no angel guardians; that we have no possible refuge but in ourselves.

Yet even in that strange day we shall only have stumbled to the threshold of 'the revelation given by the Buddha so many ages ago:

> Be ye lamps unto yourselves; be ye a refuge unto yourselves. Betake yourselves to no other refuge. The Buddhas are only teachers. Hold ye fast to the truth as to a lamp. Hold fast as a refuge to the truth. Look not for refuge to any beside yourselves.

Does the utterance shock? Yet the prospect of such a void awakening from our long fair dream of celestial aid and celestial love would never be the darkest prospect possible for man. There is a darker, also foreshadowed by Eastern thought. Science may hold in reserve for us discoveries infinitely more appalling than the realization of

Richter's dream — the dream of the dead children seeking vainly their father Jesus. In the negation of the materialist even, there was a faith of consolation — self-assurance of individual cessation, of oblivion eternal. But for the existing thinker there is no such faith. It may remain for us to learn, after having vanquished all difficulties possible to meet upon this tiny sphere, that there await us obstacles to overcome beyond it — obstacles vaster than any system of worlds — obstacles weightier than the whole inconceivable Cosmos with its centuries of millions of systems; that our task is only beginning; and that there will never be given to us even the ghost of any help, save the help of unutterable and unthinkable Time. We may have to learn that the infinite whirl of death and birth, out of which we cannot escape, is of our own creation, of our own seeking; that the forces integrating worlds are the errors of the Past; that the eternal sorrow is but the eternal hunger of insatiable desire; and that the burnt-out suns are rekindled only by the inextinguishable passions of vanished lives.

Dust

> Let the Bodhisattva look upon all things as having the nature of space, — as permanently equal to space; without essence, without substantiality.
> SADDHARMA-PUNDARÎKA

I HAVE wandered to the verge of the town; and the street I followed has roughened into a country road, and begins to curve away through rice-fields toward a hamlet at the foot of the hills. Between town and rice-fields a vague unoccupied stretch of land makes a favorite playground for children. There are trees, and spaces of grass to roll on, and many butterflies, and plenty of little stones. I stop to look at the children.

By the roadside some are amusing themselves with wet clay, making tiny models of mountains and rivers and rice-fields; tiny mud villages, also — imitations of peasants' huts — and little mud temples, and mud gardens with ponds and humped bridges and imitations of stone-lanterns (tōrō); likewise miniature cemeteries, with bits of broken stone for monuments. And they play at funerals, — burying corpses of butterflies and semi (cicadæ), and pretending to repeat Buddhist sutras over the grave. To-morrow they will not dare to do this; for to-morrow will be the first day of the festival of the Dead. During that festival it is strictly forbidden to molest insects, especially semi, some of which have on their heads little red characters said to be names of Souls.

Children in all countries play at death. Before the sense of personal identity comes, death cannot be seriously considered; and childhood thinks in this regard more correctly, perhaps, than self-conscious maturity. Of course, if these little ones were told, some bright morning, that a playfellow had gone away forever — gone away to be reborn elsewhere — there would be a very real though vague sense of loss, and much wiping of eyes with many-colored sleeves; but presently the loss would be forgotten and the playing resumed. The idea of ceasing to exist could not possibly enter a child-mind: the butterflies and birds, the flowers, the foliage, the sweet summer itself, only play at dying; — they seem to go, but they all come back again after the snow is gone. The real sorrow and fear of death arise in us only through slow accumulation of experience with doubt and pain; and these little boys and girls, being Japanese and Buddhists, will never, in any event, feel about death just as you or I do. They will find reason to fear it for somebody else's sake, but not for their own, because they will learn that they have died millions of times already, and have forgotten the trouble of it, much as one forgets the pain of successive toothaches. In the strangely penetrant light of their creed, teaching the ghostliness of all substance, granite or gossamer — just as

Dust

those lately found X-rays make visible the ghostliness of flesh — this their present world, with its bigger mountains and rivers and rice-fields, will not appear to them much more real than the mud landscapes which they made in childhood. And much more real it probably is not.

At which thought I am conscious of a sudden soft shock, a familiar shock, and know myself seized by the idea of Substance as Non-Reality.

This sense of the voidness of things comes only when the temperature of the air is so equably related to the temperature of life that I can forget having a body. Cold compels painful notions of solidity; cold sharpens the delusion of personality; cold quickens egotism; cold numbs thought, and shrivels up the little wings of dreams.

To-day is one of those warm, hushed days when it is possible to think of things as they are — when ocean, peak, and plain seem no more real than the arching of blue emptiness above them. All is mirage — my physical self, and the sunlit road, and the slow rippling of the grain under a sleepy wind, and the thatched roofs beyond the haze of the rice-fields, and the blue crumpling of the naked hills behind everything. I have the double sensation of being myself a ghost and of being haunted — haunted by the prodigious luminous Spectre of the World.

There are men and women working in those fields.

Colored moving shadows they are; and the earth under them — out of which they rose, and back to which they will go — is equally shadow. Only the Forces behind the shadow, that make and unmake, are real — therefore viewless.

Somewhat as Night devours all lesser shadow will this phantasmal earth swallow us at last, and itself thereafter vanish away. But the little shadows and the Shadow-Eater must as certainly reappear — must rematerialize somewhere and somehow. This ground beneath me is old as the Milky Way. Call it what you please — clay, soil, dust: its names are but symbols of human sensations having nothing in common with it. Really it is nameless and unnamable, being a mass of energies, tendencies, infinite possibilities; for it was made by the beating of that shoreless Sea of Birth and Death whose surges billow unseen out of eternal Night to burst in foam of stars. Lifeless it is not: it feeds upon life, and visible life grows out of it. Dust it is of Karma, waiting to enter into novel combinations — dust of elder Being in that state between birth and birth which the Buddhist calls Chū-U. It is made of forces, and of nothing else; and those forces are not of this planet only, but of vanished spheres innumerable.

Is there aught visible, tangible, measurable, that has never been mixed with sentiency? — atom that has never vibrated to pleasure or to pain? — air that has never been cry or speech? — drop that has

Dust

never been a tear? Assuredly this dust has felt. It has been everything we know; also much that we cannot know. It has been nebula and star, planet and moon, times unspeakable. Deity also it has been, — the Sun-God of worlds that circled and worshiped in other æons. "Remember, Man, thou art but dust!" — a saying profound only as materialism, which stops short at surfaces. For what is dust?

Remember, Dust, thou hast been Sun, and Sun thou shalt become again! . . . Thou hast been Light, Life, Love; — and into all these, by ceaseless cosmic magic, thou shalt many times be turned again!

For this Cosmic Apparition is more than evolution alternating with dissolution: it is infinite metempsychosis; it is perpetual palingenesis. Those old predictions of a bodily resurrection were not falsehoods; they were rather foreshadowings of a truth vaster than all myths and deeper than all religions.

Suns yield up their ghosts of flame; but out of their graves new suns rush into being. Corpses of worlds pass all to some solar funeral pyre; but out of their own ashes they are born again. This earth must die; her seas shall be Saharas. But those seas once existed in the sun; and their dead tides, revived by fire, will pour their thunder upon the coasts of another world. Transmigration — transmutation: these are not fables! What is impossible? Not the dreams of alchemists and poets; — dross may indeed be changed to gold, the jewel to the living eye, the flower into flesh. What is impossible? If seas can pass from world to sun, from sun to world again, what of the dust of dead selves — dust of memory and thought? Resurrection there is — but a resurrection more stupendous than any dreamed of by Western creeds. Dead emotions will revive as surely as dead suns and moons. Only, so far as we can just now discern, there will be no return of identical individualities. The reapparition will always be a recombination of the preëxisting, a readjustment of affinities, a reintegration of being informed with the experience of anterior being. The Cosmos is a Karma.

Merely by reason of illusion and folly do we shrink from the notion of self-instability. For what is our individuality? Most certainly it is not individuality at all: it is multiplicity incalculable. What is the human body? A form built up out of billions of living entities, an impermanent agglomeration of individuals called cells. And the human soul? A composite of quintillions of souls. We are, each and all, infinite compounds of fragments of anterior lives. And the universal process that continually dissolves and continually constructs personality has always been going on, and is even at this moment going on, in every one of us. What being ever had a totally new feeling, an absolutely new idea? All our emotions and thoughts and wishes, however chang-

Dust

ing and growing through the varying seasons of life, are only compositions and recompositions of the sensation and ideas and desires of other folk, mostly of dead people — millions of billions of dead people. Cells and souls are themselves recombinations, present aggregations of past knittings of forces, — forces about which nothing is known save that they belong to the Shadow-Makers of universes.

Whether you (by *you* I mean any other agglomeration of souls) really wish for immortality as an agglomeration, I cannot tell. But I confess that "my mind to me a kingdom is" — not! Rather it is a fantastical republic, daily troubled by more revolutions than ever occurred in South America; and the nominal government, supposed to be rational, declares that an eternity of such anarchy is not desirable. I have souls wanting to soar in air, and souls wanting to swim in water (sea-water, I think), and souls wanting to live in woods or on mountain tops. I have souls longing for the tumult of great cities, and souls longing to dwell in tropical solitude; — souls, also, in various stages of naked savagery; — souls demanding nomad freedom without tribute; — souls conservative, delicate, loyal to empire and to feudal tradition, and souls that are Nihilists, deserving Siberia; — sleepless souls, hating inaction, and hermit souls, dwelling in such meditative isolation that only at intervals of years can I feel them moving about; — souls that have faith in fetiches; — polytheistic souls; — souls proclaiming Islam; —

and souls mediæval, loving cloister shadow and incense and glimmer of tapers and the awful altitude of Gothic glooms. Coöperation among all these is not to be thought of: always there is trouble — revolt, confusion, civil war. The majority detest this state of things: multitudes would gladly emigrate. And the wiser minority feel that they need never hope for better conditions until after the total demolition of the existing social structure.

I an individual — an individual soul! Nay, I am a population — a population unthinkable for multitude, even by groups of a thousand millions! Generations of generations I am, æons of æons! Countless times the concourse now making me has been scattered, and mixed with other scatterings. Of what concern, then, the next disintegration? Perhaps, after trillions of ages of burning in different dynasties of suns, the very best of me may come together again.

If one could only imagine some explanation of the Why! The questions of the Whence and the Whither are much less troublesome, since the Present assures us, even though vaguely, of Future and Past. But the Why!

The cooing voice of a little girl dissolves my reverie. She is trying to teach a child brother how to make the Chinese character for Man — I mean

Dust

Man with a big M. First she draws in the dust a stroke sloping downwards from right to left, so:

丿

then she draws another curving downwards from left to right, thus:

乀

joining the two so as to form the perfect ji, or character, hito, meaning a person of either sex, or mankind:

人

Then she tries to impress the idea of this shape on the baby memory by help of a practical illustration — probably learned at school. She breaks a slip of wood in two pieces, and manages to balance the pieces against each other at about the same angle as that made by the two strokes of the character. "Now see," she says: "each stands only by help of the other. One by itself cannot stand. Therefore the ji is like mankind. Without help one person cannot live in this world; but by getting help and giving help everybody can live. If nobody helped anybody, all people would fall down and die."

This explanation is not philologically exact; the two strokes evolutionally standing for a pair of legs — all that survives in the modern ideograph of the whole man figured in the primitive picture-writing. But the pretty moral fancy is much more important than the scientific fact. It is also one charming example of that old-fashioned method of teaching which invested every form and every incident with ethical signification. Besides, as a mere item of moral information, it contains the essence of all earthly religion, and the best part of all earthly philosophy. A world-priestess she is, this dear little maid, with her dove's voice and her innocent gospel of one letter! Verily in that gospel lies the only possible present answer to ultimate problems. Were its whole meaning universally felt — were its whole suggestion of the spiritual and material law of love and help universally obeyed — forthwith, according to the Idealists, this seemingly solid visible world would vanish away like smoke! For it has been written that in whatsoever time all human minds accord in thought and will with the mind of the Teacher, *there shall not remain even one particle of dust that does not enter into Buddhahood.*

Buddhist Allusions in Japanese Folksong

PERHAPS only a Japanese representative of the older culture could fully inform us to what degree the mental soil of the race has been saturated and fertilized by Buddhist idealism. At all events, no European could do so; for to understand the whole relation of Far-Eastern religion to Far-Eastern life would require, not only such scholarship, but also such experience as no European could gain in a lifetime. Yet for even the Western stranger there are everywhere signs of what Buddhism has been to Japan in the past. All the arts and most of the industries repeat Buddhist legends to the eye trained in symbolism; and there is scarcely an object of handiwork possessing any beauty or significance of form — from the plaything of a child to the heirloom of a prince — which does not in some way proclaim the ancient debt to Buddhism of the craft that made it. One may discern Buddhist thoughts in the cheap cotton prints from an Ōsaka mill not less than in the figured silks of Kyōto. The reliefs upon an iron kettle, or the elephant-heads of bronze making the handles of a shopkeeper's hibachi; — the patterns of screen-paper, or the commonest ornamental woodwork of a gateway; the etchings upon a metal pipe, or the enameling upon a costly vase — may all relate, with equal eloquence, the traditions of faith. There are reflections or echoes of Buddhist teaching in the composition of a garden; — in the countless ideographs of the long vistas of shop-signs; — in the wonderfully expressive names given to certain fruits and flowers; — in the appellations of mountains, capes, waterfalls, villages — even of modern railway stations. And the new civilization would not yet seem to have much affected the influence thus manifested. Trains and steamers now yearly carry to famous shrines more pilgrims than visited them ever before in a twelvemonth; — the temple bells still, in despite of clocks and watches, mark the passing of time for the millions; — the speech of the people is still poetized with Buddhist utterances; — literature and drama still teem with Buddhist expressions; — and the most ordinary voices of the street — songs of children playing, a chorus of laborers at their toil, even cries of itinerant street-venders — often recall to me some story of saints and Bodhisattvas, or the text of some sutra.

Such an experience first gave me the idea of making a collection of songs containing Buddhist expressions or allusions. But in view of the extent of the subject I could not at once decide where to begin. A bewildering variety of Japanese songs — a variety of which the mere nomenclature would occupy pages — offers material of this description. Among noteworthy kinds may be mentioned the Utai, dramatic songs, mostly composed by high priests, of

Buddhist Allusions in Japanese Folksong

which probably no ten lines are without some allusion to Buddhism; — the Naga-uta, songs often of extraordinary length; — and the Jōruri, whole romances in verse, with which professional singers can delight their audiences for five or six hours at a time. The mere dimension of such compositions necessarily excluded them from my plan; but there remained a legion of briefer forms to choose among. I resolved at last to limit my undertaking mainly to dodoitsu — little songs of twenty-six syllables only, arranged in four lines (7, 7, 7, 5). They are more regular in construction than the street-songs treated of in a former paper; but they are essentially popular, and therefore more widely representative of Buddhist influences than many superior kinds of composition could be. Out of a very large number collected for me, I have selected between forty and fifty as typical of the class.

Perhaps those pieces which reflect the ideas of pre-existence and of future rebirths will prove especially interesting to the Western reader — much less because of poetical worth than because of comparative novelty. We have very little English verse of any class containing fancies of this kind; but they swarm in Japanese poetry even as commonplaces and conventionalisms. Such an exquisite thing as Rossetti's "Sudden Light" — bewitching us chiefly through the penetrative subtlety of a thought anathematized by all our orthodoxies for eighteen hundred years — could interest a Japanese only as the exceptional rendering, by an Occidental, of fancies and feelings familiar to the most ignorant peasant. Certainly no one will be able to find in these Japanese verses — or, rather, in my own wretchedly prosy translations of them — even a hint of anything like the ghostly delicacy of Rossetti's imagining:

> I have been here before —
> But when or how I cannot tell:
> I know the grass beyond the door,
> The sweet, keen smell,
> The sighing sound, the lights along the shore.
>
> You have been mine before —
> How long ago I may not know:
> But just when at that swallow's soar
> Your neck turned so,
> Some veil did fall — I knew it all of yore.

Yet what a queer *living* difference between such enigmatically delicate handling of thoughts classed as forbidden fruit in the Western Eden of Dreams and the every-day Japanese utterances that spring directly out of ancient Eastern faith!

> Love, it is often said, has nothing to do with reason.
> The cause of ours must be some En in a previous birth.[1]

> Even the knot of the rope tying our boats together
> Knotted was long ago by some love in a former birth.

---

[1] Iro wa shian no
Hoka to-wa iédo,
Koré mo saki-sho no
En de arō.

"En" is a Buddhist word signifying affinity — relation of cause and effect from life to life.

Buddhist Allusions in Japanese Folksong

If the touching even of sleeves be through En of a former existence,
Very much deeper must be the En that unites us now! [1]

Kwahō [2] this life must be — this dwelling with one so tender; — I am reaping now the reward of deeds in a former birth!

Many songs of this class refer to the customary vow which lovers make to belong to each other for more lives than one — a vow perhaps originally inspired by the Buddhist aphorism —

> Oya-ko wa, is-sé;
> Fūfu wa, ni-sé;
> Shujū wa, san-zé.

"The relation of parent and child is for one life; that of wife and husband, for two lives; that of master and servant, for three lives." Although the tender relation is thus limited to the time of two lives, the vow — as Japanese dramas testify, and as the letters of those who kill themselves for love bear witness — is often passionately made for seven. The following selections show a considerable variety of tone —

> [1] Sodé suri-ō no mo
> Tashō no en yo,
> Mashité futari ga
> Fukai naka.

Allusion is here made to the old Buddhist proverb: Sodé no furi-awasé mo tashō no en — "Even the touching of sleeves in passing is caused by some affinity operating from former lives."

[2] The Buddhist word "Kwahō" is commonly used instead of other synonyms for Karma (such as ingwa, innen, etc.), to signify the good, rather than the bad results of action in previous lives. But it is sometimes used in both meanings. Here there seems to be an allusion to the proverbial expression, "Kwahō no yoi hito" (literally, a person of good Kwahō), meaning a fortunate individual.

ranging from the pathetic to the satirical — in the treatment of this topic:

I have cut my hair for his sake; but the deeper relation between us
Cannot be cut in this, nor yet in another life.[1]

She looks at the portrait of him to whom for two lives she is promised:
Happy remembrances come, and each brings a smile to her face.[2]

If in this present life we never can hope for union,
Then we shall first keep house in the Lotus-Palace beyond.[3]

Have we not spoken the vow that binds for a double existence?
If we must separate now, I can only wish to die.

---

[1] Kami wa kitté mo
Ni-sé madé kaketa
Fukai enishi wa
Kiru mono ka?

Literally: "Hair have-cut although, two existences until, deep relation, cut-how-can-it-be?" By the mention of the hair-cutting we know the speaker is a woman. Her husband, or possibly betrothed lover, is dead; and, according to the Buddhist custom, she signifies her desire to remain faithful to his memory by the sacrifice of her hair. For detailed information on this subject see, in my *Glimpses of Unfamiliar Japan*, the chapter, "Of Women's Hair."

[2] Ni-sé to chigirishi
Shashin wo nagamé
Omoi-idashité
Warai-gao.

Literally: "Two existences that made alliance, photograph look-at, thinking bring-out smiling face." The use of the term shashin, photograph, shows that the poem is not old.

[3] Totémo kono yo dé
Sowaré-nu naraba
Hasu no uténa dé
Ara sétai.

Literally: "By-any-means, this-world-in, cannot-live-together if, Lotus-of Palace-in, new-housekeeping." It is with this thought that

Buddhist Allusions in Japanese Folksong

There! — oh, what shall we do? ... Pledged for a double existence, —
And now, as we sit together, the string of the samisen snaps! [1]

He woos by teaching the Law of Cause and Effect for three lives,
And makes a contract for two — the crafty-smiling priest! [2]

Every mortal has lived and is destined to live countless lives; yet the happy moments of any single existence are not therefore less precious in themselves:

Not to have met one night is verily cause for sorrow;
Since twice in a single birth the same night never comes.

But even as a summer unusually warm is apt to herald a winter of exceptional severity, so too much happiness in this life may signify great suffering in the next:

Always I suffer thus! ... Methinks, in my last existence,
Too happy I must have been — did not suffer enough.

Next in point of exotic interest to the songs expressing belief in preëxistence and rebirth, I think I should place those treating of the doctrine of ingwa, or Karma. I offer some free translations from these, together with one selection from a class of compositions more elaborate and usually much longer than the dodoitsu, called hauta. In the original, at least, lovers voluntarily die together; and the song might be called a song of jōshi.

[1] Among singing-girls it is believed that the snapping of a samisen-string under such circumstances as those indicated in the above song is an omen of coming separation.

[2] This song is of a priest who breaks the vow of celibacy.

my selection from the *hauta* — which contains a charming simile about the firefly — is by far the prettiest:

Weep not! — turn to me! . . . Nay, all my suspicions vanish!
Forgive me those words unkind: some *ingwa* controlled my tongue!

Evidently this is the remorseful pleading of a jealous lover. The next might be the answer of the girl whose tears he had caused to flow:

I cannot imagine at all by what strange manner of *ingwa*
Came I to fall in love with one so unkind as you!

Or she might exclaim:

Is this the turning of En? — am I caught in the Wheel of Karma?
That, alas! is a wheel not to be moved from the rut![1]

A more remarkable reference to the Wheel of Karma is the following:

Father and mother forbade, and so I gave up my lover; —
Yet still, with the whirl of the Wheel, the thought of him comes and goes.[2]

---

[1] Meguru en kaya?
Kuruma no watashi
Hiku ni hikarénu
Kono ingwa.

There is a play on words in the original which I have not attempted to render. The idea is of an unhappy match — either betrothal or marriage — from which the woman wishes to withdraw when too late.

[2] Oya no iken dé
Akirameta no wo
Mata mo rin-yé dé
Omoi-dasu.

The Buddhist word Rin-yé, or Rinten, has the meaning of "turning the Wheel" — another expression for passing from birth to birth. The Wheel here is the great Circle of Illusion — the whirl of Karma.

Buddhist Allusions in Japanese Folksong

This is a hauta:

Numberless insects there are that call from dawn to evening,
Crying, "I love! I love!" — but the Firefly's silent passion,
Making its body burn, is deeper than all their longing.
Even such is my love ... yet I cannot think through what ingwa
I opened my heart — alas! — to a being not sincere! [1]

If the foregoing seem productions possible only to our psychological antipodes, it is quite otherwise with a group of folk-songs reflecting the doctrine of Impermanency. Concerning the instability of all material things, and the hollowness of all earthly pleasures, Christian and Buddhist thought are very much in accord. The great difference between them appears only when we compare their teaching as to things ghostly — and especially as to the nature of the Ego. But the Oriental doctrine that the Ego itself is an impermanent compound, and that the Self is not the true Consciousness, rarely finds expression in these popular songs. For the common people the Self exists: it is a real (though multiple)

---

[1] Kaäi, kaäi to
Naku mushi yori mo
Nakanu hotaru ga
Mi wo kogasu.
Nanno ingwa dé
Jitsu naki hito ni
Shin wo akashité —
Aa kuyashi!

Literally: "'I-love-I-love'-saying-cry-insects than, better never-cry-firefly, body scorch! What Karma because-of, sincerity-not-is-man to, inmost-mind opened? — ah! regret!" ... It was formerly believed that the firefly's light really burned its own body.

personality that passes from birth to birth. Only the educated Buddhist comprehends the deeper teaching that what we imagine to be Self is wholly illusion — a darkening veil woven by Karma; and that there is no Self but the Infinite Self, the eternal Absolute. In the following dodoitsu will be found mostly thoughts or emotions according with universal experience:

Gathering clouds to the moon; — storm and rain to the flowers:
Somehow this world of woe never is just as we like.[1]

Almost as soon as they bloom, the scented flowers of the plum-tree
By the wind of this world of change are scattered and blown away.

Thinking to-morrow remains, thou heart's frail flower-of-cherry?
How knowest whether this night the tempest will not come?[2]

---

[1] Tsuki ni murakumo,
Hana ni wa arashi:
Tokaku uki-yo wa
Mama naranu.

This song especially refers to unhappy love, and contains the substance of two Buddhist proverbs: "Tsuki ni murakumo, hana ni kazé" (cloud-masses to the moon; wind to flowers); and "Mama ni naranu wa uki-yo no narai" (to be disappointed is the rule in this miserable world). "Uki-yo" (this fleeting or unhappy world) is one of the commonest Buddhist terms in use.

[2] Asu ari to
Omō kokoro no
Ada-zakura:
Yo wa ni arashi no
Fukanu monokawa?

Literally: "To-morrow-is that think heart-of perishable-cherry flower: this-night-in-storm blow-not, is-it-certain?"

Buddhist Allusions in Japanese Folksong

Shadow and shape alike melt and flow back to nothing:
He who knows this truth is the Daruma of snow.[1]

As the moon of the fifteenth night, the heart till the age fifteen:
Then the brightness wanes, and the darkness comes with love.[2]

All things change, we are told, in this world of change and sorrow;
But love's way never changes of promising never to change.[3]

Cruel the beautiful flash, — utterly heartless that lightning!
Before one can look even twice it vanishes wholly away![4]

---

[1] Kagé mo katachi mo
Kiyuréba moto no
Midzu to satoru zo
Yuki-Daruma.

Literally: "Shadow and shape also, if-melt-away, original-water is — that-understands Snow-Daruma." Daruma (Dharma), the twenty-eighth patriarch of the Zen sect, is said to have lost his legs through remaining long in the posture of meditation; and many legless toy-figures, which are so balanced that they will always assume an upright position however often placed upside-down, are called by his name. The snowmen made by Japanese children have the same traditional form. The Japanese friend who helped me to translate these verses, tells me that a ghostly meaning attaches to the word "Kagé" [shadow] in the above; — this would give a much more profound signification to the whole verse.

[2] According to the old calendar, there was always a full moon on the fifteenth of the month. The Buddhist allusion in the verse is to mayoi, the illusion of passion, which is compared to a darkness concealing the Right Way.

[3] Kawaru uki-yo ni
Kawaranu mono wa
Kawarumai to no
Koi no michi.

Literally: "Change changeable-world-in, does-not-change that-which, 'We-will-never-change'-saying of Love-of Way."

[4] Honni tsurénai
Ano inadzuma wa
Futa mé minu uchi
Kiyété yuku.

The Buddhist saying, "Inadzuma no hikari, ishi no hi" (lightning-flash and flint-spark) — symbolizing the temporary nature of all

His very sweetness itself makes my existence a burden!
Truly this world of change is a world of constant woe! [1]

Neither for youth nor age is fixed the life of the body; —
Bidding me wait for a time is the word that forever divides. [2]

Only too well I know that to meet will cause more weeping; [3]
Yet never to meet at all were sorrow too great to bear.

Too joyful in union to think, we forget that the smiles of the evening
Sometimes themselves become the sources of morning-tears.

Yet, notwithstanding the doctrine of impermanency, we are told in another dodoitsu that —

He who was never bewitched by the charming smile of a woman,
A wooden Buddha is he — a Buddha of bronze or stone! [4]

---

pleasures — is here playfully referred to. The song complains of a too brief meeting with sweetheart or lover.

[1] Words of a loving but jealous woman, thus interpreted by my Japanese friend: "The more kind he is, the more his kindness overwhelms me with anxiety lest he be equally tender to other girls who may also fall in love with him."

[2] Rō-shō fujō no
Mi dé ari nagara,
Jisetsu maté to wa
Kiré-kotoba.

Literally: "Old-young not-fixed-of body being, time-wait to-say, cutting-word." "Ros-hō fujō" is a Buddhist phrase. The meaning of the song is: "Since all things in this world are uncertain, asking me to wait for our marriage-day means that you do not really love me; — for either of us might die before the time you speak of."

[3] Allusion is made to the Buddhist text, "Shōja hitsu metsu, esha jō ri" ("Whosoever is born must die, and all who meet must as surely part"), and to the religious phrase, "Ai betsu ri ku" ("Sorrow of parting and pain of separation").

[4] Much more amusing in the original:

Adana é-gao ni
Mayowanu mono wa
Ki-Butsu — kana-Butsu —
Ishi-botoké!

"Charming-smile-by bewildered-not, he-as-for, wood-Buddha, metal-

Buddhist Allusions in Japanese Folksong

And why a Buddha of wood, or bronze, or stone? Because the living Buddha was not so insensible, as we are assured, with jocose irreverence, in the following:

"Forsake this fitful world"! —
that was { Lord Buddha's *or* upside-down } teaching!
And Ragora,[1] son of his loins? — was he forgotten indeed?

There is an untranslatable pun in the original, which, if written in Romaji, would run thus:

Uki-yo wo sutéyo t'a
Sorya { Shaka Sama / saka-sama } yo:
Ragora to iū ko wo
Wasurété ka?

"Shakamuni" is the Japanese rendering of "Sakyamuni"; "Shaka Sama" is therefore "Lord Sakya," or "Lord Buddha." But "saka-sama" is a Japanese word meaning "topsy-turvy," "upside down"; and the difference between the pronunciation of Shaka Sama and saka-sama is slight enough to have suggested the pun. Love in suspense is not usually inclined to reverence.

Even while praying together in front of the tablets ancestral,
Lovers find chance to murmur prayers never meant for the dead![2]

Buddha, stone-Buddha!" The term "Ishi-botoké" especially refers to the stone images of the Buddha placed in cemeteries. This song is sung in every part of Japan; I have heard it many times in different places.

[1] Râhula.

[2] Ekō suru toté
Hotoké no maé yé
Futari mukaité,
Konabé daté.

Literally: "Repeat prayers saying, dead-of-presence-in twain facing

The Buddhist Writings of Lafcadio Hearn

And as for interrupters:

> Hateful the wind or rain that ruins the bloom of flowers:
> Even more hateful far who obstructs the way of love.

Yet the help of the Gods is earnestly besought:

> I make my hyaku-dō, traveling Love's dark pathway,
> Ever praying to meet the owner of my heart.[1]

The interest attaching to the following typical group of love-songs will be found to depend chiefly upon the Buddhist allusions:

> In the bed of the River of Souls, or in waiting alone at evening,
> The pain differs nothing at all: to a mountain the pebble grows.[2]

— small-pan cooking!" "Hotoké" means a dead person as well as a Buddha. (See my *Glimpses of Unfamiliar Japan*: "The Household Shrine"). "Konabé daté" is an idiomatic expression signifying a lovers' tête-à-tête. It is derived from the phrase, "Chin-chin kamo nabé" ("cooking a wild duck in a pan") — the idea suggested being that of the pleasure experienced by an amorous couple in eating out of the same dish. "Chin-chin," an onomatope, expresses the sound of the gravy boiling.

[1] To perform the rite called "o-hyaku-dō" means to make one hundred visits to a temple, saying a prayer each time. The expression "dark way of Love" ("koi no yami" or "yamiji") is a Buddhist phrase; love, being due to mayoi, or illusion, is a state of spiritual darkness. The term "owner of my heart" is an attempted rendering of the Japanese word "nushi," signifying "master," "owner" — often, also, "landlord" — and, in love-matters, the lord or master of the affection inspired.

[2] Sai-no-kawara to
Nushi matsu yoi wa
Koishi, koishi ga
Yama to naru.

A more literal translation would be: "In the Sai-no-Kawara ('Dry bed of the River of Souls') and in the evening when waiting for the loved one, 'Koishi, Koishi' becomes a mountain." There is a delicate pun here — a play on the word "Koishi," which, as pronounced, though not as written, may mean either "a small stone," or "longing to see." In the bed of the phantom river, Sai-no-Kawa, the ghosts of children

Buddhist Allusions in Japanese Folksong

Who furthest after illusion wanders on Love's dark pathway
Is ever the clearest-seeing,[1] not the simple or dull.

    Coldly seen from without our love looks utter folly:
    Who never has felt mayoi never could understand!

Countless the men must be who dwell in three thousand worlds;
Yet among them all is none worthy to change for mine.[2]

    However fickle I seem, my heart is never unfaithful:
    Out of the slime itself, spotless the lotus grows.[3]

So that we stay together, even the Hell of the Blood Lake —
Even the Mountain of Swords — will signify nothing at all.[4]

---

are obliged to pile up little stones, the weight of which increases so as to tax their strength to the utmost. There is a reference here also to a verse in the Buddhist wasan of Jizō, describing the crying of the children for their parents: "Chichi koishi! haha koishi!" (See *Glimpses of Unfamiliar Japan*, vol. I, pp. 69–71.)

[1] Clearest-sighted — that is, in worldly matters.

[2] San-zen sékai ni
Otoko wa arédo,
Nushi ni mi-kayeru
Hito wa nai.

"San-zen sekai," the three thousand worlds, is a common Buddhist expression. Literally translated, the above song runs: "Three-thousand-worlds-in men are, but lover-to-exchange person is not."

[3] The familiar Buddhist simile is used more significantly here than the Western reader might suppose from the above rendering. These are supposed to be the words either of a professional singing-girl or of a jorō. Her calling is derisively termed a doro-midzu kagyō ("foul-water occupation"); and her citation of the famous Buddhist comparison in self-defense is particularly, and pathetically, happy.

[4] Chi-no-Iké-Jigoku mo,
Tsurugi-no-Yama mo,
Futari-dzuré nara
Itoi 'a sénu.

The Hell of the Blood-Lake is a hell for women; and the Mountain of Swords is usually depicted in Buddhist prints as a place of infernal punishment for men in especial.

The Buddhist Writings of Lafcadio Hearn

Not yet indeed is my body garbed in the ink-black habit; —
But as for this heart bereaved, already it is a nun.[1]

My hair, indeed, is uncut; but my heart has become a religious;
A nun it shall always be till the hour I meet him again.

But even the priest or nun is not always exempt from the power of mayoi:

I am wearing the sable garb — and yet, through illusion of longing,
Ever I lose my way — knowing not whither or where!

So far, my examples have been principally chosen from the more serious class of dodoitsu. But in dodoitsu of a lighter class the Buddhist allusions are perhaps even more frequent. The following group of five will serve for specimens of hundreds:

Never can be recalled the word too quickly spoken:
Therefore with Emma's face the lover receives the prayer.[2]

Thrice did I hear that prayer with Buddha's face; but hereafter
My face shall be Emma's face because of too many prayers.

---

[1] In the original much more pretty and much more simple:

  Sumi no koromo ni
  Mi wa yatsusanedo,
  Kokoro hitotsu wa
   Ama-hōshi.

"Ink-black koromo [priest's or nun's outer robe] in, body not clad, but heart-one nun." Hitotsu, "one," also means "solitary," "forlorn," "bereaved." Ama hōshi, literally, "nun-priest."

[2] The implication is that he has hastily promised more than he wishes to perform. Emma, or Yemma (Sansc. Yama), is the Lord of Hell and Judge of Souls; and, as depicted in Buddhist sculpture and painting, is more than fearful to look upon. There is an evident reference in this song to the Buddhist proverb: "Karu-toki no Jizō-gao; nasutoki no Emma-gao" ("Borrowing-time, the face of Jizō; repaying-time, the face of Emma").

Buddhist Allusions in Japanese Folksong

Now they are merry together; but under their boat is Jigoku.[1]
Blow quickly, thou river-wind — blow a typhoon for my sake!

Vainly, to make him stay, I said that the crows were night crows;[2]
The bell of the dawn peals doom — the bell that cannot lie.

This my desire: To kill the crows of three thousand worlds,
And then to repose in peace with the owner of my heart![3]

I have cited this last only as a curiosity. For it has a strange history, and is not what it seems — although the apparent motive was certainly suggested by some song like the one immediately preceding it. It is a song of loyalty, and was composed by Kido of Chōshū, one of the leaders in that great movement which brought about the downfall of the Shōgunate, the restoration of the Imperial power, the reconstruction of Japanese society, and the introduction and adoption of Western civilization. Kido, Saigō, and

---

[1] "Jigoku" is the Buddhist name for various hells (Sansc. narakas). The allusion here is to the proverb, "Funa-ita ichi-mai shita wa Jigoku": "Under [the thickness of] a single boat-plank is hell" — referring to the perils of the sea. This song is a satire on jealousy; and the boat spoken of is probably a roofed pleasure-boat, such as excursions are made into the sound of music.

[2] Tsuki-yo-garasu, literally, "moon-night crows." Crows usually announce the dawn by their cawing; but sometimes on moonlight nights they caw at all hours from sunset to sunrise. The bell referred to is the bell of some Buddhist temple: the aké-no-kane, or "dawn-bell," being, in all parts of Japan, sounded from every Buddhist tera. There is a pun in the original; — the expression "tsukenai," "cannot *tell* [a lie]," might also be interpreted phonetically as "cannot *strike* [a bell]."

[3] San-zen sékai no
Karasu wo koroshi
Nushi to soi-né ga
Shité mitai!

The Buddhist Writings of Lafcadio Hearn

Ōkubo are rightly termed the three heroes of the restoration. While preparing his plans at Kyōto, in company with his friend Saigō, Kido composed and sang this song as an intimation of his real sentiments. By the phrase, "ravens of the three thousand worlds," he designated the Tokugawa partisans; by the word "nushi" (lord, or heart's-master) he signified the Emperor; and by the term "soiné" (reposing together) he referred to the hoped-for condition of direct responsibility to the Throne, without further intervention of Shōgun and daimyō. It was not the first example in Japanese history of the use of popular song as a medium for the utterance of opinions which, expressed in plainer language, would have invited assassination.

While I was writing the preceding note upon Kido's song, the Buddhist phrase, "Sanzen sékai" (twice occurring, as the reader will have observed, in the present collection), suggested a few reflections with which this paper may fitly conclude. I remember that when I first attempted, years ago, to learn the outlines of Buddhist philosophy, one fact which particularly impressed me was the vastness of the Buddhist concept of the universe. Buddhism, as I read it, had not offered itself to humanity as a saving creed for one inhabited world, but as the religion of "innumerable hundreds of thousands of myriads of kôtis [1] of worlds." And the modern scientific rev-

---
[1] 1 kôti = 10,000,000.

elation of stellar evolution and dissolution then seemed to me, and still seems, like a prodigious confirmation of certain Buddhist theories of cosmical law.

The man of science to-day cannot ignore the enormous suggestions of the new story that the heavens are telling. He finds himself compelled to regard the development of what we call mind as a general phase or incident in the ripening of planetary life throughout the universe. He is obliged to consider the relation of our own petty sphere to the great swarming of suns and systems as no more than the relation of a single noctiluca to the phosphorescence of a sea. By its creed the Oriental intellect has been better prepared than the Occidental to accept this tremendous revelation, not as a wisdom that increaseth sorrow, but as a wisdom to quicken faith. And I cannot but think that out of the certain future union of Western knowledge with Eastern thought there must eventually proceed a Neo-Buddhism inheriting all the strength of Science, yet spiritually able to recompense the seeker after truth with the recompense foretold in the twelfth chapter of the Sutra of the Diamond-Cutter. Taking the text as it stands — in despite of commentators — what more could be unselfishly desired from any spiritual teaching than the reward promised in that verse — "They shall be endowed with the Highest Wonder"?

Nirvana

I

It is not possible, O Subhûti, that this treatise of the Law should be heard by beings of little faith — by those who believe in Self, in beings, in living beings, and in persons.   *The Diamond-Cutter*

THERE still widely prevails in Europe and America the idea that Nirvana signifies, to Buddhist minds, neither more nor less than absolute nothingness — complete annihilation. This idea is erroneous. But it is erroneous only because it contains half of a truth. This half of a truth has no value or interest, or even intelligibility, unless joined with the other half. And of the other half no suspicion yet exists in the average Western mind.

Nirvana, indeed, signifies an extinction. But if by this extinction of individual being we understand soul-death, our conception of Nirvana is wrong. Or if we take Nirvana to mean such reabsorption of the finite into the infinite as that predicted by Indian pantheism, again our idea is foreign to Buddhism.

Nevertheless, if we declare that Nirvana means the extinction of individual sensation, emotion, thought — the final disintegration of conscious personality — the annihilation of everything that can be included under the term "I" — then we rightly express one side of the Buddhist teaching.

Nirvana

The apparent contradiction of the foregoing statements is due only to our Occidental notion of Self. Self to us signifies feelings, ideas, memory, volition; and it can scarcely occur to any person not familiar with German idealism even to imagine that consciousness might not be Self. The Buddhist, on the contrary, declares all that we call Self to be false. He defines the Ego as a mere temporary aggregate of sensations, impulses, ideas, created by the physical and mental experiences of the race — all related to the perishable body, and all doomed to dissolve with it. What to Western reasoning seems the most indubitable of realities, Buddhist reasoning pronounces the greatest of all illusions, and even the source of all sorrow and sin.

The mind, the thoughts, and all the senses are subject to the law of life and death. With knowledge of Self and the laws of birth and death, there is no grasping, and no sense-perception. Knowing one's self and knowing how the senses act, there is no room for the idea of "I," or the ground for framing it. The thought of "Self" gives rise to all sorrows — binding the world as with fetters; but having found there is no "I" that can be bound, then all these bonds are severed.[1]

The above text suggests very plainly that the consciousness is not the Real Self, and that the mind dies with the body. Any reader unfamiliar with Buddhist thought may well ask, "What, then, is the meaning of the doctrine of Karma, the doctrine of moral progression, the doctrine of the consequence

[1] *Fo-Sho-Hing-Tsan-King.*

of acts?" Indeed, to try to study, only with the ontological ideas of the West, even such translations of the Buddhist Sutras as those given in the "Sacred Books of the East," is to be at every page confronted by seemingly hopeless riddles and contradictions. We find a doctrine of rebirth; but the existence of a soul is denied. We are told that the misfortunes of this life are punishments of faults committed in a previous life; yet personal transmigration does not take place. We find the statement that beings are reindividualized; yet both individuality and personality are called illusions. I doubt whether anybody not acquainted with the deeper forms of Buddhist belief could possibly understand the following extracts which I have made from the first volume of "The Questions of King Milinda":

The King said: "Nagasena, is there any one who after death is not reindividualized?" Nagasena answered: "A sinful being is reindividualized; a sinless one is not" (p. 50).

"Is there, Nagasena, such a thing as the soul?" "There is no such thing as soul" (pp. 86-89). [The same statement is repeated in a later chapter (p. 111), with a qualification: "*In the highest sense*, O King, there is no such thing."]

"Is there any being, Nagasena, who transmigrates from this body to another?" "No: there is not" (p. 112).

"Where there is no transmigration, Nagasena, can there be rebirth?" "Yes: there can."

"Does he, Nagasena, who is about to be reborn, know that he will be reborn?" "Yes: he knows it, O King" (p. 113).

Nirvana

Naturally the Western reader may ask — "How can there be reindividualization without a soul? How can there be rebirth without transmigration? How can there be personal foreknowledge of rebirth without personality?" But the answers to such questions will not be found in the work cited.

It would be wrong to suppose that the citations given offer any exceptional difficulty. As to the doctrine of the annihilation of Self, the testimony of nearly all those Buddhist texts now accessible to English readers is overwhelming. Perhaps the Sutra of the Great Decease furnishes the most remarkable evidence contained in the "Sacred Books of the East." In its account of the Eight Stages of Deliverance leading to Nirvana, it explicitly describes what we should be justified in calling, from our Western point of view, the process of absolute annihilation. We are told that in the first of these eight stages the Buddhist seeker after truth still retains the ideas of form — subjective and objective. In the second stage he loses the subjective idea of form, and views forms as external phenomena only. In the third stage the sense of the approaching perception of larger truth comes to him. In the fourth stage he passes beyond all ideas of form, ideas of resistance, and ideas of distinction; and there remains to him only the idea of infinite space. In the fifth stage the idea of infinite space vanishes, and the thought comes: *It is all infinite reason.* [Here is the uttermost limit, many might suppose, of pantheistic idealism; but it is only the half way resting-place on the path which the Buddhist thinker must pursue.] In the sixth stage the thought comes, "*Nothing at all exists.*" In the seventh stage the idea of nothingness itself vanishes. In the eighth stage all sensations and ideas cease to exist. And *after* this comes Nirvana.

The same sutra, in recounting the death of the Buddha, represents him as rapidly passing through the first, second, third, and fourth stages of meditation to enter into "that state of mind to which the Infinity of Space alone is present" and thence into "that state of mind to which the Infinity of Thought alone is present"; and thence into "that state of mind to which nothing at all is specially present"; and thence into "that state of mind between consciousness and unconsciousness"; and thence into "that state of mind in which the consciousness both of sensations and of ideas has wholly passed away."

For the reader who has made any serious attempt to obtain a general idea of Buddhism, such citations are scarcely necessary; since the fundamental doctrine of the concatenation of cause and effect contains the same denial of the reality of Self and suggests the same enigmas. Illusion produces action or Karma; Karma, self-consciousness; self-consciousness, individuality; individuality, the senses; the senses, contact; contact, feeling; feeling, desire; desire, union; union, conception; conception, birth; birth, sorrow and decrepitude and death. Doubtless the reader knows the doctrine of the destruction of the twelve Nidanas; and it is needless here to repeat it at length. But he may be reminded of the teaching that by the cessation of contact feeling is destroyed; by that of feeling, individuality; and by that of individuality, *self-consciousness.*

Evidently, without a preliminary solution of the riddles offered by such texts, any effort to learn the meaning of Nirvana is hopeless. Before being able to comprehend the true meaning of those sutras now made familiar to English readers by translation, it is necessary to understand that the common Occidental ideas of God and Soul, of matter, of spirit, have no existence in Buddhist philosophy; their places being occupied by concepts having no real counterparts in Western religious thought. Above all, it is necessary that the reader should expel from his mind the theological idea of Soul. The texts already quoted should have made it clear that in Buddhist philosophy there is no personal transmigration, and no individual permanent Soul.

II

O Bhagavat, the idea of a self is no idea; and the idea of a being, or a living person, or a person, is no idea. And why? Because the blessed Buddhas are freed from all ideas. *The Diamond-Cutter*

AND now let us try to understand what it is that dies, and what it is that is reborn; what it is that commits faults and what it is that suffers penalties; what passes from states of woe to states of bliss;

what enters into Nirvana after the destruction of self-consciousness; what survives "extinction" and has power to return out of Nirvana; what experiences the Four Infinite Feelings after all finite feeling has been annihilated.

It is not the sentient and conscious Self that enters Nirvana. The Ego is only a temporary aggregate of countless illusions, a phantom-shell, a bubble sure to break. It is a creation of Karma — or rather, as a Buddhist friend insists, it *is* Karma. To comprehend the statement fully, the reader should know that, in this Oriental philosophy, acts and thoughts are forces of integrating themselves into material and mental phenomena — into what we call objective and subjective appearances. The very earth we tread upon — the mountains and forests, the rivers and seas, the world and its moon, the visible universe in short — *is the integration of acts and thoughts*, is Karma, or, at least, Being conditioned by Karma.[1]

---

[1] "The aggregate actions of all sentient beings give birth to the varieties of mountains, rivers, countries, etc. . . . Their eyes, nostrils, ears, tongues, bodies — as well as their gardens, woods, farms, residences, servants, and maids — men imagine to be their own possessions; but they are, in truth, only results produced by innumerable actions." (KURODA, *Outlines of the Mahayana*.)

"Grass, trees, earth — all these shall become Buddha." (CHŪ-IN-KYŌ.)

"Even swords and things of metal are manifestations of spirit: within them exist all virtues [*or* "power"] in their fullest development and perfection." (HIZŌ-HŌ-YAKU.)

"When called sentient or non-sentient, matter is Law-Body [*or* "spiritual body"]." (CHISHŌ-HISHŌ.)

Nirvana

The Karma-Ego we call Self is mind and is body; — both perpetually decay; both are perpetually renewed. From the unknown beginning, this double phenomenon, objective and subjective, has been alternately dissolved and integrated: each integration is a birth; each dissolution a death. There is no other birth or death but the birth and death of Karma in some form or condition. But at each rebirth the reintegration is never the reintegration of the identical phenomenon, but of another to which it gives rise — as growth begets growth, as motion produces motion. So that the phantom-self changes not only as to form and condition, but as to actual personality with every reëmbodiment. There is one Reality; but there is no permanent individual, no constant personality: there is only phantom-self, and phantom succeeds to phantom, as undulation to undulation, over the ghostly Sea of Birth and Death. And even as the storming of a sea is a motion of undulation, not of translation — even as it is the form of the wave only, not the wave itself, that travels — so in the passing of lives there is only the rising and the vanishing of forms — forms mental, forms material. The fathomless Reality does not

---

"The Apparent Doctrine treats of the four great elements [earth, fire, water, air] as non-sentient. But in the Hidden Doctrine these are said to be the Sammya-Shin [Samya-Kaya], or Body-Accordant of the Nyōrai [Tathâgata]." (SOKU-SHIN-JŌ-BUTSU-GI.)

"When every phase of our mind shall be in accord with the mind of Buddha, ... then there will not be even one particle of dust that does not enter into Buddhahood." (ENGAKU-SHŌ.)

pass. "All forms," it is written in the "Kongō-hannya-haramitsu-Kyō," [1] "are unreal: he who rises above all forms is the Buddha." But what can remain to rise above all forms after the total disintegration of body and the final dissolution of mind?

Unconsciously dwelling behind the false consciousness of imperfect man — beyond sensation, perception, thought — wrapped in the envelope of what we call soul (which in truth is only a thickly woven veil of illusion), is the eternal and divine, the Absolute Reality: not a soul, not a personality, but the All-Self without selfishness — the Muga no Taiga — the Buddha enwombed in Karma. Within every phantom-self dwells this divine: yet the innumerable are but one. Within every creature incarnate sleeps the Infinite Intelligence unevolved, hidden, unfelt, unknown — yet destined from all the eternities to waken at last, to rend away the ghostly web of sensuous mind, to break forever its chrysalis of flesh, and pass to the supreme conquest of Space and Time. Wherefore it is written in the "Kegon-Kyō" ("Avatamsaka-Sutra"):

Child of Buddha, there is not even one living being that has not the wisdom of the Tathâgata. It is only because of their vain thoughts and affections that all beings are not conscious of this.... I will teach them the holy Way; — I will make them forsake their foolish thoughts, and cause them to see that the vast and deep intelligence which dwells within them is not different from the wisdom of the very Buddha.

[1] *Vagra-pragñâ pâramita-Sutra.*

Nirvana

Here we may pause to consider the correspondence between these fundamental Buddhist theories and the concepts of Western science. It will be evident that the Buddhist denial of the reality of the apparitional world is not a denial of the reality of phenomena as phenomena, nor a denial of the forces producing phenomena objectively or subjectively. For the negation of Karma as Karma would involve the negation of the entire Buddhist system. The true declaration is, that what we perceive is never reality in itself, and that even the Ego that perceives is an unstable plexus of aggregates of feelings which are themselves unstable and in the nature of illusions. This position is scientifically strong — perhaps impregnable. Of substance in itself we certainly know nothing: we are conscious of the universe as a vast play of forces only; and, even while we discern the general relative meaning of laws expressed in the action of those forces, all that which is Non-Ego is revealed to us merely through the vibrations of a nervous structure never exactly the same in any two human beings. Yet through such varying and imperfect perception we are sufficiently assured of the impermanency of all forms — of all aggregates objective or subjective.

The test of reality is persistence; and the Buddhist, finding in the visible universe only a perpetual flux of phenomena, declares the material aggregate unreal because non-persistent — unreal, at least, as a bubble, a cloud, or a mirage. Again, relation is the universal form of thought; but since relation is impermanent, how can thought be persistent?... Judged from these points of view, Buddhist doctrine is not Anti-Realism, but a veritable Transfigured Realism, finding just expression in the exact words of Herbert Spencer:

> Every feeling and thought being but transitory; — an entire life made up of such feelings and thoughts being also but transitory; — nay, the objects amid which life is passed, though less transitory, being severally in the course of losing their individualities, whether quickly or slowly — *we learn that the one thing permanent is the Unknowable Reality hidden under all these changing shapes.*

Likewise, the teaching of Buddhism, that what we call Self is an impermanent aggregate — a sensuous illusion — will prove, if patiently analyzed, scarcely possible for any serious thinker to deny. Mind, as known to the scientific psychologist, is composed of feelings and the relations between feelings; and feelings are composed of units of simple sensation which are physiologically coincident with minute nervous shocks. All the sense-organs are fundamentally alike, being evolutional modifications of the same morphological elements; — and all the senses are modifications of touch. Or, to use the simplest possible language, the organs of sense — sight, smell, taste, even hearing — have been alike developed from the skin! Even the human brain itself, by the modern testimony of histology and embryology, "is, at its first beginning, merely an infolding of the epidermic layer"; and thought, physiologically and evolutionally, is thus a modification of touch. Certain vibrations, acting through the visual apparatus, cause within the brain those motions which are followed by the sensations of light and color; — other vibrations, acting upon the auditory mechanism, give rise to the sensation of sound; — other vibrations, setting up changes in specialized tissue, produce sensations of taste, smell, touch. All our knowledge is derived and developed, directly or indirectly, from physical sensation — from touch. Of course this is no ultimate explanation, because nobody can tell us *what feels the touch*. "Everything physical," well said Schopenhauer, "is at the same time metaphysical." But science fully justifies the Buddhist position that what we call Self is a bundle of sensations, emotions, sentiments, ideas, memories, all relating to the *physical* experiences of the race and the individual, and that our wish for immortality is a wish for the eternity of this merely sensuous and selfish consciousness. And science even supports the Buddhist denial of the permanence of the sensuous Ego. "Psychology," says Wundt, "proves that not only our sense-perceptions, but the memorial images that renew them, depend for their origin upon the functionings of the organs of sense and movement.... A continuance of this sensuous consciousness must appear to her irreconcilable with the facts of her experience. And surely we may well doubt whether such continuance is an ethical requisite: more, whether the fulfillment of the wish for it, if possible, were not an intolerable destiny."

III

O Subhûti, if I had had an idea of a being, of a living being, or of a person, I should also have had an idea of malevolence. . . . A gift should not be given by any one who believes in form, sound, smell, taste, or anything that can be touched.

The Diamond-Cutter

THE doctrine of the impermanency of the conscious Ego is not only the most remarkable in Buddhist philosophy: it is also, morally, one of the most important. Perhaps the ethical value of this teaching has never yet been fairly estimated by any Western thinker. How much of human unhappiness has been caused, directly and indirectly, by opposite beliefs — by the delusion of stability — by the delusion that distinctions of character, condition, class, creed, are settled by immutable law — and the delusion of a changeless, immortal, sentient soul, destined, by divine caprice, to eternities of bliss or eternities of fire! Doubtless the ideas of a deity moved by everlasting hate — of soul as a permanent, changeless entity destined to changeless states — of sin as unatonable and of penalty as never-ending — were not without value in former savage stages of social development. But in the course of our future evolution they must be utterly got rid of; and it may be hoped that the contact of Western with Oriental thought will have for one happy result the acceleration of their decay. While even the feelings which they have developed linger with us, there can be no true spirit of tolerance, no sense of human brotherhood, no wakening of universal love.

Buddhism, on the other hand, recognizing no permanency, no finite stabilities, no distinctions of character or class or race, except as passing phenomena — nay, no difference even between gods and men — has been essentially the religion of tolerance. Demon and angel are but varying manifestations of the same Karma; — hell and heaven mere temporary halting-places upon the journey to eternal peace. For all beings there is but one law — immutable and divine: the law by which the lowest *must* rise to the place of the highest — the law by which the worst *must* become the best — the law by which the vilest *must* become a Buddha. In such a system there is no room for prejudice and for hatred. Ignorance alone is the source of wrong and pain; and all ignorance must finally be dissipated in infinite light *through the decomposition of Self.*

Certainly while we still try to cling to the old theories of permanent personality, and of a single incarnation only for each individual, we can find no moral meaning in the universe as it exists. Modern knowledge can discover no justice in the cosmic process; — the very most it can offer us by way of ethical encouragement is that the unknowable forces are not forces of pure malevolence. "Neither moral nor immoral," to quote Huxley, "but simply unmoral." Evolutional science cannot be made to accord with the notion of indissoluble personality; and if we accept its teaching of mental growth and inheritance, we must also accept its teaching of individual dissolution and of the cosmos as inexplicable. It assures us, indeed, that the higher faculties of man have been developed through struggle and pain, and will long continue to be so developed; but it also assures us that evolution is inevitably followed by dissolution — that the highest point of development is the point likewise from which retrogression begins. And if we are each and all mere perishable forms of being — doomed to pass away like plants and trees — what consolation can we find in the assurance that we are suffering for the benefit of the future? How can it concern us whether humanity become more or less happy in another myriad ages, if there remains nothing for us but to live and die in comparative misery? Or, to repeat the irony of Huxley, "what compensation does the Eohippus get for his sorrows in the fact that, some millions of years afterwards, one of his descendants wins the Derby?"

But the cosmic process may assume quite another aspect if we can persuade ourselves, like the Buddhist, that all being is Unity; that personality is but a delusion hiding reality; that all distinctions of "I" and "thou" are ghostly films spun out of perishable sensation; that even Time and Place as revealed to our petty senses are phantasms; that the past and the present and the future are veritably One. Suppose the winner of the Derby quite well able to remember having been the Eohippus? Suppose the being, once man, able to look back through all veils of death and birth, through all evolutions of evolution, even to the moment of the first faint growth of sentiency out of non-sentiency; — able to remember, like the Buddha of the Jatakas, all the experiences of his myriad incarnations, and to relate them like fairy-tales for the sake of another Ananda?

We have seen that it is not the Self but the Non-Self — the one reality underlying all phenomena — which passes from form to form. The striving for Nirvana is a struggle perpetual between false and true, light and darkness, the sensual and the supersensual; and the ultimate victory can be gained only by the total decomposition of the mental and the physical individuality. Not one conquest of self can suffice: millions of selves must be overcome. For the false Ego is a compound of countless ages — possesses a vitality enduring beyond universes. At each breaking and shedding of the chrysalis a new chrysalis appears — more tenuous, perhaps more diaphanous, but woven of like sensuous material — a mental and physical texture spun by Karma from the inherited illusions, passions, desires, pains and pleasures, of innumerable lives. But what is it that feels? — the phantom or the reality?

All phenomena of *Self*-consciousness belong to the false self — but only as a physiologist might say that sensation is a product of the sensiferous apparatus, which would not explain sensation. No more in Buddhism than in physiological psychology is there any real teaching of *two* feeling entities. In Buddhism the only entity is the Absolute; and to that entity the false self stands in the relation of a medium through which right perception is deflected and distorted — in which and because of which sentiency and impulse become possible. The unconditioned Absolute is above all relations: it has nothing of what we call pain or pleasure; it knows no difference of "I" and "thou" — no distinction of place or time. But while conditioned by the illusion of personality, it is aware of pain or pleasure, as a dreamer perceives unrealities without being conscious of their unreality. Pleasures and pains and all the feelings relating to self-consciousness are hallucinations. The false self exists only as a state of sleep exists; and sentiency and desire, and all the sorrows and passions of being, exist only as illusions of that sleep.

But here we reach a point at which science and Buddhism diverge. Modern psychology recognizes no feelings not evolutionally developed through the experiences of the race and the individual; but Buddhism asserts the existence of feelings which are immortal and divine. It declares that in this Karma-state the greater part of our sensations, perceptions, ideas, thoughts, are related only to the phantom self; — that our mental life is little more than a flow of feelings and desires belonging to selfishness; — that our loves and hates, and hopes and fears, and pleasures and pains, are illusions;[1] — but it also declares there are higher feelings, more or less latent within us, according to our degree of knowledge, which have nothing to do with the false self, and which are eternal.

Though science pronounces the ultimate nature of pleasures and pains to be inscrutable, it partly confirms the Buddhist teaching of their impermanent character. Both appear to belong rather to secondary than to primary elements of feeling, and both to be evolutions — forms of sensation developed, through billions of life-experiences, out of primal conditions in which there can have been neither real pleasure nor real pain, but only the vaguest dull sentiency. The higher the evolution the more pain, and the larger the volume of all sensation. After the state of equilibration has been reached, the volume of feeling will begin to diminish. The finer pleasures and the keener pains must first become extinct; then by gradual stages the less complex feelings, according to their complexity; till at last, in all the refrigerating planet, there will survive not even the simplest sensation possible to the lowest form of life.

But, according to the Buddhist, the highest moral feelings survive races and suns and universes. The

---

[1] "Pleasures and pains have their origin from touch; where there is no touch, they do not arise." (*Atthakavagga*, 11.)

purely unselfish feelings, impossible to grosser natures, belong to the Absolute. In generous natures the divine becomes sentient — quickens within the shell of illusion, as a child quickens in the womb (whence illusion itself is called The Womb of the Tathâgata). In yet higher natures the feelings which are not of self find room for powerful manifestation — shine through the phantom-Ego as light through a vase. Such are purely unselfish love, larger than individual being — supreme compassion — perfect benevolence: they are not of man, but of the Buddha within the man. And as these expand, all the feelings of self begin to thin and weaken. The condition of the phantom-Ego simultaneously purifies: all those opacities which darkened the reality of Mind within the mirage of mind begin to illumine; and the sense of the infinite, like a thrilling of light, passes through the dream of personality into the awakening divine.[1]

But in the case of the average seeker after truth, this refinement and ultimate decomposition of self can be effected only with lentor inexpressible. The phantom-individuality, though enduring only for the space of a single lifetime, shapes out of the sum of its innate qualities, and out of the sum of its own

---

[1] "To reach the state of the perfect and everlasting happiness is the highest Nirvana; for then all mental phenomena — such as desires, etc. — are annihilated. And as such mental phenomena are annihilated, there appears the true nature of true mind with all its innumerable functions and miraculous actions." (KURODA, *Outlines of the Mahâyâna*.)

Nirvana

particular acts and thoughts, the new combination which succeeds it — a fresh individuality — another prison of illusion for the Self-without-selfishness.[1] As name and form, the false self dissolves; but its impulses live on and recombine; and the final destruction of those impulses — the total extinction of their ghostly vitality — may require a protraction of effort through billions of centuries. Perpetually from the ashes of burnt-out passions subtler passions are born — perpetually from the graves of illusions new illusions arise. The most powerful of human passions is the last to yield: it persists far into superhuman conditions. Even when its grosser forms have passed away, its tendencies still lurk in those feelings originally derived from it or interwoven with it — the sensation of beauty, for example, and the delight of the mind in graceful things. On earth these are classed among the higher feelings. But in a supramundane state their indulgence is fraught with peril: a touch or a look may cause the broken fetters of sensual bondage to reform. Beyond all worlds of sex there are strange zones in which thoughts and memories become tangible and visible objective facts — in which emotional fancies are materialized — in which the least unworthy wish may prove creative.

It may be said, in Western religious phraseology,

[1] It is on the subject of this propagation and perpetuation of characters that the doctrine of Karma is in partial agreement with the modern scientific teaching of the hereditary transmission of tendencies.

that throughout the greater part of this vast pilgrimage, and in all the zones of desire, the temptations increase according to the spiritual strength of resistance. With every successive ascent there is a further expansion of the possibilities of enjoyment, an augmentation of power, a heightening of sensation. Immense the reward of self-conquest; but whosoever strives for that reward strives after emptiness. One must not desire heaven as a state of pleasure; it has been written, "Erroneous thoughts as to the joys of heaven are still entwined by the fast cords of lust." One must not wish to become a god or an angel. "Whatsoever brother, O Bhikkus" — the teacher said — "may have adopted the religious life thinking, to himself, 'By this morality I shall become an angel,' his mind does not incline to zeal, perseverance, exertion." Perhaps the most vivid exposition of the duty of the winner of happiness is that given in the Sutra of the Great King of Glory. This great king, coming into possession of all imaginable wealth and power, abstains from enjoyments, despises splendors, refuses the caresses of a queen dowered with "the beauty of the gods," and bids her demand of him, out of her own lips, that he forsake her. She, with dutiful sweetness, but not without natural tears, obeys him; and he passes at once out of existence. Every such refusal of the prizes gained by virtue helps to cause a still more fortunate birth in a still loftier state of being. But no state should be desired; and it is only after the wish for Nirvana itself has ceased that Nirvana can be attained.

And now we may venture for a little while into the most fantastic region of Buddhist ontology — since, without some definite notion of the course of psychical evolution therein described, the suggestive worth of the system cannot be fairly judged. Certainly I am asking the reader to consider a theory about what is beyond the uttermost limit of possible human knowledge. But as much of the Buddhist doctrine as can be studied and tested within the limit of human knowledge is found to accord with scientific opinion better than does any other religious hypothesis; and some of the Buddhist teachings prove to be incomprehensible anticipations of modern scientific discovery — can it, therefore, seem unreasonable to claim that even the pure fancies of a faith so much older than our own, and so much more capable of being reconciled with the widest expansions of nineteenth-century thought, deserve at least respectful consideration?

IV

Non existence is only the entrance to the Great Vehicle.
Daibon-Kyōi
And in which way is it, Siha, that one speaking truly could say of me: "The Samana Gotama maintains annihilation; — he teaches the doctrine of annihilation"? I proclaim, Siha, the annihilation of lust, of illwill, of delusion; I proclaim the annihilation of the manifold conditions (of heart) which are evil and not good. *Mahavagga*, VI, 31. 7

"NIN mité, hō toké" (see first the person, then preach

the law) is a Japanese proverb signifying that Buddhism should be taught according to the capacity of the pupil. And the great systems of Buddhist doctrine are actually divided into progressive stages (five usually), to be studied in succession, or otherwise, according to the intellectual ability of the learner. Also there are many varieties of special doctrine held by the different sects and sub-sects — so that, to make any satisfactory outline of Buddhist ontology, it is necessary to shape a synthesis of the more important and non-conflicting among these many tenets. I need scarcely say that popular Buddhism does not include concepts such as we have been examining. The people hold to the simpler creed of a veritable transmigration of souls. The people understand Karma only as the law that makes the punishment or reward of faults committed in previous lives. The people do not trouble themselves about Nehan or Nirvana;[1] but they think much about heaven (Gokuraku), which the members of many sects believe can be attained immediately after this life by the spirits of the good. The followers of the greatest and richest of the modern sects — the Shinshū — hold that, by the invocation of Amida, a righteous person can pass at once after

[1] Scarcely a day passes that I do not hear such words uttered as ingwa, gokuraku, gōshō — or other words referring to Karma, heaven, future life, past life, etc. But I have never heard a man or woman of the people use the word "Nehan"; and whenever I have ventured to question such about Nirvana, I found that its philosophical meaning was unknown. On the other hand, the Japanese scholar speaks of Nehan as the reality — of heaven, either as a temporary condition or as a parable.

death to the great Paradise of the West — the Paradise of the Lotus-Flower-Birth. I am taking no account of popular beliefs in this little study, nor of doctrines peculiar to any one sect only.

But there are many differences in the higher teaching as to the attainment of Nirvana. Some authorities hold that the supreme happiness can be won, or at least seen, even on this earth; while others declare that the present world is too corrupt to allow of a perfect life, and that only by winning, through good deeds, the privilege of rebirth into a better world, can men hope for opportunity to practice that holiness which leads to the highest bliss. The latter opinion, which posits the superior conditions of being in other worlds, better expresses the general thought of contemporary Buddhism in Japan.

The conditions of human and of animal being belong to what are termed the Worlds of Desire (Yoku-Kai) — which are four in number. Below these are the states of torment or hells (Jigoku), about which many curious things are written; but neither the Yoku-Kai nor the Jigoku need be considered in relation to the purpose of this little essay. We have only to do with the course of spiritual progress from the world of men up to Nirvana — assuming, with modern Buddhism, that the pilgrimage through death and birth must continue, for the majority of mankind at least, even after the attainment of the highest conditions possible upon this globe. The way rises from terrestrial conditions to other and superior worlds — passing first through the Six Heavens of Desire (Yoku-Ten); — thence through the Seventeen Heavens of Form (Shiki-Kai); — and lastly through the Four Heavens of Formlessness (Mushiki-Kai), beyond which lies Nirvana.

The requirements of physical life — the need of food, rest, and sexual relations — continue to be felt in the Heavens of Desire — which would seem to be higher physical worlds rather than what we commonly understand by the expression "heavens." Indeed, the conditions in some of them are such as might be supposed to exist in planets more favored than our own — in larger spheres warmed by a more genial sun. And some Buddhist texts actually place them in remote constellations — declaring that the Path leads from star to star, from galaxy to galaxy, from universe to universe, up to the Limit of Existence.[1]

In the first of the heavens of this zone, called the Heaven of the Four Kings (Shi-Tennō-Ten), life lasts five times longer than life on this earth according to number of years, and each year there is equal to fifty terrestrial years. But its inhabitants eat and drink, and marry and give in marriage, much after the fashion of mankind. In the succeeding heaven

[1] This astronomical localization of higher conditions of being, or of other "Buddha-fields," may provoke a smile; but it suggests undeniable possibilities. There is no absurdity in supposing that potentialities of life and growth and development really pass, with nebular diffusion and concentration, from expired systems to new systems. Indeed, not to suppose this, in our present state of knowledge, is scarcely possible for the rational mind.

Nirvana

(Sanjiu-san-Ten), the duration of life is doubled, while all other conditions are correspondingly improved; and the grosser forms of passion disappear. The union of the sexes persists, but in a manner curiously similar to that which a certain Father of the Christian Church wished might become possible — a simple embrace producing a new being. In the third heaven (called Emma-Ten), where longevity is again doubled, the slightest touch may create life. In the fourth, or Heaven of Contentment (Tochita-Ten), longevity is further increased. In the fifth, or Heaven of the Transmutation of Pleasure (Keraku-Ten), strange new powers are gained. Subjective pleasures become changed at will into objective pleasures; — thoughts as well as wishes become creative forces; — and even the act of seeing may cause conception and birth. In the sixth heaven (Také-jizai-Ten), the powers obtained in the fifth heaven are further developed; and the subjective pleasures transmuted into objective can be presented to others, or shared with others — like material gifts. But the look of an instant — one glance of the eye — may generate a new Karma.

The Yoku-Kai are all heavens of sensuous life — heavens such as might answer to the dreams of artists and lovers and poets. But those who are able to traverse them without falling (and a fall, be it observed, is not difficult) pass into the Supersensual Zone, first entering the Heavens of Luminous Observation of Existence and of Calm Meditation upon

Existence (Ujin-ushi-shōryo, or Kakkwan). These are in number three — each higher than the preceding — and are named The Heaven of Sanctity, The Heaven of Higher Sanctity, and The Heaven of Great Sanctity. After these come the heavens called the Heavens of Luminous Observation of Non-Existence and of Calm Meditation upon Non-Existence (Mūjin-mushi-shōryo). These also are three; and the names of them in their order signify, Lesser Light, Light Unfathomable, and Light Making Sound, or, Light-Sonorous. Here there is attained the highest degree of supersensuous joy possible to temporary conditions. Above are the states named Riki-shōryo, or the Heavens of the Meditation of the Abandonment of Joy. The names of these states in their ascending order are, Lesser Purity, Purity Unfathomable, and Purity Supreme. In them neither joy nor pain, nor forceful feeling of any sort exist: there is a mild negative pleasure only — the pleasure of heavenly Equanimity.[1] Higher than these heavens are the eight spheres of Calm Meditation upon the Abandonment of all Joy and Pleasure (Riki-raku-shōryo). They are called The Cloudless, Holiness-Manifest, Vast Results, Empty of Name, Void of Heat, Fair-Appearing, Vision-Per-

---

[1] One is reminded by this conception of Mr. Spencer's beautiful definition of Equanimity: "Equanimity may be compared to white light, which, though composed of numerous colors, is colorless; while pleasurable and painful moods of mind may be compared to the modifications of light that result from increasing the proportions of some rays, and decreasing the proportions of others." (*Principles of Psychology*.)

Nirvana

fecting, and The Limit of Form. Herein pleasure and pain, and name and form, pass utterly away. But there remain ideas and thoughts.

He who can pass through these supersensual realms enters at once into the Mushiki-Kai — the spheres of Formlessness. These are four. In the first state of the Mushiki-Kai, all sense of individuality is lost: even the thought of name and form becomes extinct, and there survives only the idea of Infinite Space, or Emptiness. In the second state of the Mushiki-Kai, this idea of space vanishes; and its place is filled by the Idea of Infinite Reason. But this idea of reason is anthropomorphic: it is an illusion; and it fades out in the third state of the Mushiki-Kai, which is called the "State-of-Nothing-to-take-hold-of," or Mū-sho-ū-shō-jō. Here is only the Idea of Infinite Nothingness. But even this condition has been reached by the aid of the action of the personal mind. This action ceases: then the fourth state of the Mushiki-Kai is reached — the Hisō-hihisō-shō, or the state of "neither-namelessness-nor-not-namelessness." Something of personal mentality continues to float vaguely here — the very uttermost expiring vibration of Karma — the last vanishing haze of being. It melts; — and the immeasurable revelation comes. The dreaming Buddha, freed from the last ghostly bond of Self, rises at once into the "infinite bliss" of Nirvana.[1]

---

[1] The expression "infinite bliss" as synonymous with Nirvana is taken from the *Questions of King Milinda*.

But every being does not pass through all the states above enumerated: the power to rise swiftly or slowly depends upon the acquisition of merit as well as upon the character of the Karma to be overcome. Some beings pass to Nirvana immediately after the present life; some after a single new birth; some after two or three births; while many rise directly from this world into one of the Supersensuous Heavens. All such are called Chō — the Leapers, — of whom the highest class reach Nirvana at once after their death as men or women. There are two great divisions of Chō — the Fu-Kwan, or Never-Returning-Ones,[1] and the Kwan, Returning Ones, or *revenants*. Sometimes the return may be in the nature of a prolonged retrogression; and, according to a Buddhist legend of the origin of the world, the first men were beings who had fallen from the Kwō-on-Ten, or Heaven of Sonorous Light. A remarkable fact about the whole theory of progression is that the progression is not conceived of (except in very rare cases) as an advance in straight lines, but as an advance by undulations — a psychical rhythm of motion. This is exemplified by the curious Buddhist classification of the different short courses by which the Kwan or *revenants* may hope to reach Nirvana. These short courses are divided into Even and Uneven; — the

[1] In the Sutra of the Great Decease we find the instance of a woman reaching this condition: "The Sister Nanda, O Ananda, by the destruction of the five bonds that bind people to this world, has become an inhabitant of the highest heaven — there to pass entirely away — thence never to return."

former includes an equal number of heavenly and of earthly rebirths; while in the latter class the heavenly and the earthly intermediate rebirths are not equal in number. There are four kinds of these intermediate stages. A Japanese friend has drawn for me the accompanying diagrams, which explain the subject clearly. Fantastic this may be called; but it harmonizes with the truth that all progress is necessarily rhythmical.

Though all beings do not pass through every stage of the great journey, all beings who attain to the highest enlightenment, by any course whatever, acquire certain faculties not belonging to particular conditions of birth, but only to particular conditions of psychical development. These are, the Roku-Jindzū (Abhidjñâ), or Six Supernatural Powers:[1] (1) Shin-Kyō-Tsū, the power of passing anywhither through any obstacles — through solid walls, for example; (2) Tengen-Tsū, the power of infinite vision; (3) Tenni-Tsū, the power of infinite hearing; (4) Tashin-Tsū, the power of knowing the thoughts of all other beings; (5) Shuku-jū-Tsū, the power of remembering former births; (6) Rojin-Tsū, infinite wisdom with the power of entering at will into Nirvana. The Roku-Jindzū first begin to develop in the

[1] Different Buddhist systems give different enumerations of these mysterious powers whereof the Chinese names literally signify: (1) Calm-Meditation-outward-pouring-no-obstacle-wisdom: (2) Heaven-Eye-no-obstacle-wisdom; (3) Heaven-Ear-no-obstacle-wisdom; (4) Other-minds-no-obstacle-wisdom; (5) Former-States-no-obstacle-wisdom; (6) Leak-Extinction-no-obstacle-wisdom.

The Buddhist Writings of Lafcadio Hearn

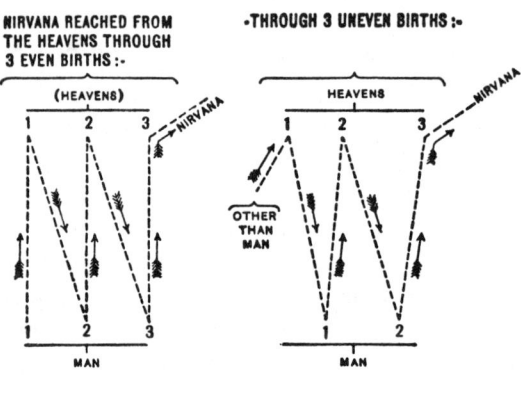

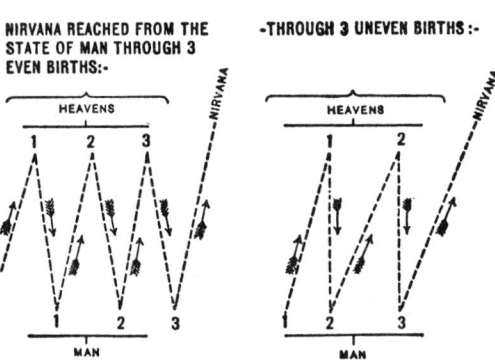

Nirvana

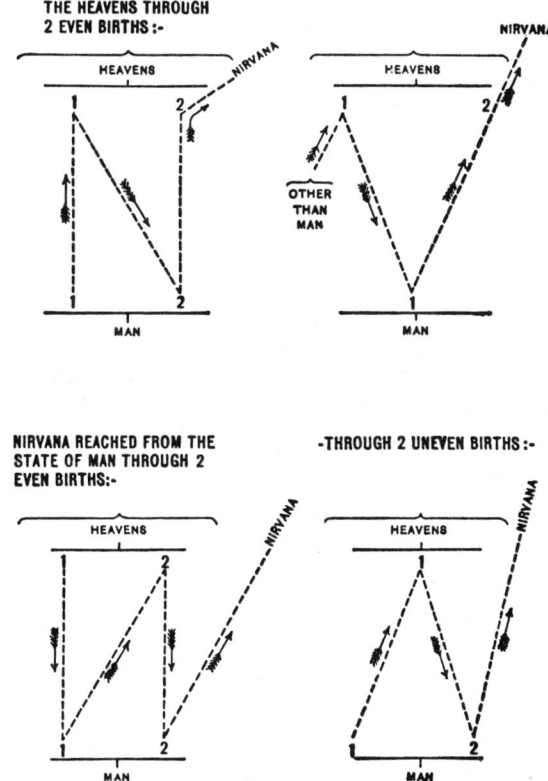

state of Shōmon (Sravaka), and expand in the higher conditions of Engaku (Pratyeka-Buddha) and of Bosatsu (Bodhisattva or Mahâsattva). The powers of the Shōmon may be exerted over two thousand worlds; those of the Engaku or Bosatsu, over three thousand; — but the powers of Buddhahood extend over the total cosmos. In the first state of holiness, for example, comes the memory of a certain number of former births, together with the capacity to foresee a corresponding number of future births; — in the next higher state the number of births remembered increases; — and in the state of Bosatsu all former births are visible to memory. But the Buddha sees not only all of his own former births, but likewise all births that ever have been or can be — and all the thoughts and acts, past, present, or future, of all past, present, or future beings.... Now these dreams of supernatural power merit attention because of the ethical teaching in regard to them — the same which is woven through every Buddhist hypothesis, rational or unthinkable — the teaching of self-abnegation. The Supernatural Powers must never be used for personal pleasure, but only for the highest beneficence — the propagation of doctrine, the saving of men. Any exercise of them for lesser ends might result in their loss — would certainly signify retrogression in the path.[1] To show them

[1] Beings who have reached the state of Engaku or of Bosatsu are not supposed capable of retrogression, or of any serious error; but it is otherwise in lower spiritual states.

Nirvana

for the purpose of exciting admiration or wonder were to juggle wickedly with what is divine; and the Teacher himself is recorded to have once severely rebuked a needless display of them by a disciple.[1]

This giving up not only of one life, but of countless lives — not only of one world, but of innumerable worlds — not only of natural but also of supernatural pleasures — not only of selfhood but of godhood — is certainly not for the miserable privilege of ceasing to be, but for a privilege infinitely outweighing all that even paradise can give. Nirvana is no cessation, but an emancipation. It means only the passing of conditioned being into unconditioned being — the fading of all mental and physical phantoms into the light of Formless Omnipotence and Omniscience. But the Buddhist hypothesis holds some suggestion of the persistence of that which has once been able to remember all births and states of limited being, — the persistence of the identity of the Buddhas even in Nirvana, notwithstanding the teaching that all Buddhas are one. How reconcile this doctrine of monism with the assurance of various texts that the being who enters Nirvana can, when so desirous, reassume an earthly personality? There are some very remarkable texts on this subject in the Sutra of the Lotus of the Good Law: those for instance in which the Tathâgata Prabhûtarâtna is pictured as sitting *"perfectly extinct upon his throne,"* and speaking before a vast assembly to

[1] See a curious legend in the Vinaya texts — *Kullavagga*, v, 8, 2.

which he has been introduced as "the great Seer who, *although perfectly extinct for many kôtis of æons,* now comes to hear the Law." These texts themselves offer us the riddle of multiplicity in unity; for the Tathâgata Prabhûtarâtna and the myriads of other extinct Buddhas who appear simultaneously, are said to have been all incarnations of but a single Buddha.

A reconciliation is offered by the hypothesis of what might be called a *pluristic monism* — a sole reality composed of groups of consciousness, at once independent and yet interdependent — or, to speak of pure mind in terms of matter, *an atomic spiritual ultimate.* This hypothesis, though not doctrinably enunciated in Buddhist texts, is distinctly implied both by text and commentary. The Absolute of Buddhism is one as ether is one. Ether is conceivable only as a composition of units.[1] The Absolute

[1] This position, it will be observed, is very dissimilar from that of Hartmann, who holds that "all plurality of individuation belongs to the sphere of phenomenality" (vol. II, page 233 of English translation). One is rather reminded of the thought of Galton that human beings "may contribute more or less unconsciously to the manifestation of a far higher life than our own — somewhat as the individual cells of one of the more complex animals contribute to the manifestation of its higher order of personality." (*Hereditary Genius,* p. 361.) Another thought of Galton's, expressed on the same page of the work just quoted from, is still more strongly suggestive of the Buddhist concept: "We must not permit ourselves to consider each human or other personality as something supernaturally added to the stock of nature, but rather as a segregation of what already existed, under a new shape, and as a regular consequence of previous conditions. . . . Neither must we be misled by the word 'individuality.' . . . We may look upon each individual as something not wholly detached from its parent source, — as a wave that

Nirvana

is conceivable only (according to any attempt at a synthesis of the Japanese doctrines) as composed of Buddhas. But here the student finds himself voyaging farther, perhaps, beyond the bar of the thinkable than Western philosophers have ever ventured. All are One; — each by union becomes equal with All! We are not only bidden to imagine the ultimate reality as composed of units of conscious being — but to believe each unit permanently equal to every other *and infinite in potentiality*.[1] The central reality of every living creature is a pure Buddha: the visible form and thinking self, which encell it, being but Karma. With some degree of truth it might be

has been lifted and shaped by normal conditions in an unknown and illimitable ocean."

The reader should remember that the Buddhist hypothesis does not imply either individuality or personality in Nirvana, but simple entity — not a spiritual *body*, in our meaning of the term, but only a divine consciousness. "Heart," in the sense of divine mind, is a term used in some Japanese texts to describe such entity. In the *Dai-Nichi Kyō Sô* (Commentary on the Dai-Nichi Sutra), for example, is the statement: "When all seeds of Karma-life are entirely burnt out and annihilated, then the *vacuum-pure* Bodhi-heart is reached." (I may observe that Buddhist metaphysicians use the term "vacuum-bodies" to describe one of the high conditions of entity.) The following, from the fifty-first volume of the work called *Daizō-hō-sū* will also be found interesting: "By experience the Tathâgata possesses all forms — forms for multitude numberless as the dust-grains of the universe. . . . The Tathâgata gets himself born in such places as he desires, or in accord with the desire of others, and there saves [literally, "carries over" — that is, over the Sea of Birth and Death] all sentient beings. Wheresoever his will finds an abiding point, there is he embodied: this is called Will-Birth Body. . . . The Buddha makes Law his body, and remains pure as empty space: this is called Law-Body."

[1] Half of this Buddhist thought is really embodied in Tennyson's line —
"Boundless inward, in the atom; boundless outward, in the Whole."

said that Buddhism substitutes for our theory of a universe of physical atoms the hypothesis of a universe of psychical units. Not that it necessarily denies our theory of physical atoms, but that it assumes a position which might be thus expressed in words: "What you call atoms are really combinations, unstable aggregates, essentially impermanent, and therefore essentially unreal. Atoms are but Karma." And this position is suggestive. We know nothing whatever of the ultimate nature of substance and motion: but we have scientific evidence that the known has been evolved from the unknown; that the atoms of our elements *are* combinations; and that what we call matter and force are but different manifestations of a single and infinite Unknown Reality.

There are wonderful Buddhist pictures which at first sight appear to have been made, like other Japanese pictures, with bold free sweeps of a skilled brush, but which, when closely examined, prove to have been executed in a much more marvelous manner. The figures, the features, the robes, the aureoles — also the scenery, the colors, the effects of mist or cloud — all, even to the tiniest detail of tone or line, have been produced by groupings of microscopic Chinese characters — tinted according to position, and more or less thickly massed according to need of light or shade. In brief, these pictures are composed entirely out of texts of Sutras: they are mosaics of minute ideographs — each ideograph a

Nirvana

combination of strokes, and the symbol at once of a sound and of an idea.

Is our universe so composed? — an endless phantasmagory made only by combinations of combinations of combinations of combinations of units finding quality and form through unimaginable affinities; — now thickly massed in solid glooms; now palpitating in tremulosities of light and color; always and everywhere grouped by some stupendous art into one vast mosaic of polarities; — yet each unit in itself a complexity inconceivable, and each in itself also a symbol only, a character, a single ideograph of the undecipherable text of the Infinite Riddle? ... Ask the chemists and the mathematicians.

V

> ... All beings that have life shall lay
> Aside their complex form, — that aggregation
> Of *mental* and material qualities
> That gives them, or in heaven or on earth,
> Their fleeting individuality.
>
> *The Book of the Great Decease*

IN every teleological system there are conceptions which cannot bear the test of modern psychological analysis, and in the foregoing unfilled outline of a great religious hypothesis there will doubtless be recognized some "ghosts of beliefs haunting those mazes of verbal propositions in which metaphysicians habitually lose themselves." But truths will be perceived also — grand recognitions of the law of ethical evolution, of the price of progress, and of our relation to the changeless Reality abiding beyond all change.

The Buddhist estimate of the enormity of that opposition to moral progress which humanity must overcome is fully sustained by our scientific knowledge of the past and perception of the future. Mental and moral advance has thus far been effected only through constant struggle against inheritances older than reason or moral feeling — against the instincts and the appetites of primitive brute life. And the Buddhist teaching, that the average man can hope to leave his worse nature behind him only after the lapse of millions of future lives, is much more of a truth than of a theory. Only through millions of births have we been able to reach even this our present imperfect state; and the dark bequests of our darkest past are still strong enough betimes to prevail over reason and ethical feeling. Every future forward pace upon the moral path will have to be taken against the massed effort of millions of ghostly wills. For those past selves which priest and poet have told us to use as steps to higher things are not dead, nor even likely to die for a thousand generations to come: they are too much alive; — they have still power to clutch the climbing feet — sometimes even to fling back the climber into the primeval slime.

Again, in its legend of the Heavens of Desire — progress through which depends upon the ability of triumphant virtue to refuse what it has won —

Nirvana

Buddhism gives us a wonder-story full of evolutional truth. The difficulties of moral self-elevation do not disappear with the amelioration of material social conditions; — in our own day they rather increase. As life becomes more complex, more multiform, so likewise do the obstacles to ethical advance — so likewise do the results of thoughts and acts. The expansion of intellectual power, the refinement of sensibility, the enlargement of the sympathies, the intensive quickening of the sense of beauty — all multiply ethical dangers just as certainly as they multiply ethical opportunities. The highest material results of civilization, and the increase of possibilities of pleasure, exact an exercise of self-mastery and a power of ethical balance, needless and impossible in older and lower states of existence.

The Buddhist doctrine of impermanency is the doctrine also of modern science: either might be uttered in the words of the other. "Natural knowledge," wrote Huxley in one of his latest and finest essays, "tends more and more to the conclusion that 'all the choir of heaven and furniture of the earth' are the transitory forms of parcels of cosmic substance wending along the road of evolution from nebulous potentiality — through endless growths of sun and planet and satellite — through all varieties of matter — through infinite diversities of life and thought — possibly through modes of being of which we neither have a conception nor are competent to form any — back to the indefinable latency from which they arose. Thus the most obvious attribute of the Cosmos is its impermanency." [1]

And, finally, it may be said that Buddhism not only presents remarkable accordance with nineteenth century thought in regard to the instability of all integrations, the ethical signification of heredity, the lesson of mental evolution, the duty of moral progress, but it also agrees with science in repudiating equally our doctrines of materialism and of spiritualism, our theory of a Creator and of special creation, and our belief in the immortality of the soul. Yet, in spite of this repudiation of the very foundations of Occidental religion, it has been able to give us the revelation of larger religious possibilities — the suggestions of a universal scientific creed nobler than any which has ever existed. Precisely in that period of our own intellectual evolution when faith in a personal God is passing away — when the belief in an individual soul is becoming impossible — when the most religious minds shrink from everything that we have been calling religion — when the universal doubt is an ever-growing weight upon ethical aspiration — light is offered from the East. There we find ourselves in presence of an older and a vaster faith — holding no gross anthropomorphic conceptions of the immeasurable Reality, and denying the existence of soul, but nevertheless inculcating a system of morals superior to any other, and maintaining a hope which no possible

[1] *Evolution and Ethics.*

Nirvana

future form of positive knowledge can destroy. Reenforced by the teaching of science, the teaching of this more ancient faith is that for thousands of years we have been thinking inside-out and upside-down. The only reality is One; — all that we have taken for Substance is only Shadow; — the physical is the unreal; — *and the outer-man is the ghost.*

Within the Circle

NEITHER personal pain nor personal pleasure can be really expressed in words. It is never possible to communicate them in their original form. It is only possible, by vivid portrayal of the circumstances or conditions causing them, to awaken in sympathetic minds some kindred qualities of feeling. But if the circumstances causing the pain or the pleasure be totally foreign to common human experience, then no representation of them can make fully known the sensations which they evoked. Hopeless, therefore, any attempt to tell the real pain of seeing my former births. I can say only that no combination of suffering possible to *individual* being could be likened to such pain — the pain of countless lives interwoven. It seemed as if every nerve of me had been prolonged into some monstrous web of sentiency spun back through a million years — and as if the whole of that measureless woof and warp, over all its shivering threads, were pouring into my consciousness, out of the abysmal past, some ghastliness without name — some horror too vast for human brain to hold. For, as I looked backward, I became double, quadruple, octuple; — I multiplied by arithmetical progression; — I became hundreds and thousands — and feared with the terror of thousands — and despaired with

Within the Circle

the anguish of thousands — and shuddered with the agony of thousands; yet knew the pleasure of none. All joys, all delights appeared but mists or mockeries: only the pain and the fear were real — and always, always growing. Then in the moment when sentiency itself seemed bursting into dissolution, one divine touch ended the frightful vision, and brought again to me the simple consciousness of the single present. Oh! how unspeakably delicious that sudden shrinking back out of multiplicity into unity! — that immense, immeasurable collapse of Self into the blind oblivious numbness of individuality!

"To others also," said the voice of the divine one who had thus saved me — "to others in the like state it has been permitted to see something of their prëexistence. But no one of them ever could endure to look far. Power to see all former births belongs only to those eternally released from the bonds of Self. Such exist outside of illusion — outside of form and name; and pain cannot come nigh them.

"But to you, remaining in illusion, not even the Buddha could give power to look back more than a little way.

"Still you are bewitched by the follies of art and of poetry and of music — the delusions of color and form — the delusions of sensuous speech, the delusions of sensuous sound.

"Still that apparition called Nature — which is but another name for emptiness and shadow — deceives and charms you, and fills you with dreams of longing for the things of sense.

"But he who truly wishes to know, must not love this phantom Nature — must not find delight in the radiance of a clear sky — nor in the sight of the sea — nor in the sound of the flowing of rivers — nor in the forms of peaks and woods and valleys — nor in the colors of them.

"He who truly wishes to know must not find delight in contemplating the works and the deeds of men, nor in hearing their converse, nor in observing the puppet-play of their passions and of their emotions. All this is but a weaving of smoke — a shimmering of vapors — an impermanency — a phantasmagory.

"For the pleasures that men term lofty or noble or sublime are but larger sensualisms, subtler falsities: venomous fair-seeming flowerings of selfishness — all rooted in the elder slime of appetites and desires. To joy in the radiance of a cloudless day — to see the mountains shift their tintings to the wheeling of the sun — to watch the passing of waves, the fading of sunsets — to find charm in the blossoming of plants or trees: all this is of the senses. Not less truly of the senses is the pleasure of observing actions called great or beautiful or heroic — since it is one with the pleasure of imagining those things for which men miserably strive in this miserable world: brief love and fame and honor — all of which are empty as passing foam.

Within the Circle

"Sky, sun, and sea; — the peaks, the woods, the plains; — all splendors and forms and colors — are spectres. The feelings and the thoughts and the acts of men — whether deemed high or low, noble or ignoble — all things imagined or done for any save the eternal purpose, are but dreams born of dreams and begetting hollowness. To the clear of sight, all feelings of self — all love and hate, joy and pain, hope and regret, are alike shadows; — youth and age, beauty and horror, sweetness and foulness, are not different; — death and life are one and the same; and Space and Time exist but as the stage and the order of the perpetual Shadow-play.

"All that exists in Time must perish. To the Awakened there is no Time or Space or Change — no night or day — no heat or cold — no moon or season — no present, past, or future. Form and the names of form are alike nothingness: Knowledge only is real; and unto whomsoever gains it, the universe becomes a ghost. But it is written: 'He who hath overcome Time in the past and the future must be of exceedingly pure understanding.'

"Such understanding is not yours. Still to your eyes the shadow seems the substance — and darkness, light — and voidness, beauty. And therefore to see your former births could give you only pain."

I asked:
"Had I found strength to look back to the begin-

ning — back to the verge of Time — could I have read the Secret of the universe?"

"Nay," was answer made. "Only by Infinite Vision can the Secret be read. Could you have looked back incomparably further than your power permitted, then the Past would have become for you the Future. And could you have endured even yet more, the Future would have orbed back for you into the Present."

"Yet why?" I murmured, marveling.... "What is the Circle?"

"Circle there is none," was the response; — "Circle there is none but the great phantom-whirl of birth and death to which, by their own thoughts and deeds, the ignorant remain condemned. But this has being only in Time; and Time itself is illusion."

A Question in the Zen Texts

I

MY friend opened a thin yellow volume of that marvelous text which proclaims at sight the patience of the Buddhist engraver. Movable Chinese types may be very useful; but the best of which they are capable is ugliness itself when compared with the beauty of the old block-printing.

"I have a queer story for you," he said.
"A Japanese story?"
"No — Chinese."
"What is the book?"
"According to Japanese pronunciation of the Chinese characters of the title, we call it 'Mu-Mon-Kwan,' which means, 'The Gateless Barrier.' It is one of the books especially studied by the Zen sect, or sect of Dhyâna. A peculiarity of some of the Dhyâna texts — this being a good example — is that they are not explanatory. They only suggest. Questions are put; but the student must think out the answers for himself. He must *think* them out, but not write them. You know that Dhyâna represents human effort to reach, through meditation, zones of thought beyond the range of verbal expression; and any thought once narrowed into utterance loses all Dhyâna quality.... Well, this story is supposed to be true; but it is used only for a Dhyâna

question. Thereare three different Chinese versions of it; and I can give you the substance of the three."

Which he did as follows:

II

THE story of the girl Ts'ing, which is told in the "Lui-shwo-li-hwan-ki," cited by the "Ching-tang-luh," and commented upon in the "Wu-mu-kwan" (called by the Japanese "Mu-Mon-Kwan"), which is a book of the Zen sect:

There lived in Han-yang a man called Chang-Kien, whose child-daughter, Ts'ing, was of peerless beauty. He had also a nephew called Wang-Chau — a very handsome boy. The children played together, and were fond of each other. Once Kien jestingly said to his nephew: "Some day I will marry you to my little daughter." Both children remembered these words; and they believed themselves thus betrothed.

When Ts'ing grew up, a man of rank asked for her in marriage; and her father decided to comply with the demand. Ts'ing was greatly troubled by this decision. As for Chau, he was so much angered and grieved that he resolved to leave home, and go to another province. The next day he got a boat ready for his journey, and after sunset, without bidding farewell to any one, he proceeded up the river. But in the middle of the night he was startled by a voice calling to him, "Wait! — it is I!" — and he saw a girl running along the bank toward the boat. It was Ts'ing. Chau was unspeakably delighted. She sprang into the boat; and the lovers found their way safely to the province of Chuh.

In the province of Chuh they lived happily for six years; and they had two children. But Ts'ing could not forget her parents, and often longed to see them again.

At last she said to her husband: "Because in former

A Question in the Zen Texts

time I could not bear to break the promise made to you, I ran away with you and forsook my parents — although knowing that I owed them all possible duty and affection. Would it not now be well to try to obtain their forgiveness?"

"Do not grieve yourself about that," said Chau; — "we shall go to see them."

He ordered a boat to be prepared; and a few days later he returned with his wife to Han-yang.

According to custom in such cases, the husband first went to the house of Kien, leaving Ts'ing alone in the boat. Kien welcomed his nephew with every sign of joy and said:

"How much I have been longing to see you! I was often afraid that something had happened to you."

Chau answered respectfully:

"I am distressed by the undeserved kindness of your words. It is to beg your forgiveness that I have come."

But Kien did not seem to understand. He asked:

"To what matter do you refer?"

"I feared," said Chau, "that you were angry with me for having run away with Ts'ing. I took her with me to the province of Chuh."

"What Ts'ing was that?" asked Kien.

"Your daughter Ts'ing," answered Chau, beginning to suspect his father-in-law of some malevolent design.

"What are you talking about?" cried Kien, with every appearance of astonishment. "My daughter Ts'ing has been sick in bed all these years — ever since the time when you went away."

"Your daughter Ts'ing," returned Chau, becoming angry, "has not been sick. She has been my wife for six years; and we have two children; and we have both returned to this place only to seek your pardon. Therefore please do not mock us!"

For a moment the two looked at each other in silence.

Then Kien arose, and motioning to his nephew to follow, led the way to an inner room where a sick girl was lying. And Chau, to his utter amazement, saw the face of Ts'ing — beautiful, but strangely thin and pale.

"She cannot speak," explained the old man; "but she can understand." And Kien said to her, laughingly: "Chau tells me that you ran away with him, and that you gave him two children."

The sick girl looked at Chau, and smiled; but remained silent.

"Now come with me to the river," said the bewildered visitor to his father-in-law. "For I can assure you — in spite of what I have seen in this house — that your daughter Ts'ing is at this moment in my boat."

They went to the river; and there, indeed, was the young wife, waiting. And seeing her father, she bowed down before him, and besought his pardon.

Kien said to her:

"If you really be my daughter, I have nothing but love for you. Yet though you seem to be my daughter, there is something which I cannot understand.... Come with us to the house."

So the three proceeded toward the house. As they neared it, they saw that the sick girl — who had not before left her bed for years — was coming to meet them, smiling as if much delighted. And the two Ts'ings approached each other. But then — nobody could ever tell how — they suddenly melted into each other, and became one body, one person, one Ts'ing — even more beautiful than before, and showing no sign of sickness or of sorrow.

Kien said to Chau:

"Ever since the day of your going, my daughter was dumb, and most of the time like a person who had taken too much wine. Now I know that her spirit was absent."

Ts'ing herself said:

"Really I never knew that I was at home. I saw Chau

A Question in the Zen Texts

going away in silent anger; and the same night I dreamed that I ran after his boat.... But now I cannot tell which was really I — the I that went away in the boat, or the I that stayed at home."

III

"THAT is the whole of the story," my friend observed. "Now there is a note about it in the 'Mu-Mon-Kwan' that may interest you. This note says: 'The fifth patriarch of the Zen sect once asked a priest — "In the case of the separation of the spirit of the girl Ts'ing, which was the true Ts'ing?"' It was only because of this question that the story was cited in the book. But the question is not answered. The author only remarks: 'If you can decide which was the real Ts'ing, then you will have learned that to go out of one envelope and into another is merely like putting up at an inn. But if you have not yet reached this degree of enlightenment, take heed that you do not wander aimlessly about the world. Otherwise, when Earth, Water, Fire, and Wind shall suddenly be dissipated, you will be like a crab with seven hands and eight legs, thrown into boiling water. And in that time do not say that you were never told about the *Thing*.'... Now the *Thing* —"

"I do not want to hear about the Thing," I interrupted — "nor about the crab with seven hands and eight legs. I want to hear about the clothes."

"What clothes?"

"At the time of their meeting, the two Ts'ings would have been differently dressed — very differently, perhaps; for one was a maid, and the other a wife. Did the clothes of the two also blend together? Suppose that one had a silk robe and the other a robe of cotton, would these have mixed into a texture of silk and cotton? Suppose that one was wearing a blue girdle, and the other a yellow girdle, would the result have been a green girdle? ... Or did one Ts'ing simply slip out of her costume, and leave it on the ground, like the cast-off shell of a cicada?"

"None of the texts say anything about the clothes," my friend replied: "so I cannot tell you. But the subject is quite irrelevant, from the Buddhist point of view. The doctrinal question is the question of what I suppose you would call the personality of Ts'ing."

"And yet it is not answered," I said.

"It is best answered," my friend replied, "by not being answered."

"How so?"

"Because there is no such thing as personality."

The Literature of the Dead

> Shindaréba koso ikitaré.
> Only because of having died, does one enter into life.
> *Buddhist proverb*

I

BEHIND my dwelling, but hidden from view by a very lofty curtain of trees, there is a Buddhist temple, with a cemetery attached to it. The cemetery itself is in a grove of pines, many centuries old: and the temple stands in a great quaint lonesome garden. Its religious name is "Ji-shō-in"; but the people call it "Kobudera," which means the "Gnarled," or "Knobby" Temple, because it is built of undressed timber — great logs of hinoki, selected for their beauty or strangeness of shape, and simply prepared for the builder by the removal of limbs and bark. But such gnarled and knobby wood is precious: it is of the hardest and most enduring, and costs far more than common building-material — as might be divined from the fact that the beautiful alcoves and the choicest parts of Japanese interiors are finished with wood of a similar kind. To build Kobudera was an undertaking worthy of a prince; and, as a matter of history, it was a prince who erected it, for a place of family worship. There is a doubtful tradition that two designs were submitted to him by the architect, and that he chose the more fantastic one under the innocent impression that undressed timber would prove cheap. But whether it owes its existence to a mistake or not, Kobudera remains one of the most interesting temples of Japan. The public have now almost forgotten its existence; — but it was famous in the time of Iyemitsu; and its appellation, Ji-shō-in, was taken from the kaimyō of one of the great Shogun's ladies, whose superb tomb may be seen in its cemetery. Before Meiji, the temple was isolated among woods and fields; but the city has now swallowed up most of the green spaces that once secluded it, and has pushed out the ugliest of new streets directly in front of its gate.

This gate — a structure of gnarled logs, with a tiled and tilted Chinese roof — is a fitting preface to the queer style of the temple itself. From either gable-end of the gate-roof, a demon-head, grinning under triple horns, looks down upon the visitor.[1]

---

[1] Such figures are really elaborate tiles, and are called "onigawara," or "demon-tiles." It may naturally be asked why demon-heads should be ever placed above Buddhist gateways. Originally they were not intended to represent demons, in the Buddhist sense, but guardian-spirits whose duty it was to drive demons away. The onigawara were introduced into Japan either from China or Korea — not improbably Korea; for we read that the first roof-tiles made in Japan were manufactured shortly after the introduction of the new faith by Korean priests, and under the supervision of Shōtoku Taishi, the princely founder and supporter of Japanese Buddhism. They were baked at Koizumi-mura, in Yamato; — but we are not told whether there were any of this extraordinary shape among them. It is worth while remarking that in Korea to-day you can see hideous faces painted upon house-doors — even upon the gates of the royal palace; and these, intended merely to frighten away evil spirits, suggest the real origin of the demon-tiles. The Japanese, on first seeing such tiles, called them demon-tiles because the faces upon them resembled those conventionally given to Buddhist demons; and now that their history has been forgotten, they are popu-

The Literature of the Dead

Within, except at the hours of prayer, all is green silence. Children do not play in the court — perhaps because the temple is a private one. The ground is everywhere hidden by a fine thick moss of so warm a color that the brightest foliage of the varied shrubbery above it looks sombre by contrast; and the bases of walls, the pedestals of monuments, the stonework of the bell-tower, the masonry of the ancient well, are muffled with the same luminous growth. Maples and pines and cryptomerias screen the façade of the temple; and, if your visit be in autumn, you may find the whole court filled with the sweet heavy perfume of the mokusei[1] blossom. After having looked at the strange temple, you would find it worth while to enter the cemetery, by the black gate on the west side of the court.

I like to wander in that cemetery — partly because in the twilight of its great trees, and in the silence of centuries which has gathered about them, one can forget the city and its turmoil, and dream but of space and time — but much more because it is full of beauty, and of the poetry of great faith. Indeed of such poetry it possesses riches quite exceptional. Each Buddhist sect has its own tenets,

larly supposed to represent demon-guardians. There would be nothing contrary to Buddhist faith in the fancy; — for there are many legends of good demons. Besides, in the eternal order of divine law, even the worst demon must at last become a Buddha.

[1] *Osmanthus fragrans.* This is one of the very few Japanese plants having richly perfumed flowers.

rites, and forms; and the special character of these is reflected in the iconography and epigraphy of its burial-grounds — so that for any experienced eye a Tendai graveyard is readily distinguishable from a Shingon graveyard, or a Zen graveyard from one belonging to a Nichiren congregation. But at Kobudera the inscriptions and the sculptures peculiar to several Buddhist sects can be studied side by side. Founded for the Hokké, or Nichiren rite, the temple nevertheless passed, in the course of generations, under the control of other sects — the last being the Tendai; — and thus its cemetery now offers a most interesting medley of the emblems and the epitaphic formularies of various persuasions. It was here that I first learned, under the patient teaching of an Oriental friend, something about the Buddhist literature of the dead.

No one able to feel beauty could refuse to confess the charm of the old Buddhist cemeteries — with their immemorial trees, their evergreen mazes of shrubbery trimmed into quaintest shapes, the carpet-softness of their mossed paths, the weird but unquestionable art of their monuments. And no great knowledge of Buddhism is needed to enable you, even at first sight, to understand something of this art. You would recognize the lotus chiseled upon tombs or water-tanks, and would doubtless observe that the designs of the pedestals represent a lotus of eight petals — though you might not know that

The Literature of the Dead

these eight petals symbolize the Eight Intelligences. You would recognize the manji, or swastika, figuring the Wheel of the Law — though ignorant of its relation to the Mahâyâna philosophy. You would perhaps be able to recognize also the images of certain Buddhas — though not aware of the meaning of their attitudes or emblems in relation to mystical ecstasy or to the manifestation of the Six Supernatural Powers. And you would be touched by the simple pathos of the offerings — the incense and the flowers before the tombs, the water poured out for the dead — even though unable to divine the deeper pathos of the beliefs that make the cult. But unless an excellent Chinese scholar as well as a Buddhist philosopher, all book-knowledge of the great religion would still leave you helpless in a world of riddles. The marvelous texts — the exquisite Chinese scriptures chiseled into the granite of tombs, or limned by a master-brush upon the smooth wood of the sotoba — will yield their secrets only to an interpreter of no common powers. And the more you become familiar with their aspect, the more the mystery of them tantalizes — especially after you have learned that a literal translation of them would mean, in the majority of cases, exactly nothing!

What strange thoughts have been thus recorded and yet concealed? Are they complex and subtle as the characters that stand for them? Are they beautiful also like those characters — with some undreamed of, surprising beauty, such as might inform the language of another planet?

II

As for sublety and complexity, much of this mortuary literature is comparable to the Veil of Isis. Behind the mystery of the Text — in which almost every character has two readings — there is the mystery of the phrase; and again behind this are successions of riddles belonging to a gnosticism older than all the wisdom of the Occident, and deep as the abysses of Space. Fortunately the most occult texts are also the least interesting, and bear little relation to the purpose of this essay. The majority are attached, not to the sculptured, but to the written and impermanent literature of cemeteries — not to the stone monuments, but to the sotoba: those tall narrow laths of unpainted wood which are planted above the graves at fixed, but gradually increasing intervals, during a period of one hundred years.[1]

The uselessness of any exact translation of these

[1] The word "sotoba" is identical with the Sanscrit "stûpa." Originally a mausoleum, and later a simple monument — commemorative or otherwise — the stûpa was introduced with Buddhism into China, and thence, perhaps by way of Korea, into Japan. Chinese forms of the stone stûpa are to be found in many of the old Japanese temple-grounds. The wooden sotoba is only a symbol of the stûpa; and the more elaborate forms of it plainly suggest its history. The slight carving along its upper edges represents that superimposition of cube, sphere, crescent, pyramid, and body-pyriform (symbolizing the Five Great Elements), which forms the design of the most beautiful funeral monuments.

The Literature of the Dead

inscriptions may be exemplified by a word-for-word rendering of two sentences written upon the sotoba used by the older sects. What meaning can you find in such a term as "Law-sphere-substance-nature-wisdom," or such an invocation as "Ether, Wind, Fire, Water, Earth!" — for an invocation it really is? To understand these words one must first know that, in the doctrine of the mystical sects, the universe is composed of Five Great Elements which are identical with Five Buddhas; that each of the Five Buddhas contains the rest; and that the Five are One by essence, though varying in their phenomenal manifestations.

The name of an element has thus three significations. The word Fire, for example, means flame as objective appearance; it means flame also as the manifestation of a particular Buddha; and it likewise means the special quality of wisdom or power attributed to that Buddha. Perhaps this doctrine will be more easily understood by the help of the following Shingon classification of the Five Elements in their Buddhist relations:

I. Hō-kai-tai-shō-chi

(Sanscrit, Dhârma-dhâtu-prakrit-gñâna), or "Law-sphere-substance-nature-wisdom"; signifying the wisdom that becomes the substance of things. This is the element Ether. Ether personified is Dai-Nichi-Nyōrai, the "Great Sun-Buddha" (Mahâvairokana Tathâgata), who "holds the seal of Wisdom."

II. Dai-en-kyō-chi

(Adarsana-gñâna), or "Great-round-mirror-wisdom"; that is to say, the divine power making images manifest. This is the element Earth. Earth personified is Ashuku Nyōrai, the "Immovable Tathâgata" (Akshobhya).

III. Byō-dō-shō-chi

(Samatâ-gñâna), "Even-equal-nature-wisdom"; that is, the wisdom making no distinction of persons or of things. The element Fire. Personified, Fire is Hō-shō Nyōrai, or "Gem-Birth" Buddha (Ratnasambhava Tathâgata), presiding over virtue and happiness.

IV. Myō-kwan-zatsu-chi

(Pratyavekshana-gñâna), "Wondrously-observing-considering-wisdom"; that is, the wisdom distinguishing clearly truth from error, destroying doubts, and presiding over the preaching of the Law. The element Water. Water personified is Amida Nyōrai, the Buddha of Immeasurable Light (Amitâbha Tathâgata).

V. Jō-shō-sa-chi

(Krityânushthâna-gñâna), the "Wisdom-of-accomplishing-what-is-to-be-done"; that is to say, the divine wisdom that helps beings to reach Nirvana. The element Air. Air personified is Fu-kū-jō-ju, the "Unfailing-of-Accomplishment" — more commonly called Fuku-Nyōrai (Amoghasiddhi, or Sâkyamuni).[1]

---

[1] These relations of the elements to the Buddhas named are not, however, permanently fixed in the doctrine — for obvious philosophical reasons. Sometimes Sakyamuni is identified with Ether, and Amitâbha with Air, etc., etc. In the above enumeration I have followed the order taken by Professor Bunyiu Nanjio, who nevertheless suggests that this order is not to be considered perpetual.

The Literature of the Dead

Now the doctrine that each of the Five Buddhas contains the rest, and that all are essentially One, is symbolized in these texts by an extraordinary use of characters called "Bon-ji" — which are recognizably Sanscrit letters. The name of each element can be written with any one of four characters — all having for Buddhists the same meaning, though differing as to sound and form. Thus the characters standing for Fire would read, according to Japanese pronunciation, Ra, Ran, Raän, and Raku; — and the characters signifying Ether, Kya, Ken, Keën, and Kyaku. By different combinations of the twenty characters making the five sets, different supernatural powers and different Buddhas are indicated; and the indication is further helped by an additional symbolic character, called "Shū-ji," or "seed-word," placed immediately after the names of the elements.

The reader will now comprehend the meaning of the invocatory "Ether, Wind, Fire, Water, Earth!" and of the strange names of divine wisdom written upon sotoba; but the enigmas offered by even a single sotoba may be much more complicated than the foregoing examples suggest. There are unimaginable acrostics; there are rules, varying according to sect, for the position of texts in relation to the points of the compass; and there are kabalisms based upon the multiple values of certain Chinese ideographs. The whole subject of esoteric inscriptions would require volumes to explain; and the reader will not be sorry, I fancy, to abandon it at this point in favor of texts possessing a simpler and a more humane interest.

The really attractive part of Buddhist cemetery-literature mostly consists of sentences taken from the sutras or the sastras; and the attraction is due not only to the intrinsic beauty of the faith which these sentences express, but also to the fact that they will be found to represent, in epitome, a complete body of Buddhist doctrine. Like the mystical inscriptions above mentioned, they belong to the sotoba, not to the gravestones; but, while the invocations usually occupy the upper and front part of the sotoba, these sutra-texts are commonly written upon the back.

In addition to scriptural and invocatory texts, each sotoba bears the name of the giver, the kaimyō of the dead, and the name of a commemorative anniversary. Sometimes a brief prayer is also inscribed, or a statement of the pious purpose inspiring the erection of the sotoba. Before considering the scripture-texts proper, in relation to their embodiment of doctrine, I submit examples of the general character and plan of sotoba inscriptions. They are written upon both sides of the wood, be it observed; but I have not thought it necessary to specify which texts belong to the front, and which to the back of the sotoba — since the rules concerning such position differ according to sect:

The Literature of the Dead

I. Sotoba of the Nichiren Sect

(Invocation)

Ether, Wind, Fire, Water, Earth! — Hail to the Sutra of the Lotus of the Good Law!

(Commemorative text)

To-day, the service of the third year has been performed in order that our lay-brother [kaimyō] may be enabled to cut off the bonds of illusion, to open the Eye of Enlightenment, to remain free from all pain, and to enter into bliss.

(Sastra text)

MYŌ-HŌ-KYŌ-RIKI-SOKU-SHIN-JŌ-BUTSU!

Even this body [of flesh] by the virtue of the Sutra of the Excellent Law, enters into Buddhahood.

II. Sotoba of the Nichiren Sect

(Invocation)

Hail to the Sutra of the Lotus of the Good Law!

(Commemorative text)

The rite of feeding the hungry spirits having been fulfilled, and the service for the dead having been performed, this sotoba is set up in commemoration of the service and the offerings made with prayer for the salvation of Buddha on behalf of — (kaimyō follows).

(Prayer — with English translation)
Gan i shi kudoku
Fu-gyū o issai
Gatō yo shujō
Kai-gu jō butsudo.

By virtue of this good action I beseech that the merit of it may be extended to all, and that we and all living beings may fulfill the Way of Buddha.[1]

---

[1] The above prayer is customarily said after having read a sutra, or copied a sacred text, or caused a Buddhist service to be performed.

The fifth day of the seventh month of the thirtieth year of Meiji, by—— ——, this sotoba has been set up.

III. SOTOBA OF THE JŌ DO SECT

(Invocation)

Hail to the Buddha Amida!

(Commemorative mention)

This for the sake of — (here kaimyō follows).

(Sutra text)

The Buddha of the Golden Mouth, who possesses the Great-Round-Mirror-Wisdom,[1] has said: "The glorious light of Amida illuminates all the worlds of the Ten Directions, and takes into itself and never abandons all living beings who fix their thoughts upon that Buddha!"

IV. SOTOBA OF THE ZEN SECT

(Sastra text)

The Dai-en-kyō-chi-kyō declares: "By entering deeply into meditation, one may behold the Buddhas of the Ten Directions."

(Commemorative text)

That the noble Elder Sister [2] Chi-Shō-In-Kō-Un-Tei-Myō,[3] now dwelling in the House of Shining Wisdom, may instantly attain to Bodhi.[4]

---

[1] Dai-en-kyō-chi (Adarsana-gñâna). Amida is the Japanese form of the name Amitâbha.

[2] "Great (or Noble) Elder Sister" is the meaning of the title dai-shi affixed to the kaimyō of a woman. In the rite of the Zen sect dai-shi always signifies a married woman; shin-nyo, a maid.

[3] This kaimyō, or posthumous name, literally signifies: Radiant Chastity-Beaming-Through-Luminous-Clouds.

[4] The Supreme Wisdom; the state of Buddhahood.

The Literature of the Dead

(Prayer)
Let whomsoever looks upon this sotoba be forever delivered from the Three Evil Ways.[1]

(Record)
In the thirtieth year of Meiji, on the first day of the fifth month, by the house of Inouyé, this sotoba has been set up.

The foregoing will doubtless suffice as specimens of the ordinary forms of inscription. The Buddha praised or invoked is always the Buddha especially revered by the sect from whose sutra or sastra the quotation is chosen; — sometimes also the divine power of a Bodhisattva is extolled, as in the following Zen inscription:

The Sutra of Kwannon says: "In all the provinces of all the countries in the Ten Directions, there is not even one temple where Kwannon is not self-revealed."

Sometimes the scripture text more definitely assumes the character of a praise-offering, as the following juxtaposition suggests:

The Buddha of Immeasurable Light illuminates all worlds in the Ten Directions of Space.

This for the sake of the swift salvation into Buddhahood of our lay-brother named the Great-Secure-Retired-Scholar.

Sometimes we also find a verse of praise or an invocation addressed to the apotheosized spirit of the founder of the sect — a common example being furnished by the sotoba of the Shingon rite:

[1] San-Akudō — the three unhappy conditions of Hell, of the World of Hungry Spirits (Pretas), and of Animal Existence.

The Buddhist Writings of Lafcadio Hearn

Hail to the Great Teacher Haijō-Kongō! [1]

Rarely the little prayer for the salvation of the dead assumes, as in the following beautiful example, the language of unconscious poetry:

This for the sake of our noble Elder Sister ——. May the Lotus of Bliss by virtue of these prayers be made to bloom for her, and to bear the fruit of Buddhahood! [2]

But usually the prayers are of the simplest, and differ from each other only in the use of peculiar Buddhist terms:

This for the sake of the true happiness of our lay-brother [kaimyō], that he may obtain the Supreme Perfect Enlightenment.

This tower is set up for the sake of ——, that he may obtain complete Sambodhi. [3]

This precious tower, and these offerings for the sake of —— ——, — that he may obtain the Anattra-Sammyak-Sambodhi. [4]

One other subject of interest belonging to the merely commemorative texts of sotoba remains to be mentioned — the names of certain Buddhist services for the dead. There are two classes of such services: those performed within one hundred days

---

[1] "Haijō Kongō" means "the Diamond of Universal Enlightenment": it is the honorific appellation of Kūkai or Kobodaishi, founder of the Shingon-Shū.

[2] From a Zen sotoba.

[3] In Japanese "Sanbodai." The term "tower" refers of course to the sotoba, the symbol of a real tower, or at least of the desire to erect such a monument, were it possible.

[4] In Japanese, " Anuka-tara-sanmaku-sanbodai" — the supreme form of Buddhist enlightenment.

after death, and those celebrated at fixed intervals during a term of one hundred years — on the first, second, seventh, thirteenth, seventeenth, twenty-fourth, thirty-third, fiftieth, and one hundredth anniversaries of the death. In the Zen rite these commemorative services — perhaps we might call them masses — have singular mystical names by which they are recorded upon the sotoba of the sect — such as Lesser Happiness, Greater Happiness, Broad Repose, The Bright Caress, and The Great Caress.

But we shall now turn to the study of the scripture-texts proper — those citations from sutra or sastra which form the main portion of a sotoba-writing; expounding the highest truth of Buddhist belief, or speaking the deepest thought of Eastern philosophy.

III

AT the beginning of my studies in the Kobudera cemetery, I was not less impressed by the quiet cheerfulness of the sotoba-texts than by their poetry and their philosophy. In none did I find even a shadow of sadness: the greater number were utterances of a faith that seemed to me wider and deeper than our own — sublime proclamations of the eternal and infinite nature of Thought, the unity of all mind, and the certainty of universal salvation. And other surprises awaited me in this strange literature. Texts or fragments of texts, that at first rendering appeared of the simplest, would yield to learned commentary profundities of significance absolutely startling. Phrases, seemingly artless, would suddenly reveal a dual suggestiveness — a twofold idealism — a beauty at once exoteric and mystical. Of this latter variety of inscription the following is a good example:

The flower having bloomed last night, the World has become fragrant.[1]

In the language of the higher Buddhism, this means that through death a spirit has been released from the darkness of illusion, even as the perfume of a blossom is set free at the breaking of the bud, and that the divine Absolute, or World of Law, is refreshed by the new presence, as a whole garden might be made fragrant by the blooming of some precious growth. But in the popular language of Buddhism, the same words signify that in the Lotus-Lake of Paradise another magical flower has opened for the Apparitional Rebirth into highest bliss of the being loved and lost on earth, and that Heaven rejoices for the advent of another Buddha.

But I desire rather to represent the general result of my studies than to point out the special beauties of this epitaphic literature: and my purpose will be most easily attained by arranging and considering the inscriptions in a certain doctrinal order.

[1] From a sotoba of the Jōdo sect.

The Literature of the Dead

A great variety of sotoba-texts refer, directly or indirectly, to the Lotus-Flower Paradise of Amida — or, as it is more often called, the Paradise of the West. The following are typical:

The Amida-Kyō says: "All who enter into that country enter likewise into that state of virtue from which there can be no turning back." [1]

The Text of Gold proclaims: "In that world they receive bliss only: therefore that world is called Gokuraku— exceeding bliss." [2]

Hail unto the Lord Amida Buddha! The Golden Mouth has said, "All living beings that fix their thoughts upon the Buddha shall be received and welcomed into his Paradise; — never shall they be forsaken." [3]

But texts like these, though dear to popular faith, make no appeal to the higher Buddhism, which admits heaven as a temporary condition only, not to be desired by the wise. Indeed, the Mahâyâna texts, describing Sukhâvatî, themselves suggest its essentially illusive character — a world of jewel-lakes and perfumed airs and magical birds, but a world also in which the voices of winds and waters and

[1] From a sotoba of the Jōdo sect. The Amida-Kyō, or Sutra of Amida, is the Japanese [Chinese] version of the smaller Sukhâvatî-Vyûha Sutra.

[2] Gokuraku is the common word in Japan for the Buddhist heaven. The above inscription, translated for me from a sotoba of the Jōdo sect, is an abbreviated form of a verse in the Smaller Sukhâvatî-Vyûha (see *Buddhist Mahâyâna Texts:* "Sacred Books of the East"), which Max Müller has thus rendered in full: "In that world Sukhâvatî, O Sâriputra, there is neither bodily nor mental pain for living beings. The sources of happiness are innumerable there. For that reason is that world called Sukhâvatî, the happy."

[3] From a sotoba of the Jōdo sect.

singers perpetually preach the unreality of self and the impermanency of all things. And even the existence of this Western Paradise might seem to be denied in other sotoba-texts of deeper significance — such as this:

Originally there is no East or West: where then can South or North be?[1]

"Originally" — that is to say, in relation to the Infinite. The relations and the ideas of the Conditioned cease to exist for the Unconditioned. Yet this truth does not really imply denial of other worlds of relation — states of bliss to which the strong may rise, and states of pain to which the weak may descend. It is a reminder only. All conditions are impermanent, and so, in the profounder sense, unreal. The Absolute — the Supreme Buddha — is the sole Reality. This doctrine appears in many sotoba-inscriptions:

The Blue Mountain of itself remains eternally unmoved: the White Clouds come of themselves and go.[1]

By "the Blue Mountain" is meant the Sole Reality of Mind; — by "the White Clouds," the phenomenal universe. Yet the universe exists but as a dream of Mind:

If any one desire to obtain full knowledge of all the Buddhas of the past, the present, and the future, let him learn to comprehend the true nature of the World of Law.

[1] Sotoba of the Jōdo sect.

The Literature of the Dead

Then will he perceive that all things are but the production of Mind.[1]

By the learning and the practice of the True Doctrine, the Non-Apparent becomes [for us] the only Reality."[1]

The universe is a phantom, and a phantom likewise the body of man, together with all emotions, ideas, and memories that make up the complex of his sensuous Self. But is this evanescent Self the whole of man's inner being? Not so, proclaim the sotoba:

All living beings have the nature of Buddha. The Nyōrai,[2] eternally living, is alone unchangeable.[3]

The Kegon-Kyō[4] declares: "In all living creatures there exists, and has existed from the beginning, the Real-Law Nature: all by their nature contain the original essence of Buddha."

Sharing the nature of the Unchangeable, we share the Eternal Reality. In the highest sense, man also is divine:

The Mind becomes Buddha: the Mind itself is Buddha.[5]

In the Engaku-Kyō[6] it is written: "Now for the first time I perceive that all living beings have the original Buddha-nature — wherefore Birth and Death and Nir-

---

[1] Sotoba of the Zen sect. [2] Tathâgata. [3] Sotoba of the Zen sect.
[4] Avatamsaka Sutra. This text is also from a Zen sotoba.
[5] From a tombstone of the Jōdo sect. The text is evidently from the Chinese version of the Amitâyur-Dhyâna-Sutra (see *Buddhist Mahâyâna Texts:* "Sacred Books of the East"). It reads in the English version thus: "In fine, it is your mind that becomes Buddha; — nay, it is your mind that is indeed Buddha."
[6] Pratveka-Buddha sastra? From a sotoba of the Zen sect.

vana have become for me as a dream of the night that is gone."

Yet what of the Buddhas who successively melt into Nirvana, and nevertheless "return in their order"? Are they, too, phantoms? — is their individuality also unreal? Probably the question admits of many different answers — since there is a Buddhist Realism as well as a Buddhist Idealism; but, for present purposes, the following famous text is a sufficient reply:

NAMU ITSU SHIN SAN-ZE SHŌ BUTSU!

Hail to all the Buddhas of the Three Existences,[1] who are but one in the One Mind![2]

In relation to the Absolute, no difference exists even between gods and men:

The Golden Verse of the Jō-sho-sa-chi [3] says: "This doctrine is equal and alike for all; there is neither superior nor inferior, neither above nor below."

Nay, according to a still more celebrated text, there is not even any difference of personality:

JI TA HŌ KAI BYŌ DŌ RI YAKU

The "I" and the "Not-I" are not different in the World of Law: both are favored alike.[4]

---

[1] San-ze, or mitsu-yo — the Past, Present, and Future.

[2] "Mind" is here expressed by the character "shin" or "kokoro." The text is from a Zen sotoba, but is used also, I am told, by the mystical sects of Tendai and Shingon.

[3] Krityânushthâna-gñâna. The text is from a sotoba of the Shingon sect.

[4] More literally, "Self and Other": i.e., the Ego and the Non-Ego in the meaning of "I" and "Thou." There is no "I" and "Thou" in Buddhahood. This text was copied from a Zen sotoba.

The Literature of the Dead

And a still more wonderful text, from a Zen sotoba (to my thinking, the most remarkable of all Buddhist texts), declares that the world itself, phantom though it be, is yet not different from Mind:

SŌ MOKU KOKU DŌ SHITSU KAI JŌ BUTSU
Grass, trees, countries, the earth itself, — all these shall enter wholly into Buddhahood.

Literally, "shall become Buddha"; that is, they shall enter into Buddhahood or Nirvana. All that we term matter will be transmuted therefore into Mind — Mind with the attributes of Infinite Sentiency, Infinite Vision, and Infinite Knowledge. As phenomenon, matter is unreal; but transcendentally it belongs by its ultimate nature to the Sole Reality.

Such a philosophical position is likely to puzzle the average reader. To call matter and mind but two aspects of the Ultimate Reality will not seem irrational to students of Herbert Spencer. But to say that matter is a phenomenon, an illusion, a dream, explains nothing; — as phenomenon it exists, and having a destiny attributed to it, must be considered objectively. Equally unsatisfying is the statement that phenomena are aggregates of Karma. What is the nature of the particles of the aggregate? Or, in plainest language, what is the illusion made of?

Not in the original Buddhist scriptures, and still less in the literature of Buddhist cemeteries, need the reply be sought. Such questions are dealt with in the sastras rather than in the sutras; — also in various Japanese commentaries upon both. A friend has furnished me with some very curious and unfamiliar Shingon texts containing answers to the enigma.

The Shingon sect, I may observe, is a mystical sect, which especially proclaims the identity of mind and substance, and boldly carries out the doctrine to its furthest logical consequences. Its founder and father Kū-kai, better known as Kōbōdaishi, declared in his book "Hizōki" that matter is not different in essence from spirit. "As to the doctrine of grass, trees, and things non-sentient becoming Buddhas," he writes, "I say that the refined forms [ultimate nature] of spiritual bodies consist of the Five Great Elements; that Ether [1] consists of the Five Great Elements; and that the refined forms of bodies spiritual, of ether, of plants, of trees, consequently pervade all space. This ether, these plants and trees, are themselves spiritual bodies. To the eye of flesh, plants and trees appear to be gross matter. But to the eye of the Buddha *they are composed of minute spiritual entities*. Therefore, even without any change in their substance, there can be no error or impropriety in our calling them Buddhas."

[1] The Chinese word literally means "void" — as in the expression "Void Supreme," to signify the state of Nirvana. But the philosophical reference here is to the ultimate substance, or primary matter; and the rendering of the term by "Ether" (rather in the Greek than the modern sense, of course) has the sanction of Bunyiu Nanjio, and the approval of other eminent Sanscrit and Chinese scholars.

The Literature of the Dead

The use of the term "non-sentient" in the foregoing would seem to involve a contradiction; but this is explained away by a dialogue in the book "Shi-man-gi":

Q. Are not grass and trees sometimes called sentient?
A. They can be so called.
Q. But they have also been called non-sentient: how can they be called sentient?
A. In all substance from the beginning exists the impress of the wisdom-nature of the Nyōrai (Tathâgata): therefore to call such things sentient is not error.

"Potentially sentient," the reader might conclude; but this conclusion would be wrong. The Shingon thought is not of a potential sentiency, but of a latent sentiency which, although to us non-apparent and non-imaginable, is nevertheless both real and actual. Commenting upon the words of Kōbōdaishi above cited, the great priest Yū-kai not only reiterates the opinion of his master, but asserts that it is absurd to deny that plants, trees, and what we call inanimate objects, can practice virtue! "Since Mind," he declares, "pervades the whole World of Law, the grasses, plants, trees, and earth pervaded by it must all have mind, and must turn their mind to Buddhahood and practice virtue. Do not doubt the doctrine of our sect, regarding the Non-Duality of the Pervading and the Pervaded, merely because of the distinction made in common parlance between Matter and Mind." As for *how* plants or stones can practice virtue, the sutras indeed have nothing to say. But that is because the sutras, being intended for man, teach only what man should know and do.

The reader will now, perhaps, be better able to follow out the really startling Buddhist hypothesis of the nature of matter to its more than startling conclusion. (It must not be contemned because of the fantasy of five elements; for these are declared to be only modes of one ultimate.) All forms of what we call matter are really but aggregates of spiritual units; and all apparent differences of substance represent only differences of combination among these units. The differences of combination are caused by special tendencies and affinities of the units; — the tendency of each being the necessary result of its particular evolutional history (using the term "evolutional" in a purely ethical sense). All integrations of apparent substance — the million suns and planets of the universe — represent only the affinities of such ghostly ultimates; and every human act or thought registers itself through enormous time by some knitting or loosening of forces working for good or evil.

Grass, trees, earth, and all things seem to us what they are not, simply because the eye of flesh is blind. Life itself is a curtain hiding reality — somewhat as the vast veil of day conceals from our sight the countless orbs of Space. But the texts of the cemeteries proclaim that the purified mind, even

The Literature of the Dead

while prisoned within the body, may enter for moments of ecstasy into union with the Supreme:

The One Bright Moon illuminates the mind in the meditation called Zenjō.[1]

The "One Bright Moon" is the Supreme Buddha. By the pure of heart He may even be seen:

Hail unto the Wondrous Law! By attaining to the state of single-mindedness we behold the Buddha.[2]

Greater delight there is none:

Incomparable the face of the Nyōrai — surpassing all beauty in this world! [3]

But to see the face of one Buddha is to see all:

The Dai-en-kyō-chi-kyō [4] says: "By entering deeply into the meditation Zenjō, one may see all the Buddhas of the Ten Directions of Space."

The Golden Mouth has said: "He whose mind can discern the being of one Buddha may easily behold three, four, five Buddhas — nay, all the Buddhas of the Three Existences." [5]

Which mystery is thus explained:

The Myō-kwan-satsu-chi-kyō [6] has said: "The mind that detaches itself from all things becomes the very mind of Buddha." [7]

---

[1] Literally: "illuminates the Zenjō-mind." Zenjō is the Sanscrit Dhyâna. It is believed that in real Dhyâna the mind can hold communication with the Absolute. From a sotoba of the Zen sect.
[2] From a sotoba of the Tendai sect.   [3] From a Jōdo sotoba.
[4] Literally: "the Great-Round-Mirror-Wisdom-Sutra." Sanscrit, Adarsana-gñâna. From a Zen sotoba.
[5] Sotoba of the Zen sect.   [6] Pratyavekshana-gñâna.
[7] From a Zen sotoba.

The Buddhist Writings of Lafcadio Hearn

Visitors to the older Buddhist temples of Japan can scarcely fail to notice the remarkable character of the gilded aureoles attached to certain images. These aureoles, representing circles, disks, or ovals of glory, contain numbers of little niches shaped like archings or whirls of fire, each enshrining a Buddha or a Bodhisattva. A verse of the Amitâyur-Dhyâna Sutra might have suggested this symbolism to the Japanese sculptors:

In the halo of that Buddha there are Buddhas innumerable as the sands of the Ganga.[1]

Icon and verse alike express that doctrine of the One in Many suggested by the foregoing sotoba-texts; and the assurance that he who sees one Buddha can see all, may further be accepted as signifying that he who perceives one great truth fully, will be able to perceive countless truths.

But even to the spiritually blind the light must come at last. A host of cemetery texts proclaim the Infinite Love that watches all, and the certainty of ultimate and universal salvation:

Possessing all the Virtues and all the Powers, the Eyes of the Infinite Compassion behold all living creatures.[2]

The Kongō-takara-tō-mei [3] proclaims: "All living beings in the Six States of Existence [4] shall be delivered

---

[1] *Buddhist Mahâyâna Texts: Sacred Books of the East*, XLIX, 180.

[2] From a sotoba of the Zen sect.

[3] Literally: "the Inscription of the Tower of Diamond" — name of a Buddhist text.

[4] The Six States of Existence are Heaven, Man, Demons, Hell, Hungry Spirits (Pretas), and Animals. The above is from a Zen sotoba.

The Literature of the Dead

from the bonds of attachment; their minds and their bodies alike shall be freed from desire; and they shall obtain the Supreme Enlightenment."

The Sutra says: "Changing the hearts of all beings, I cause them to enter upon the Way of Buddhahood." [1]

Yet the supreme conquest can be achieved only by self-effort:

Through the destruction of the Three Poisons [2] one may rise above the Three States of Existence.

The Three Existences signify time past, present, and future. To rise above (more literally, to "emerge from") the Three Existences means therefore to pass beyond Space and Time — to become one with the Infinite. The conquest of Time is indeed possible only for a Buddha; but all shall become Buddhas. Even a woman, while yet a woman, may reach Buddhahood, as this Nichiren text bears witness, inscribed above the grave of a girl:

KAI YŌ KEN PI RYŌ-NYO JŌ BUTSU

All beheld from afar the Dragon Maiden become a Buddha.

The reference is to the beautiful legend of Sâgara, the daughter of the Nâga-king, in the "Myō-hō-rengé-kyō." [3]

---

[1] Sotoba of the Nichiren sect.
[2] San-doku or Mitsu-no-doku, viz.: Anger, Ignorance, and Desire. From a Zen sotoba.
[3] Japanese title of the Saddhârma-Pundarika Sutra. See, for legend, chap. XI of Kern's translation in the *Sacred Books of the East* series.

IV

THOUGH not representing, nor even suggesting, the whole range of sotoba-literature, the foregoing texts will sufficiently indicate the quality of its philosophical interest. The inscriptions of the haka, or tombs, have another kind of interest; but before treating of these, a few words should be said about the tombs themselves. I cannot attempt detail, because any description of the various styles of such monuments would require a large and profusely illustrated volume; while the study of their sculptures belongs to the enormous subject of Buddhist iconography — foreign to the purpose of this essay.

There are hundreds — probably thousands — of different forms of Buddhist funeral monuments — ranging from the unhewn boulder, with a few ideographs scratched on it, of the poorest village graveyard, to the complicated turret (kagé-kio) enclosing a shrine with images, and surmounted with a spire of umbrella-shaped disks or parasols (Sanscrit: tchâtras) — possibly representing the old Chinese stûpa. The most common class of haka are plain. A large number of the better class have lotus designs chiseled upon some part of them: either the pedestal is sculptured so as to represent lotus-petals; or a single blossom is cut in relief or intaglio on the face of the tablet; or (but this is rare) a whole lotus-plant, leaves and flowers, is designed in relief upon one or two sides of the monument. In the

The Literature of the Dead

costly class of tombs symbolizing the Five Buddhist Elements, the eight-petaled lotus-symbol may be found repeated, with decorative variations, upon three or four portions of their elaborate structure. Occasionally we find beautiful reliefs upon tombstones — images of Buddhas or Bodhisattvas; and not unfrequently a statue of Jizō may be seen erected beside a grave. But the sculptures of this class are mostly old; — the finest pieces in the Kobudera cemetery, for example, were executed between two and three hundred years ago. Finally I may observe that the family crest or mon of the dead is cut upon the front of the tomb, and sometimes also upon the little stone tank set before it.

The inscriptions very seldom include any texts from the holy books. On the front of the monument, below the chiseled crest, the kaimyō is graven, together, perhaps, with a single mystical character — Sanscrit or Chinese; on the left side is usually placed the record of the date of death; and on the right, the name of the person or family erecting the tomb. Such is now, at least, the ordinary arrangement; but there are numerous exceptions; and as the characters are most often disposed in vertical columns, it is quite easy to put all the inscriptions upon the face of a very narrow monument. Occasionally the real name is also cut upon some part of the stone — together, perhaps, with some brief record of the memorable actions of the dead. Excepting the kaimyō, and the sect-invocation often accompanying it, the inscriptions upon the ordinary class of tombs are secular in character; and the real interest of such epigraphy is limited to the kaimyō. By kai-myō (sîla-name) is meant the Buddhist name given to the spirit of the dead, according to the custom of all sects except the Ikkō or Shinshū. In a special sense the term kai, or sîla, refers to precepts of conduct;[1] in a general sense it might be rendered as "salvation by works." But the Shinshū allows no kai to any mortal; it does not admit the doctrine of immediate salvation by works, but only by faith in Amida; and the posthumous appellations which it bestows are therefore called, not kai-myō, but hō-myō, or "Law-names."

Before Meiji the social rank occupied by any one during life was suggested by the kaimyō. The use, with a kaimyō, of the two characters reading "in den," and signifying "temple-dweller," or "mansion dweller" — or of the more common single character "in" signifying "temple" or "mansion," was a privilege reserved to the nobility and gentry. Class-distinctions were further indicated by suffixes.

[1] There is a great variety of sîla; — five, eight, and ten for different classes of laity; two hundred and fifty for priests; — five hundred for nuns, etc., etc. Be it here observed that the posthumous Buddhist name given to the dead must not be studied as referring always to conduct in this world, but rather as referring to sîla in another world. The kaimyō is thus a title of spiritual initiation. Some Japanese Buddhist sects hold what are called "Ju-Kai-E" ("sîla-giving assemblies"), at which the initiated are given kaimyō of another sort — sîla-names of admission as neophytes.

The Literature of the Dead

Koji — a term partly corresponding to our "lay-brother" — and Daishi, "great elder-sister," were honorifically attached to the kaimyō of the samurai and the aristocracy; while the simpler appellations of Shinshi and Shinnyo, respectively signifying "faithful [believing] man," "faithful woman," followed the kaimyō of the humble. These forms are still used; but the distinctions they once maintained have mostly passed away, and the privilege of the knightly "in den," and its accompaniments, is free to any one willing to pay for it. At all times the words "Dōji" and "Dōnyo" seem to have been attached to the kaimyō of children. Dō, alone, means a lad, but when combined with ji or nyo it means "child" in the adjectival sense; — so that we may render Dōji as "Child-son," and Dōnyo as "Child-daughter." Children are thus called who die before reaching their fifteenth year — the majority-year by the old samurai code; a lad of fifteen being deemed fit for war-service. In the case of children who die within a year after birth, the terms "Gaini" and "Gainyo" occasionally replace "Dōji" and "Dōnyo." The syllable Gai here represents a Chinese character meaning "suckling."

Different Buddhist sects have different formulas for the composition of the kaimyō and its addenda; — but this subject would require a whole special treatise; and I shall mention only a few sectarian customs. The Shingon sect sometimes put a Sanscrit character — the symbol of a Buddha — before their kaimyō; — the Shin head theirs with an abbreviation of the holy name Sakyamuni; — the Nichiren often preface their inscriptions with the famous invocation, "Namu myō hō rengé kyō" ("Hail to the Sutra of the Lotus of the Good Law!") — sometimes followed by the words "Senzo daidai" ("forefathers of the generations"); — the Jōdo, like the Ikkō, use an abbreviation of the name Sakyamuni, or, occasionally, the invocation "Namu Amida Butsu!" — and they compose their four-character kaimyō with the aid of two ideographs signifying "honour" or "fame"; — the Zen sect contrive that the first and the last character of the kaimyō, when read together, shall form a particular Buddhist term, or mystical phrase — except when the kaimyō consists of only two characters.

Probably the word "mansion" in kaimyō-inscriptions would suggest to most Western readers the idea of heavenly mansions. But the fancy would be at fault. The word has no celestial signification; yet the history of its epitaphic use is curious enough. Anciently, at the death of any illustrious man, a temple was erected for the special services due to his spirit, and also for the conservation of relics or memorials of him. Confucianism introduced into Japan the ihai, or mortuary tablet, called by the Chinese shin-shu;[1] and a portion of the temple was set apart to serve as a chapel for the ihai, and the ancestral cult. Any such memorial temple was called

[1] That is, according to the Japanese reading of the Chinese characters.

The Literature of the Dead

"in," or "mansion" — doubtless because the august spirit was believed to occupy it at certain periods; — and the term yet survives in the names of many celebrated Buddhist temples — such as the Chion-In, of Kyōtō. With the passing of time, this custom was necessarily modified; for as privileges were extended and aristocracies multiplied, the erection of a separate temple to each notable presently became impossible. Buddhism met the difficulty by conferring upon every individual of distinction the posthumous title of "in-den" — and affixing to this title the name of an imaginary temple or "mansion." So that to-day, in the vast majority of kaimyō, the character "in" refers only to the temple that would have been built had circumstances permitted, but now exists only in the pious desire of those who love and reverence the departed.

Nevertheless the poetry of these in-names does possess some real meaning. They are nearly all of them names such as would be given to real Buddhist temples — names of virtues and sanctities and meditations — names of ecstasies and powers and splendors and luminous immeasurable unfoldings — names of all ways and means of escape from the Six States of Existence and the sorrow of "peopling the cemeteries again and again."

The general character and arrangement of kaimyō can best be understood by the aid of a few typical specimens. The first example is from a beautiful tomb in the cemetery of Kobudera, which is sculptured with a relief representing the Bodhisattva Mahâsthâma (Seishi Bosatsu) meditating. All the text in this instance has been cut upon the face of the monument, to left and right of the icon. Transliterated into Romaji it reads thus:

(Kaimyō)
Tei-Sho-In, Hō-sō Myō-shin, *Daishi*
(Record)
Shōtoku Ni, Jin shin Shimotsuki, jiu-ku nichi
(Translation)
Great Elder-Sister, Wonderful-Reality-Appearing-at-the-Window-of-Law, dwelling in the Mansion of the Pine of Chastity.

The nineteenth day of the Month of Frost,[1] second year of Shōtoku [2] — the year being under the Dragon of Elder Water.

For the sake of clearness, I have printed the posthumous name proper (Hō-sō Myō-shin) in small capitals, and the rest in italics. The first three characters of the inscription — Tei-Shō-In — form the name of the temple, or "mansion." The pine, both in religious and secular poetry, is a symbol of changeless conditions of good, because it remains freshly green in all seasons. The use of the term "Reality" in the kaimyō indicates the state of unity with the Absolute; — by "Window-of-Law" (Law here signi-

[1] By the old calendar, the eleventh month was the Month of Frost.
[2] The second year of the period Shōtoku corresponds to 1712 A.D. (For the meaning of the phrase "Dragon of Elder Water" the reader will do well to consult Professor Rein's *Japan*, pp. 434–36.)

The Literature of the Dead

fying the Buddha-state) must be understood that exercise of virtue through which even in this existence some perception of Infinite Truth may be obtained. I have already explained the final word, Daishi ("great elder-sister").

Less mystical, but not less beautiful, is this Nichiren kaimyō sculptured upon the grave of a young samurai:

  Ko-shin In, Ken-dō Nichi-ki, Koji.

[Koji —
Bright-Sun-on-the-Way-of-the-Wise, in the Mansion of Luminous Mind.] [1]

On the same stone is carven the kaimyō of the wife:

  Shin-kyō In, Myō-en Nichi-ko, Daishi.

[Daishi —
Spherically-Wondrous-Sunbeam, in the Mansion of the Mirror of the Heart.]

Perhaps the reader will now be able to find interest in the following selection of kaimyō, translated for me by Japanese scholars. The inscriptions are of various rites and epochs; but I have arranged them only by class and sex:

  [MASCULINE KAIMYŌ]

Koji —
Law-Nature-Eternally-Complete, in the Mansion of the Mirror of Light.

---

[1] This beautiful kaimyō is identical with that placed upon the monument of my dear friend Nishida, buried in the Nichiren cemetery of Chōmanji, in Matsué.

Koji —
Lone-Moon-above-Snowy-Peak, in the Mansion of Quiet Light.

Koji —
Wonderful-Radiance-of-Luminous-Sound, in the Mansion of the Day-dawn of Mind.

Koji —
Pure-Lotus-bloom-of-the-Heart, in the Mansion of Shining Beginnings.

Koji —
Real-Earnestness-Self-sufficing-within, in the Mansion of Mystery Penetration.

Koji —
Wonderful-Brightness-of-the-Clouds-of-Law, in the Mansion of Wisdom-Illumination.

Koji —
Law-Echo-proclaiming-Truth, in the Mansion of Real Zeal.

Koji —
Ocean-of-Reason-Calmly-Full, in the Mansion of Self-Nature.

Koji —
Effective-Benevolence-Hearing-with-Pure-Heart-the-Supplications-of-the-Poor — dwelling in the Mansion of the Virtue of Pity.

Koji —
Perfect-Enlightenment-beaming-tranquil-Glory — in the Mansion of Supreme Comprehension.

Koji —
Autumnal-Prospect-Clear-of-Cloud — of the Household of Sakyamuni — in the Mansion of the Obedient Heart.

The Literature of the Dead

Koji —
Illustrious-Brightness — of the Household of the Buddha — in the Mansion of Conspicuous Virtue.
Koji —
Daily-Peace-Home-Prospering, in the Mansion of Spherical Completeness.
Shinshi —
Prosperity-wide-shining-as-the-Moon-of-Autumn.
Shinshi —
Vow-abiding-wondrously-without-fault.
Shinshi —
Vernal-Mountain-bathed-in-the-Light-of-the-Law.
Shinshi —
Waking-to-Dhyâna-at-the-Bell-Peal-of-the Wondrous-Dawn.
Shinshi —
Winter-Mountain-Chastity-Mind.[1]

[FEMININE KAIMYÖ]
Daishi —
Moon-Dawn-of-the-Mountain-of-Light, dwelling in the August Mansion of Self-witness.[2]

[1] Signifying: "believing man of mind as chastely pure as the snow upon a peak in winter."
[2] This is the kaimyō of the lady for whose sake the temple of Kobudera was built; and the words "Mansion of Self-witness" here refer to the temple itself, which is thus named (Ji-Shō In). The Chinese text reads: "Ji-Shō-In den, Kwo-zan Kyō-kei, Daishi"; literally, "Great Elder-Sister, Dawn-Katsura-of-Luminous-Mountain, dwelling in the August Mansion of Self-witness." The katsura (*olea fragrans*) is a tree mysteriously connected, in Japanese poetical fancy, with the moon; and its name is often used, as here, to signify the moon. Katsura-no-hana, or "katsura-flower," is a poetical term for moonlight. This kaimyō is remarkable in having the honorific term "August" prefixed to the name of the mansion or temple — a sign of the high rank of the dead lady. The full date inscribed is "twenty-eighth day of Mid-Autumn" (the old eighth month) "of the seventeenth year of Kwansei" (1640 A.D.).

Daishi –
 Wondrous-Lotus-of-Fleckless-Light, in the Mansion of the Moonlike Heart.

Daishi —
 Wonderful-Chastity-Responding-with-Pure-Mind-to-the-Summons-of-Duty — in the Mansion of the Great Sea of Compassion.

Daishi —
 Lotus-Heart-of-Wondrous-Apparition — in the Mansion of Luminous Perfume.

Daishi —
 Clear-Light-of-the-Spotless-Moon, in the Mansion of Spring-time-Eve.

Kaishi —
 Pure-Mind-as-a-Sun-of-Compassion, in the Mansion of Real Light.

Daishi —
 Wondrous-Lotus-of-Fragrance-Ethereal, in the Mansion of Law-Nature.

Shinnyo —
 Rejoicing-in-the-Way-of-the-Infinite.

Shinnyo —
 Excellent-Courage to-follow-Wisdom-to-the-End.

Shinnyo —
 Winter-Moon-shedding-purest-Light.

Shinnyo —
 Luminous-Shadow-in-the-Plumflower-Chamber.

Shinnyo —
 Virtue-fragrant-as-the-Odor-of-the-Lotus.

The Literature of the Dead

[CHILDREN'S KAIMYŌ — MALE]
Dai-Dōji[1] —
Instantly-Attaining-to-the-Perfect-Peace, dwelling in the August Mansion of Purity.
Dai-Dōji [2] —
Permeating-Lucidity-of-the-Pure-Grove, dwelling in the August Mansion of Blossom-Fragrance.
Gaini —
Frost-Glimmer.
Dōji —
Dewy-Light.
Dōji —
Dream-of-Spring.
Dōji —
Spring-Frost.
Dōji —
Ethereal-Nature.
Dōji —
Rain-of-the-Law-from-translucent-Clouds.

[CHILDREN'S KAIMYŌ — FEMALE]
Dai-Dōnyo [3] —
Bright-Shining-Height-of-Wisdom, dwelling in the August Mansion of Fragrant Trees.

[1] The prefix "dai" (great) before the ordinary term "dōji" (male child) is of rare occurrence. Probably the lad was of princely birth. The grave is in a reserved part of the Kobudera cemetery; and the year-date of death is "the fourth of Enkyō" — corresponding to 1747.
[2] The tomb bearing this kaimyō is set beside that inscribed with the kaimyō preceding. Probably the boys were brothers. In both instances we have the honorific prefix "dai," and the term "August" qualifying the mansion-name. The year-date of death is "the second of Kwan-en" (1749).
[3] Probably a princely child — sister apparently of the highborn boys before referred to. She is buried beside them in Kobudera. Observe here again the use of the prefix "dai" — this time before the term

Gainyo —
 Snowy-Bubble.

Gainyo —
 Shining-Phantasm.

Dōnyo —
 Plumflower-Light.

Dōnyo —
 Dream-Phantasm.

Dōnyo —
 Chaste-Spring.

Dōnyo —
 Wisdom-Mirror-of-Flawless-Appearing.

Dōnyo —
 Wondrous-Excellence-of-Fragrant-Snow.

After having studied the sotoba-texts previously cited, the reader should be able to divine the meaning of most of the kaimyō above given. At all events he will understand such frequently repeated terms as "Moon," "Lotus," "Law." But he may be puzzled by other expressions; and some further explanation will, perhaps, not be unwelcome.

Besides expressing a pious hope for the higher happiness of the departed, or uttering some assurance of special conditions in the spiritual world, a great number of kaimyō also refer, directly or indirectly, to the character of the vanished personality. Thus a man of widely recognized integrity, and strong

"dōnyo," "child-girl" or "child-daughter." Perhaps the dai here would be better rendered by "grand" than by "great." Notice that the term "August" precedes the mansion-name in this case also. The date of death is given as "the sixth year of Hōreki" (1756).

The Literature of the Dead

moral purpose, may — like my dead friend — be not unfitly named: "Bright-Sun-on-the-Way-of-the Wise." The child-daughter or the young wife, especially remembered for sweetness of character, may be commemorated by some such posthumous name as "Plumflower-Light," or "Luminous-Shadow-of-the-Plumflower-Chamber"; — the word "plumflower" in either case at once suggesting the quality of the virtue of the dead, because this blossom in Japan is the emblem of feminine moral charm — more particularly faithfulness to duty and faultless modesty. Again the memory of any person noted for deeds of charity may be honored by such a kaimyō as, "Effective-Benevolence-Listening-with-Pure-Heart-to-the-Supplications-of-the-Poor." Finally I may observe that the kaimyō-terms expressing altitude, luminosity, and fragrance have most often a moral-exemplary signification. But in all countries epitaphic literature has its conventional hypocrisies or extravagances. Buddhist kaimyō frequently contain a great deal of religious flattery; and beautiful posthumous names are often given to those whose lives were the reverse of beautiful.

When we find among feminine kaimyō such appellations as "Wondrous-Lotus," or "Beautiful-as-the-Lotus-of-the-Dawn," we may be sure in the generality of cases that the charm, to which reference is so made, was ethical only. Yet there are exceptions; and the more remarkable of these are furnished by the kaimyō of children. Names like "Dream-of-

The Buddhist Writings of Lafcadio Hearn

Spring," "Radiant-Phantasm," "Snowy-Bubble," do actually refer to the lost form — or at least to the supposed parental idea of vanished beauty and grace. But such names also exemplify a peculiar consolatory application of the Buddhist doctrine of Impermanency. We might say that through the medium of these kaimyō the bereaved are thus soothed in the loftiest language of faith:

"Beautiful and brief was the being of your child — a dream of spring, a radiant passing vision — a snowy bubble. But in the order of eternal law all forms must pass; material permanency there is none: only the divine Absolute dwelling in every being — only the Buddha in the heart of each of us — forever endures. Be this great truth at once your comfort and your hope!"

Extraordinary examples of the retrospective significance sometimes given to posthumous names, are furnished by the kaimyō of the Forty-Seven Rōnin buried at Sengakuji in Tōkyō. (Their story is now well known to all the English-reading world through Mitford's eloquent and sympathetic version of it in the "Tales of Old Japan.") The noteworthy peculiarity of these kaimyō is that each contains the two words, "dagger" and "sword" — used in a symbolic sense, but having also an appropriate military suggestiveness. Ōishi Kuranosuké Yoshiwo, the leader, is alone styled "Koji"; — the kaimyō of his followers have the humbler suffix "Shinshi." Ōishi's

The Literature of the Dead

kaimyō reads: "Dagger-of-Emptiness-and-stainless-Sword, in the Mansion of Earnest Loyalty." I need scarcely call attention to the historic meaning of the mansion-name. Three of the kaimyō of his followers will serve as examples of the rest. That of Masé Kyudayu Masaake is: "Dagger-of-Fame-and-Sword of-the-Way [or Doctrine]." The kaimyō of Ōishi Sezayémon Nobukiyo is: "Dagger of Magnanimity-and-Sword-of-Virtue." And the kaimyō of Horibei Yasubei is: "Dagger-of-Cloud-and-Sword-of-Brightness."

The first and the last of these four kaimyō will be found obscure; and several more of the forty-seven inscriptions are equally enigmatic at first sight. Usually in a kaimyō the word "Emptiness," or "Void," signifies the Buddhist state of absolute spiritual purity — the state of Unconditioned Being. But in the kaimyō of Ōishi Kuranosuké the meaning of it, though purely Buddhist, is very different. By "emptiness" here, we must understand "illusion," "unreality" — and the full meaning of the phrase "dagger-emptiness" is: "Wisdom that, seeing the emptiness of material forms, pierces through illusion as a dagger." In Horibei Yasubei's kaimyō we must similarly render the word "cloud" by "illusion"; and "Dagger-of-Cloud" should be interpreted, "Illusion-penetrating Dagger of Wisdom." The wisdom that perceives the emptiness of phenomena is the sharply-dividing or distinguishing wisdom, is Myō-kwan-zatsu-chi (Pratyavekshana-gñâna).

V

POSSIBLY I have presumed too much upon the patience of my readers; yet I feel that these studies can yield scarcely more than the glimpse of a subject wide and deep as a sea. If they should arouse any Western interest in the philosophy and the poetry of Buddhist epitaphic literature, then they will certainly have accomplished all that I could reasonably hope.

Not improbably I shall be accused, as I have been on other occasions, of trying to make Buddhist texts "more beautiful than they are." This charge usually comes from persons totally ignorant of the originals, and betrays a spirit of disingenuousness with which I have no sympathy. Whoever confesses religion to have been a developing influence in the social and moral history of races — whoever grants that respect is due to convictions which have shaped the nobler courses of human conduct for thousands of years — whoever acknowledges that in any great religion something of eternal truth must exist — will hold it the highest duty of a translator to interpret the concepts of an alien faith as generously as he would wish his own thoughts or words interpreted by his fellow-men. In the rendering of Chinese sentences this duty presents itself under a peculiar aspect. Any attempt at literal translation would result in the production either of nonsense, or of a succession of ideas totally foreign to Far-Eastern

The Literature of the Dead

thought. The paramount necessity in treating such texts is to discover and to expound the thought conveyed to Oriental minds by the original ideographs — which are very different things indeed from "written words." The translations given in this essay were made by Japanese scholars, and, in their present form, have the approval of competent critics.

As I write these lines a full moon looks into my study over the trees of the temple-garden, and brings me the recollection of a little Buddhist poem:

> From the foot of the mountain, many are the paths ascending in shadow; but from the cloudless summit all who climb behold the self-same Moon.

The reader who knows the truth shrined in this little verse will not regret an hour passed with me among the tombs of Kobudera.

Of Moon Desire

I

He was two years old when — as ordained in the law of perpetual recurrence — he asked me for the Moon.

Unwisely I protested:

"The Moon I cannot give you because it is too high up. I cannot reach it."

He answered:

"By taking a very long bamboo, you probably could reach it, and knock it down."

I said:

"There is no bamboo long enough."

He suggested:

"By standing on the ridge of the roof of the house, you probably could poke it with the bamboo."

Whereat I found myself constrained to make some approximately truthful statements concerning the nature and position of the Moon.

This set me thinking. I thought about the strange fascination that brightness exerts upon living creatures in general — upon insects and fishes and birds and mammals — and tried to account for it by some inherited memory of brightness as related to food, to water, and to freedom. I thought of the countless generations of children who have asked for the Moon, and of the generations of parents who have

Of Moon Desire

laughed at the asking. And then I entered into the following meditation:

Have we any right to laugh at the child's wish for the Moon? No wish could be more natural; and as for its incongruity — do not we, children of a larger growth, mostly nourish wishes quite as innocent — longings that if realized could only work us woe — such as desire for the continuance after death of that very sense-life, or individuality, which once deluded us all into wanting to play with the Moon, and often subsequently deluded us in far less pleasant ways?

Now foolish as may seem, to merely empirical reasoning, the wish of the child for the Moon, I have an idea that the highest wisdom commands us to wish for very much more than the Moon — even for more than the Sun and the Morning-Star and all the Host of Heaven.

II

I REMEMBER when a boy lying on my back in the grass, gazing into the summer blue above me, and wishing that I could melt into it — become a part of it. For these fancies I believe that a religious tutor was innocently responsible: he had tried to explain to me, because of certain dreamy questions, what he termed "the folly and the wickedness of pantheism" — with the result that I immediately became a pantheist, at the tender age of fifteen. And my imaginings presently led me not only to want the sky for a playground, but also to become the sky!

Now I think that in those days I was really close to a great truth — touching it, in fact, without the faintest suspicion of its existence. I mean the truth that the wish *to become* is reasonable in direct ratio to its largeness — or, in other words, that the more you wish to be, the wiser you are; while the wish *to have* is apt to be foolish in proportion to its largeness. Cosmic law permits us very few of the countless things that we wish to have, but will help us to become all that we can possibly wish to be. Finite, and in so much feeble, is the wish to have: but infinite in puissance is the wish to become; and every mortal wish to become must eventually find satisfaction. By wanting to be, the monad makes itself the elephant, the eagle, or the man. By wanting to be, the man should become a god. Perhaps on this tiny globe, lighted only by a tenth-rate yellow sun, he will not have time to become a god; but who dare assert that his wish cannot project itself to mightier systems illuminated by vaster suns, and there reshape and invest him with the forms and powers of divinity? Who dare even say that his wish may not expand him beyond the Limits of Form, and make him one with Omnipotence? And Omnipotence, without asking, can have much brighter and bigger playthings than the Moon.

Probably everything is a mere question of wishing — providing that we wish, not to have, but to be.

Of Moon Desire

Most of the sorrow of life certainly exists because of the wrong kind of wishing and because of the contemptible pettiness of the wishes. Even to wish for the absolute lordship and possession of the entire earth were a pitifully small and vulgar wish. We must learn to nourish very much bigger wishes than that! My faith is that we must wish to become the total universe with its thousands of millions of worlds — and more than the universe, or a myriad universes — and more even than Space and Time.

III

Possibly the power for such wishing must depend upon our comprehension of the ghostliness of substance. Once men endowed with spirit all forms and motions and utterances of Nature: stone and metal, herb and tree, cloud and wind — the lights of heaven, the murmuring of leaves and waters, the echoes of the hills, the tumultuous speech of the sea. Then becoming wiser in their own conceit, they likewise became of little faith; and they talked about "the Inanimate" and "the Inert" — which are nonexistent — and discoursed of Force as distinct from Matter, and of Mind as distinct from both. Yet we now discover that the primitive fancies were, after all, closer to probable truth. We cannot indeed think of Nature to-day precisely as did our forefathers; but we find ourselves obliged to think of her in very much weirder ways; and the later revelations of our science have revitalized not a little of the primitive thought, and infused it with a new and awful beauty. And meantime those old savage sympathies with savage Nature that spring from the deepest sources of our being — always growing with our growth, strengthening with our strength, more and more unfolding with the evolution of our higher sensibilities — would seem destined to sublime at last into forms of cosmical emotion expanding and responding to infinitude.

Have you never thought about those immemorial feelings? . . . Have you never, when looking at some great burning, found yourself exulting without remorse in the triumph and glory of fire? — never unconsciously coveted the crumbling, splitting, iron-wrenching, granite-cracking force of its imponderable touch? — never delighted in the furious and terrible splendor of its phantasmagories — the ravening and bickering of its dragons — the monstrosity of its archings — the ghostly soaring and flapping of its spires? Have you never, with a hill-wind pealing in your ears, longed to ride that wind like a ghost — to scream round the peaks with it — to sweep the face of the world with it? Or, watching the lifting, the gathering, the muttering rush and thunder-burst of breakers, have you felt no impulse kindred to that giant motion — no longing to leap with that wild white tossing, and to join in that mighty shout? . . . And all such ancient emotional sympathies with Nature's familiar forces

Of Moon Desire

— do they not prelude, with their modern æsthetic developments, the future growth of rarer sympathies with incomparably subtler forces, and of longings to be limited only by our power to know? Know ether — shivering from star to star; — comprehend its sensitivities, its penetrancies, its transmutations; — and sympathies ethereal will evolve. Know the forces that spin the suns; — and already the way has been reached of becoming one with them.

And, furthermore, is there no suggestion of such evolvement in the steady widening through all the centuries of the thoughts of their world-priests and poets? — in the later sense of Life-as-Unity absorbing or transforming the ancient childish sense of life-personal? — in the tone of the new rapture in world-beauty, dominating the elder worship of beauty-human? — in the larger modern joy evoked by the blossoming of dawns, the blossoming of stars — by all quiverings of color, all shudderings of light? And is not the thing-in-itself, the detail, the appearance, being ever less and less studied for its mere power to charm, and ever more and more studied as a single character in that Infinite Riddle of which all phenomena are but ideographs?

Nay! — surely the time must come when we shall desire to be all that is, all that ever has been known — the past and the present and the future in one — all feeling, striving, thinking, joying, sorrowing — and everywhere the Part — and everywhere the Whole. And before us, with the waxing of the wish, perpetually the Infinities shall widen.

And I — even I! — by virtue of that wish, shall become all forms, all forces, all conditions: Ether, Wind, Fire, Water, Earth — all motion visible or viewless — all vibration named of light, of color, of sonority, of torrefaction — all thrillings piercing substance — all oscillations picturing in blackness, like the goblin-vision of the X-rays. By virtue of that wish I shall become the Source of all becoming and of all ceasing — the Power that shapes, the Power that dissolves — creating, with the shadows of my sleep, the life that shall vanish with my wakening. And even as phosphor-lampings in currents of midnight sea, so shall shimmer and pulse and pass, in mine Ocean of Death and Birth, the burning of billions of suns, the whirling of trillions of worlds. . . .

IV

"WELL," said the friend to whom I read this reverie, "there is some Buddhism in your fancies — though you seem to have purposely avoided several important points of doctrine. For instance, you must know that Nirvana is never to be reached by wishing, but by *not* wishing. What you call the 'wish-to-become' can only help us, like a lantern, along the darker portions of the Way. As for wanting the Moon — I think that you must have seen many old Japanese pictures of apes clutching at the

Of Moon Desire

reflection of the Moon in water. The subject is a Buddhist parable: the water is the phantom-flux of sensations and ideas; the Moon — not its distorted image — is the sole Truth. And your Western philosopher was really teaching a Buddhist parable when he proclaimed man but a higher kind of ape. For in this world of illusion, man is truly still the ape, trying to seize on water the shadow of the Moon."

"Ape, indeed," I made answer — "but an ape of gods — even that divine Ape of the Ramayana who may clutch the Sun!"

Footprints of the Buddha

I

I WAS recently surprised to find, in Anderson's catalogue of Japanese and Chinese paintings in the British Museum, this remarkable statement: "It is to be noted that in Japan the figure of the Buddha is never represented by the feet, or pedestal alone, as in the Amravâtî remains, and many other Indian art-relics." As a matter of fact the representation is not even rare in Japan. It is to be found not only upon stone monuments, but also in religious paintings — especially certain kakemono suspended in temples. These kakemono usually display the footprints upon a very large scale, with a multitude of mystical symbols and characters. The sculptures may be less common; but in Tōkyō alone there are a number of Butsu-soku-séki, or "Buddha-foot stones," which I have seen — and probably several which I have not seen. There is one at the temple of Ekō-In, near Ryōgoku-bashi; one at the temple of Dentsu-In, in Koishikawa; one at the temple of Denbō-In, in Asakusa; and a beautiful example at Zōjōji in Shiba. These are not cut out of a single block, but are composed of fragments cemented into the irregular traditional shape, and capped with a heavy slab of Nebukawa granite, on the polished surface of which the design is engraved in lines about one tenth of an inch in depth. I should judge the average height of these pedestals to be about two feet four inches, and their greatest diameter about three feet. Around the footprints there are carved (in most of the examples) twelve little bunches of leaves and buds of the Bodai-jū ("Bodhidruma"), or Bodhi-tree of Buddhist legend. In all cases the footprint design is about the same; but the monuments are different in quality and finish. That of Zōjōji — with figures of divinities cut in low relief on its sides — is the most ornate and costly of the four. The specimen at Ekō-In is very poor and plain.

The first Butsu-soku-séki made in Japan was that erected at Tōdaiji, in Nara. It was designed after a similar monument in China, said to be the faithful copy of an Indian original. Concerning this Indian original, the following tradition is given in an old Buddhist book : [1]

In a temple of the province of Makada [Maghada] there is a great stone. The Buddha once trod upon this stone; and the prints of the soles of his feet remain upon its surface. The length of the impressions is one foot and eight inches,[2] and the width of them a little more than six inches. On the sole-part of each footprint there is the impression of a wheel; and upon each of the prints of the

---

[1] The Chinese title is pronounced by Japanese as *Sei-iki-ki*. "Sei-Iki" (the Country of the West) was the old Japanese name for India; and thus the title might be rendered, "The Book about India." I suppose this is the work known to Western scholars as *Si-yu-ki*.

[2] "One shaku and eight sun." But the Japanese foot and inch are considerably longer than the English.

Footprints of the Buddha

ten toes there is a flower-like design, which sometimes radiates light. When the Buddha felt that the time of his Nirvana was approaching, he went to Kushina [Kusinârâ], and there stood upon that stone. He stood with his face to the south. Then he said to his disciple Anan [Ananda]: "In this place I leave the impression of my feet, to remain for a last token. Although a king of this country will try to destroy the impression, it can never be entirely destroyed." And indeed it has not been destroyed unto this day. Once a king who hated Buddhism caused the top of the stone to be pared off, so as to remove the impression; but after the surface had been removed, the footprints reappeared upon the stone.

Concerning the virtue of the representation of the footprints of the Buddha, there is sometimes quoted a text from the "Kwan-butsu-sanmai-kyō" ["Buddha-dhyâna-samâdhi-sâgara-sutra"], thus translated for me:

In that time Shaka ["Sâkyamuni"] lifted up his foot. ... When the Buddha lifted up his foot all could perceive upon the sole of it the appearance of a wheel of a thousand spokes.... And Shaka said: "Whosoever beholds the sign upon the sole of my foot shall be purified from all his faults. Even he who beholds the sign after my death shall be delivered from all the evil results of all his errors."

Various other texts of Japanese Buddhism affirm that whoever looks upon the footprints of the Buddha "shall be freed from the bonds of error, and conducted upon the Way of Enlightenment."

An outline of the footprints as engraved on one of the Japanese pedestals [1] should have some interest

[1] A monument at Nara exhibits the S'rîpâda in a form differing considerably from the design upon the Tōkyō pedestals.

even for persons familiar with Indian sculptures of the S'rîpâda. The drawing below, showing both footprints, has been made after the tracing at Dentsu-In, where the footprints have the full legendary dimension.

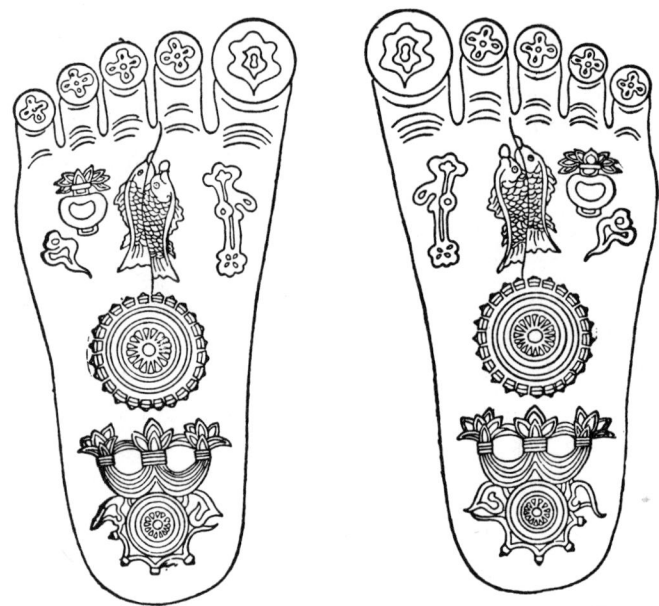

S'RÎPÂDA-TRACING AT DENTSU-IN, KOISHIKAWA, TŌKYŌ

It will be observed that there are only seven emblems: these are called in Japan the "Shichi-Sō," or "Seven Appearances." I got some information about them from the "Shō-Ekō-Hō-Kwan" — a book used by the Jōdo sect. This book also contains rough woodcuts of the footprints; and one of

Footprints of the Buddha

them I reproduce here for the purpose of calling attention to the curious form of the emblems upon the toes. They are said to be modifications of the manji, or swastika (卍); but I doubt it. In the Butsu-soku-séki-tracings, the corresponding figures

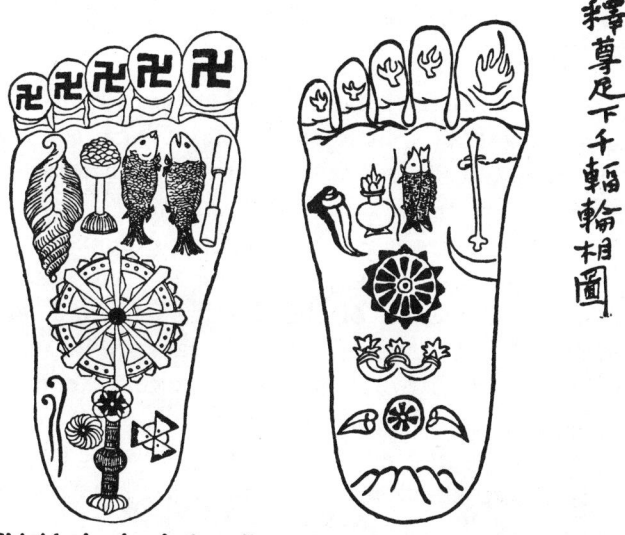

S'rîpâda showing the Swastika
(*From the* BUKKYŌ-HYAKKWA-ZENSHO)

(*From the* SHŌ-EKŌ-HŌ-KWAN)

suggest the "flower-like design" mentioned in the tradition of the Maghada stone; while the symbols in the book-print suggest fire. Indeed their outline so much resembles the conventional flamelet-design of Buddhist decoration, that I cannot help thinking them originally intended to indicate the traditional luminosity of the footprints. Moreover, there is a text in the book called "Hō-Kai-Shidai" that lends support to this supposition:

> The sole of the foot of the Buddha is flat — like the base of a toilet-stand. . . . Upon it are lines forming the appearance of a wheel of a thousand spokes. . . . The toes are slender, round, long, straight, graceful, *and somewhat luminous.*

The explanation of the Seven Appearances which is given by the "Shō-Ekō-Hō-Kwan" cannot be called satisfactory; but it is not without interest in relation to Japanese popular Buddhism. The emblems are considered in the following order:

I. *The Swastika* The figure upon each toe is said to be a modification of the manji [1] (卍); and although I doubt whether this is always the case, I have observed that on some of the large kakemono representing the footprints, the emblem really *is* the swastika — not a flamelet nor a flower-shape. [2] The Japanese commentator explains the swastika as a symbol of "everlasting bliss."

II. *The Fish* (*Gyo*). The fish signifies a freedom from all restraints. As in the water a fish moves easily in any direction, so in the Buddha-state the fully-emancipated knows no restraints or obstructions.

---
[1] Literally: "The thousand-character" sign.
[2] On some monuments and drawings there is a sort of disk made by a single line in spiral, on each toe — together with the image of a small wheel.

Footprints of the Buddha

III. *The Diamond-Mace* (Jap. "Kongō-sho"; — Sansc. "Vadjra"). Explained as signifying the divine force that "strikes and breaks all the lusts (bonnō) of the world."

IV. *The Conch-Shell* (Jap. "Hora") *or Trumpet.* Emblem of the preaching of the Law. The book "Shin-zoku-butsu-ji-hen" calls it the symbol of the voice of the Buddha. The "Dai-hi-kyō" calls it the token of the preaching and of the power of the Mâhâyâna doctrine. The "Dai-Nichi-Kyō" says:

At the sound of the blowing of the shell, all the heavenly deities are filled with delight, and come to hear the Law.

V. *The Flower-Vase* (Jap. "Hanagamé"). Emblem of murō — a mystical word which might be literally rendered as "not-leaking" — signifying that condition of supreme intelligence triumphant over birth and death.

VI. *The Wheel-of-a-Thousand-Spokes* (Sansc. "Tchakra"). This emblem, called in Japanese "Senfuku-rin-sō," is curiously explained by various quotations. The "Hokké-Monku" says:

The effect of a wheel is to crush something; and the effect of the Buddha's preaching is to crush all delusions, errors, doubts, and superstitions. Therefore preaching the doctrine is called, "turning the Wheel." . . .

The "Sei-Ri-Ron" says:

Even as the common wheel has its spokes and its hub, so in Buddhism there are many branches of the Hasshi Shōdo ("Eight-fold Path," or eight rules of conduct).

VII. *The Crown of Brahmâ.* Under the heel of the Buddha is the Treasure-Crown (Hō-Kwan) of Brahmâ (Bon-Ten-O) — in symbol of the Buddha's supremacy above the gods.

But I think that the inscriptions upon any of these Butsu-soku-séki will be found of more significance than the above imperfect attempts at an explanation of the emblems. The inscriptions upon the monument at Dentsu-In are typical. On different sides of the structure — near the top, and placed by rule so as to face certain points of the compass — there are engraved five Sanscrit characters which are symbols of the Five Elemental Buddhas, together with scriptural and commemorative texts. These latter have been translated for me as follows:

The "Ho-ko-hon-nyo-kyo" says: "In that time, from beneath his feet, the Buddha radiated a light having the appearance of a wheel of a thousand spokes. And all who saw that radiance became strictly upright, and obtained the Supreme Enlightenment."

The "Kwan-Butsu-sanmai-kyo" says: "Whosoever looks upon the footprints of the Buddha shall be freed from the results even of innumerable thousands of imperfections."

The "Butsu-setsu-mu-ryo-ju-kyo" says: "In the land that the Buddha treads in journeying, there is not even one person in all the multitude of the villages who is not benefited. Then throughout the world there is peace and good will. The sun and the moon shine clear and bright. Wind and rain come only at a suitable time. Calamity and pestilence cease. The country prospers; the people are free from care. Weapons become useless. All men

Footprints of the Buddha

reverence religion, and regulate their conduct in all matters with earnestness and modesty."

[Commemorative Text]

The Fifth Month of the Eighteenth Year of Meiji, all the priests of this temple made and set up this pedestal-stone, bearing the likeness of the footprints of the Buddha, and placed the same within the main court of Dentsu-In, in order that the seed of holy enlightenment might be sown for future time, and for the sake of the advancement of Buddhism.

Taijo, priest — being the sixty-sixth chief-priest by succession of this temple — has respectfully composed.

Junyu, the minor priest, has reverentially inscribed.

II

STRANGE facts crowd into memory as one contemplates those graven footprints — footprints giant-seeming, yet less so than the human personality of which they remain the symbol. Twenty-four hundred years ago, out of solitary meditation upon the pain and the mystery of being, the mind of an Indian pilgrim brought forth the highest truth ever taught to men, and in an era barren of science anticipated the uttermost knowledge of our present evolutional philosophy regarding the secret unity of life, the endless illusions of matter and of mind, and the birth and death of universes. He, by pure reason — and he alone before our time — found answers of worth to the questions of the Whence, the Whither, and the Why; — and he made with these answers another and a nobler faith than the creed of his fathers. He spoke, and returned to his dust; and the people worshiped the prints of his dead feet, because of the love that he had taught them. Thereafter waxed and waned the name of Alexander, and the power of Rome, and the might of Islam; — nations arose and vanished; — cities grew and were not; — the children of another civilization, vaster than Rome's, begirdled the earth with conquest, and founded far-off empires, and came at last to rule in the land of that pilgrim's birth. And these, rich in the wisdom of four and twenty centuries, wondered at the beauty of his message, and caused all that he had said and done to be written down anew in languages unborn at the time when he lived and taught. Still burn his footprints in the East; and still the great West, marveling, follows their gleam to seek the Supreme Enlightenment. Even thus, of old, Milinda the king followed the way to the house of Nagasena — at first only to question, after the subtle method of the Greeks; yet, later, to accept with noble reverence the nobler method of the Master.

Japanese Buddhist Proverbs

As representing that general quality of moral experience which remains almost unaffected by social modifications of any sort, the proverbial sayings of a people must always possess a special psychological interest for thinkers. In this kind of folklore the oral and the written literature of Japan is rich to a degree that would require a large book to exemplify. To the subject as a whole no justice could be done within the limits of a single essay. But for certain classes of proverbs and proverbial phrases something can be done within even a few pages; and sayings related to Buddhism, either by allusion or derivation, form a class which seems to me particularly worthy of study. Accordingly, with the help of a Japanese friend, I have selected and translated the following series of examples — choosing the more simple and familiar where choice was possible, and placing the originals in alphabetical order to facilitate reference. Of course the selection is imperfectly representative; but it will serve to illustrate certain effects of Buddhist teaching upon popular thought and speech.

1. Akuji mi ni tomaru.
All evil done clings to the body.[1]

[1] The consequence of any evil act or thought never — so long as karma endures — will cease to act upon the existence of the person guilty of it.

The Buddhist Writings of Lafcadio Hearn

2. Atama soru yori kokoro wo soré.
Better to shave the heart than to shave the head.[1]

3. Au wa wakaré no hajimé.
Meeting is only the beginning of separation.[2]

4. Banji wa yumé.
All things [3] are merely dreams.

5. Bonbu mo satoréba hotoké nari.
Even a common man by obtaining knowledge becomes a Buddha.[4]

6. Bonnō kunō.
All lust is grief.[5]

7. Buppō to wara-ya no amé, dété kiké.
One must go outside to hear Buddhist doctrine or the sound of rain on a straw roof.[6]

8. Busshō en yori okoru.

[1] Buddhist nuns and priests have their heads completely shaven. The proverb signifies that it is better to correct the heart — to conquer all vain regrets and desires — than to become a religious. In common parlance the phrase "to shave the head" means to become a monk or a nun.

[2] Regret and desire are equally vain in this world of impermanency; for all joy is the beginning of an experience that must have its pain. This proverb refers directly to the sutra-text — "Shōja hitsumetsu é-shajori" ("All that live must surely die; and all that meet will surely part").

[3] Literally: "ten thousand things."

[4] The only real differences of condition are differences in knowledge of the highest truth.

[5] All sensual desire invariably brings sorrow.

[6] There is an allusion here to the condition of the shukké (priest): literally: "one who has left his house." The proverb suggests that the higher truths of Buddhism cannot be acquired by those who continue to live in the world of follies and desires.

Japanese Buddhist Proverbs

Out of karma-relation even the divine nature itself grows.[1]

9. Enkō ga tsuki wo toran to suru ga gotoshi.
Like monkeys trying to snatch the moon's reflection on water.[2]

10. En naki shujō wa doshi gatashi.
To save folk having no karma-relation would be difficult indeed![3]

11. Fujō seppō suru hōshi wa, hiraraké ni umaru.
The priest who preaches foul doctrine shall be reborn as a fungus.

12. Gaki mo ninzu.
Even gaki (prêtas) can make a crowd.[4]

[1] There is good as well as bad karma. Whatever happiness we enjoy is not less a consequence of the acts and thoughts of previous lives, than is any misfortune that comes to us. Every good thought and act contributes to the evolution of the Buddha-nature within each of us. Another proverb [No. 10] — "En naki shujō wa doshi gatashi" — further illustrates the meaning of this one.

[2] Allusion to a parable, said to have been related by the Buddha himself, about some monkeys who found a well under a tree, and mistook for reality the image of the moon in the water. They resolved to seize the bright apparition. One monkey suspended himself by the tail from a branch overhanging the well, a second monkey clung to the first, a third to the second, a fourth to the third, and so on — till the long chain of bodies had almost reached the water. Suddenly the branch broke under the unaccustomed weight; and all the monkeys were drowned.

[3] No karma-relation would mean an utter absence of merit as well as of demerit.

[4] Literally: "Even gaki are a multitude [or, population]." This is a popular saying used in a variety of ways. The ordinary meaning is to the effect that no matter how poor or miserable the individuals composing a multitude, they collectively represent a respectable force. Jocosely the saying is sometimes used of a crowd of wretched or tired-looking people — sometimes of an assembly of weak boys desiring to make some

13. Gaki no mé ni midzu miézu.
To the eyes of gaki water is viewless.¹

14. Goshō wa daiji.
The future life is the all-important thing.²

15. Gun-mō no tai-zō wo saguru ga gotoshi.
Like a lot of blind men feeling a great elephant.³

16. Gwai-men nyo-Bosatsu; nai shin nyo-Yasha.
In outward aspect a Bodhisattva; at innermost heart a demon.⁴

17. Hana wa né ni kaeru.
The flower goes back to its root.⁵

18. Hibiki no koë ni ozuru ga gotoshi.
Even as the echo answers to the voice.⁶

demonstration — sometimes of a miserable-looking company of soldiers. Among the lowest classes of the people it is not uncommon to call a deformed or greedy person a "gaki."

¹ Some authorities state that those prêtas who suffer especially from thirst, as a consequence of faults committed in former lives, are unable to see water. This proverb is used in speaking of persons too stupid or vicious to perceive a moral truth.

² The common people often use the curious expression "gosho-daiji" as an equivalent for "extremely important."

³ Said of those who ignorantly criticize the doctrines of Buddhism. The proverb alludes to a celebrated fable in the *Avadânas*, about a number of blind men who tried to decide the form of an elephant by feeling the animal. One, feeling the leg, declared the elephant to be like a tree; another, feeling the trunk only, declared the elephant to be like a serpent; a third, who felt only the side, said that the elephant was like a wall; a fourth, grasping the tail, said that the elephant was like a rope, etc.

⁴ Yasha (Sanscrit, "Yaksha"), a man-devouring demon.

⁵ This proverb is most often used in reference to death — signifying that all forms go back into the nothingness out of which they spring. But it may also be used in relation to the law of cause-and-effect.

⁶ Referring to the doctrine of cause-and-effect. The philosophical

Japanese Buddhist Proverbs

19. Hito wo tasukéru ga shukké no yuku.
The task of the priest is to save mankind.

20. Hi wa kiyurédomo tō-shin wa kiyédzu.
Though the flame be put out, the wick remains.[1]

21. Hotoké mo motowa bonbu.
Even the Buddha was originally but a common man.

22. Hotoké ni naru mo shami wo heru.
Even to become a Buddha one must first become a novice.

23. Hotoké no kao mo sando.
Even a Buddha's face — only three times.[2]

24. Hotoké tanondé Jigoku é yuku.
Praying to Buddha one goes to hell.[3]

25. Hotoké tsukutté tamashii irédzu.
Making a Buddha without putting in the soul.[4]

beauty of the comparison will be appreciated only if we bear in mind that even the *tone* of the echo repeats the tone of the voice.

[1] Although the passions may be temporarily overcome, their sources remain. A proverb of like meaning is, "Bonnō no inu oëdomo sarazu": "Though driven away, the Dog of Lust cannot be kept from coming back again."

[2] This is a short popular form of the longer proverb, "Hotoké no kao mo sando nazuréba, hara wo tatsu": "Stroke even the face of a Buddha three times, and his anger will be roused."

[3] The popular saying, "Oni no Nembutsu" — "a devil's praying" — has a similar meaning.

[4] That is to say, making an image of the Buddha without giving it a soul. This proverb is used in reference to the conduct of those who undertake to do some work, and leave the most essential part of the work unfinished. It contains an allusion to the curious ceremony called "Kai-gen," or "Eye-Opening." This Kai-gen is a kind of consecration, by virtue of which a newly-made image is supposed to become animated by the real presence of the divinity represented.

26. Ichi-ju no kagé, ichi-ga no nagaré, tashō no en.
Even [the experience of] a single shadow or a single flowing of water, is [made by] the karma-relations of a former life.[1]

27. Ichi-mō shū-mō wo hiku.
One blind man leads many blind men.[2]

28. Ingwa na ko.
A karma-child.[3]

29. Ingwa wa, kuruma no wa.
Cause-and-effect is like a wheel.[4]

30. Innen ga fukai.
The karma-relation is deep.[5]

---

[1] Even so trifling an occurrence as that of resting with another person under the shadow of a tree, or drinking from the same spring with another person, is caused by the karma-relations of some previous existence.

[2] From the Buddhist work *Dai-chi-dō-ron*. The reader will find a similar proverb in Rhys-David's "*Buddhist Suttas*" (*Sacred Books of the East*), p. 173 — together with a very curious parable, cited in a footnote, which an Indian commentator gives in explanation.

[3] A common saying among the lower classes in reference to an unfortunate or crippled child. Here the word "ingwa" is used especially in the retributive sense. It usually signifies evil karma; "kwahō" being the term used in speaking of meritorious karma and its results. While an unfortunate child is spoken of as "a child of ingwa," a very lucky person is called a "kwahō-mono" — that is to say, an instance, or example of kwaho.

[4] The comparison of karma to the wheel of a wagon will be familiar to students of Buddhism. The meaning of this proverb is identical with that of the *Dhammapada* verse: "If a man speaks or acts with an evil thought, pain follows him as the wheel follows the foot of the ox that draws the carriage."

[5] A saying very commonly used in speaking of the attachment of lovers, or of the unfortunate results of any close relation between two persons.

Japanese Buddhist Proverbs

31. Inochi wa fū-zen no tomoshibi.
Life is a lamp-flame before a wind.[1]

32. Issun no mushi ni mo, gobu no tamashii.
Even a worm an inch long has a soul half-an-inch long.[2]

33. Iwashi[3] no atama mo shinjin kara.
Even the head of an iwashi, by virtue of faith, [will have power to save, or heal].

34. Jigō-jitoku.[4]
The fruit of one's own deeds [in a previous state of existence].

35. Jigoku dé hotoké.
Like meeting with a Buddha in hell.[5]

36. Jigoku Gokuraku wa kokoro ni ari.
Hell and Heaven are in the hearts of men.[6]

[1] Or, "like the flame of a lamp exposed to the wind." A frequent expression in Buddhist literature is "the Wind of Death."
[2] Literally: "has a soul of five bu" — five bu being equal to half of the Japanese inch. Buddhism forbids all taking of life, and classes as *living* things (Ujō) all forms having sentiency. The proverb, however — as the use of the word "soul" (tamashii) implies — reflects popular belief rather than Buddhist philosophy. It signifies that any life, however small or mean, is entitled to mercy.
[3] The iwashi is a very small fish, much resembling a sardine. The proverb implies that the object of worship signifies little, so long as the prayer is made with perfect faith and pure intention.
[4] Few popular Buddhist phrases are more often used than this. "Jigō" signifies one's own acts or thoughts; "jitoku," to bring upon one's self — nearly always in the sense of misfortune, when the word is used in the Buddhist way. "Well, it is a matter of Jigō-jitoku," people will observe on seeing a man being taken to prison; meaning, "He is reaping the consequence of his own faults."
[5] Refers to the joy of meeting a good friend in time of misfortune. The above is an abbreviation. The full proverb is, "Jigoku dé hotoké ni ōta yo da."
[6] A proverb in perfect accord with the higher Buddhism.

37. Jigoku mo sumika.
Even Hell itself is a dwelling-place.[1]

38. Jigoku ni mo shiru hito.
Even in hell old acquaintances are welcome.

39. Kagé no katachi ni shitagau gotoshi.
Even as the shadow follows the shape.[2]

40. Kané wa Amida yori hikaru.
Money shines even more brightly than Amida.[3]

41. Karu-toki no Jizō-gao; nasu-toki no Emma-gao.
Borrowing-time, the face of Jizō; repaying-time, the face of Emma.[4]

42. Kiité Gokuraku, mité Jigoku.
Heard of only, it is Paradise; seen, it is Hell.[5]

43. Kōji mon wo idézu: akuji sen ri wo hashiru.
Good actions go not outside of the gate: bad deeds travel a thousand ri.

[1] Meaning that even those obliged to live in hell must learn to accommodate themselves to the situation. One should always try to make the best of circumstances. A proverb of kindred signification is, "Sumeba, Miyako": "Wheresoever one's home is, that is the Capital [or, Imperial City]."
[2] Referring to the doctrine of cause-and-effect. Compare with verse 2 of the *Dhammapada*.
[3] Amitâbha, the Buddha of Immeasurable Light. His image in the temples is usually gilded from head to foot. There are many other ironical proverbs about the power of wealth — such as "Jigoku no sata mo kané shidai": "Even the Judgments of Hell may be influenced by money."
[4] Emma is the Chinese and Japanese Yama — in Buddhism the Lord of Hell, and the Judge of the Dead. The proverb is best explained by the accompanying drawings, which will serve to give an idea of the commoner representations of both divinities.
[5] Rumor is never trustworthy.

Japanese Buddhist Proverbs

44. Kokoro no koma ni tadzuna wo yuru-suna.
Never let go the reins of the wild colt of the heart.

Jizō

45. Kokoro no oni ga mi wo séméru.
The body is tortured only by the demon of the heart.[1]

46. Kokoro no shi to wa naré; kokoro wo shi to sezaré.
Be the teacher of your heart: do not allow your heart to become your teacher.

---

[1] Or "mind." That is to say that we suffer only from the consequences of our own faults. The demon torturer in the Buddhist hell says to his victim: "Blame not me! — I am only the creation of your own deeds and thoughts: you made me for this!" (Compare with No. 36.)

47. Kono yo wa kari no yado.
This world is only a resting-place.[1]

EMMA DAI-Ō

48. Kori wo chiribamé; midzu ni égaku.
To inlay ice; to paint upon water.[2]

[1] "This world is but a travelers' inn," would be an almost equally correct translation. "Yado" literally means a lodging, shelter, inn; and the word is applied often to those wayside resting-houses at which Japanese travelers halt during a journey. "Kari" signifies temporary, transient, fleeting — as in the common Buddhist saying, "Kono yo kari no yo": "This world is a fleeting world." Even Heaven and Hell represent to the Buddhist only halting places upon the journey to Nirvâna.

[2] Refers to the vanity of selfish effort for some merely temporary end.

Japanese Buddhist Proverbs

49.   Korokoro to
    Naku wa yamada no
        Hototogisu,
    Chichi nitéya aran,
    Haha nitéya aran.

The bird that cries korokoro in the mountain rice-field I know to be a hototogisu; — yet it may have been my father; it may have been my mother.[1]

50. Ko wa Sangai no kubikase.
A child is a neck-shackle for the Three States of Existence.[2]

51. Kuchi wa wazawai no kado.
The mouth is the front-gate of all misfortune.[3]

52. Kwahō wa, nété maté.
If you wish for good luck, sleep and wait.[4]

[1] This verse-proverb is cited in the Buddhist work *Wōjō Yōshū*, with the following comment: "Who knows whether the animal in the field, or the bird in the mountain-wood, has not been either his father or his mother in some former state of existence?" The hototogisu is a kind of cuckoo.

[2] That is to say, The love of parents for their child may impede their spiritual progress — not only in this world, but through all their future states of being — just as a kubikasé, or Japanese cangue, impedes the movements of the person upon whom it is placed. Parental affection, being the strongest of earthly attachments, is particularly apt to cause those whom it enslaves to commit wrongful acts in the hope of benefiting their offspring. The term "Sangai" here signifies the three worlds of Desire, Form, and Formlessness — all the states of existence below Nirvâna. But the word is sometimes used to signify the Past, the Present, and the Future.

[3] That is to say, The chief cause of trouble is unguarded speech. The word "Kado" means always the *main* entrance to a residence.

[4] "Kwahō," a purely Buddhist term, signifying good fortune as the result of good actions in a previous life, has come to mean in common parlance good fortune of any kind. The proverb is often used in a sense similar to that of the English saying: "Watched pot never boils." In a

53. Makanu tané wa haënu.
Nothing will grow, if the seed be not sown.[1]

54. Matéba, kanrō no hiyori.
If you wait, ambrosial weather will come.[2]

55. Meidō no michi ni Ō wa nashi.
There is no King on the Road of Death.[3]

56. Mekura hebi ni ojizu.
The blind man does not fear the snake.[4]

57. Mitsuréba, kakuru.
Having waxed, wanes.[5]

58. Mon zen no kozō narawanu kyō wo yomu.
The shop-boy in front of the temple-gate repeats the sutra which he never learned.[6]

strictly Buddhist sense it would mean, "Do not be too eager for the reward of good deeds."

[1] Do not expect harvest, unless you sow the seed. Without earnest effort no merit can be gained.

[2] Kanrō, the sweet dew of Heaven, or amrita. All good things come to him who waits.

[3] Literally: "on the Road of Meidō." The Meidō is the Japanese Hades — the dark under-world to which all the dead must journey.

[4] The ignorant and the vicious, not understanding the law of cause-and-effect, do not fear the certain results of their folly.

[5] No sooner has the moon waxed full than it begins to wane. So the height of prosperity is also the beginning of fortune's decline.

[6] "Kozō" means "acolyte" as well as "shop-boy," "errand-boy," or "apprentice"; but in this case it refers to a boy employed in a shop situated near or before the gate of a Buddhist temple. By constantly hearing the sutra chanted in the temple, the boy learns to repeat the words. A proverb of kindred meaning is, "Kangaku-In no suzumé wa, Mōgyū wo sayézuru": "The sparrows of Kangaku-In [an ancient seat of learning] chirp the Mōgyū" — a Chinese text formerly taught to young students. The teaching of either proverb is excellently expressed by a third: "Narau yori wa naréro": "Rather than study [an art], get

Japanese Buddhist Proverbs

59. Mujō no kazé wa, toki erabazu.
The Wind of Impermanency does not choose a time. [1]

60. Neko mo Busshō ari.
In even a cat the Buddha-nature exists. [2]

61. Néta ma ga Gokuraku.
The interval of sleep is Paradise. [3]

62. Nijiu-go Bosatsu mo soré-soré nó yaku.
Even each of the Twenty-five Bodhisattvas has his own particular duty to perform.

63. Nin mité, hō toké.
[First] see the person, [then] preach the doctrine. [4]

64. Ninshin ukégataku Buppō aigatashi.
It is not easy to be born among men, and to meet with [the good fortune of hearing the doctrine of] Buddhism. [5]

accustomed to it"; that is to say, "keep constantly in contact with it." Observation and practice are even better than study.

[1] Death and Change do not conform their ways to human expectation.

[2] Notwithstanding the legend that only the cat and the mamushi (a poisonous viper) failed to weep for the death of the Buddha.

[3] Only during sleep can we sometimes cease to know the sorrow and pain of this world. (Compare with No. 83.)

[4] The teaching of Buddhist doctrine should always be adapted to the intelligence of the person to be instructed. There is another proverb of the same kind — " Ki ni yorité, hō wo toké": "According to the understanding [of the person to be taught], preach the Law."

[5] Popular Buddhism teaches that to be born in the world of mankind, and especially among a people professing Buddhism, is a very great privilege. However miserable human existence, it is at least a state in which some knowledge of divine truth may be obtained; whereas the beings in other and lower conditions of life are relatively incapable of spiritual progress.

65. Oni mo jiu-hachi.
Even a devil [is pretty] at eighteen.[1]

66. Oni mo mi, narétaru ga yoshi.
Even a devil, when you become accustomed to the sight of him, may prove a pleasant acquaintance.

67. Oni ni kanabō.
An iron club for a demon.[2]

68. Oni no nyōbo ni kijin.
A devil takes a goblin to wife.[3]

69. Onna no ké ni wa dai-zō mo tsunagaru.
With one hair of a woman you can tether even a great elephant.

70. Onna wa Sangai ni iyé nashi.
Women have no homes of their own in the Three States of Existence.

71. Oya no ingwa ga ko ni mukuü.
The karma of the parents is visited upon the child.[4]

[1] There are many curious sayings and proverbs about the oni, or Buddhist devil — such as "Oni no mé ni mo namida," "tears in even a devil's eyes"; — "Oni no kakuran," "devil's cholera" (said of the unexpected sickness of some very strong and healthy person), etc., etc. The class of demons called "Oni," properly belong to the Buddhist hells, where they act as torturers and jailers. They are not to be confounded with the Ma, Yasha, Kijin, and other classes of evil spirits. In Buddhist art they are represented as beings of enormous strength, with the heads of bulls and of horses. The bull-headed demons are called "Go-zu"; the horse-headed "Mé-zu."

[2] Meaning that great power should be given only to the strong.

[3] Meaning that a wicked man usually marries a wicked woman.

[4] Said of the parents of crippled or deformed children. But the popular idea here expressed is not altogether in accord with the teachings of the higher Buddhism.

Japanese Buddhist Proverbs

72. Rakkwa éda ni kaerazu.
The fallen blossom never returns to the branch.[1]

73. Raku wa ku no tané; ku wa raku no tané.
Pleasure is the seed of pain; pain is the seed of pleasure.

74. Rokudō wa, mé no maë.
The Six Roads are right before your eyes.[2]

75. Sangai mu-an.
There is no rest within the Three States of Existence.

76. Sangai ni kaki nashi; — Rokudō ni hotori nashi.
There is no fence to the Three States of Existence; — there is no neighborhood to the Six Roads.[3]

77. Sangé ni wa sannen no tsumi mo hōrobu.
One confession effaces the sins of even three years.

78. Sannin yoréba, kugai.
Where even three persons come together, there is a world of pain.[4]

[1] That which has been done never can be undone: the past cannot be recalled. This proverb is an abbreviation of the longer Buddhist text: "Rakkwa éda ni kaerazu; ha-kyō futatabi terasazu": "The fallen blossom never returns to the branch; the shattered mirror never again reflects."

[2] That is to say, Your future life depends upon your conduct in this life; and you are thus free to choose for yourself the place of your next birth.

[3] Within the Three States (Sangai), or universes, of Desire, Form, and Formlessness; and within the Six Worlds, or conditions of being — Jigokudō (Hell), Gakidō (Pretas), Chikushōdō (Animal Life), Shuradō (World of Fighting and Slaughter), Ningendō (Mankind), Tenjodō (Heavenly Spirits) — all existence is included. Beyond there is only Nirvâna. "There is no fence," "no neighborhood" — that is to say, no limit beyond which to escape — no middle-path between any two of these states. We shall be reborn into some one of them according to our karma. (Compare with No. 74.)

[4] "Kugai" (literally: "bitter world") is a term often used to describe the life of a prostitute.

79. San nin yoréba, Monjū no chié.
Where three persons come together, there is the wisdom of Monjū.[1]

80. Shaka ni sekkyō.
Preaching to Sâkyamuni.

81. Shami kara chōrō.
To become an abbot one must begin as a novice.

82. Shindaréba, koso ikitaré.
Only by reason of having died does one enter into life.[2]

83. Shiranu ga, hotoké; minu ga, Gokuraku.
Not to know is to be a Buddha; not to see is Paradise.

84. Shōbo ni kidoku nashi.
There is no miracle in true doctrine.[3]

85. Shō-chié wa Bodai no samatagé.
A little wisdom is a stumbling-block on the way to Buddhahood.[4]

[1] Monjū Bosatsu [Mañdjus'ri Bodhisattva) figures in Japanese Buddhism as a special divinity of wisdom. The proverb signifies that three heads are better than one. A saying of like meaning is, "Hiza to mo dankō": "Consult even with your own knee"; that is to say, Despise no advice, no matter how humble the source of it.

[2] I never hear this singular proverb without being reminded of a sentence in Huxley's famous essay, *On the Physical Basis of Life:* "The living protoplasm not only ultimately dies and is resolved into its mineral and lifeless constituents, but is always dying, and, strange as the paradox may sound, *could not live unless it died.*"

[3] Nothing can happen except as a result of eternal and irrevocable law.

[4] "Bodai" is the same word as the Sanscrit "Bodhi," signifying the supreme enlightenment — the knowledge that leads to Buddhahood; but it is often used by Japanese Buddhists in the sense of divine bliss, or the Buddha-state itself.

Japanese Buddhist Proverbs

86. Shōshi no kukai hetori nashi.
There is no shore to the bitter Sea of Birth and Death.[1]

87. Sodé no furi-awasé mo tashō no en.
Even the touching of sleeves in passing is caused by some relation in a former life.

88. Sun zen; shaku ma.
An inch of virtue; a foot of demon.[2]

89. Tanoshimi wa kanashimi no motoi.
All joy is the source of sorrow.

90. Tondé hi ni iru natsu no mushi.
So the insects of summer fly to the flame.[3]

91. Tsuchi-botoké no midzu-asobi.
Clay-Buddha's water-playing.[4]

92. Tsuki ni murakumo, hana ni kazé.
Cloud-wrack to the moon; wind to flowers.[5]

93. Tsuyu no inochi.
Human life is like the dew of morning.

---

[1] Or, "the Pain-Sea of Life and Death."

[2] Ma (Sanscrit, Mârakâyikas) is the name given to a particular class of spirits who tempt men to evil. But in Japanese folklore the Ma have a part much resembling that occupied in Western popular superstition by goblins and fairies.

[3] Said especially in reference to the result of sensual indulgence.

[4] That is to say, "As dangerous as for a clay Buddha to play with water." Children often amuse themselves by making little Buddhist images of mud, which melt into shapelessness, of course, if placed in water.

[5] The beauty of the moon is obscured by masses of clouds; the trees no sooner blossom than their flowers are scattered by the wind. All beauty is evanescent.

94. U-ki wa, kokoro ni ari.
Joy and sorrow exist only in the mind.

95. Uri no tsuru ni nasubi wa naranu.
Egg-plants do not grow upon melon-vines.

96. Uso mo hōben.
Even an untruth may serve as a device.[1]

97. Waga ya no hotoké tattoshi.
My family ancestors were all excellent Buddhas.[2]

98. Yuki no haté wa, Nehan.
The end of snow is Nirvâna.[3]

99. Zen ni wa zen no mukui; aku ni wa aku no mukui.
Goodness [or, virtue] is the return for goodness; evil is the return for evil.[4]

[1] That is, a pious device for effecting conversion. Such a device is justified especially by the famous parable of the third chapter of the *Saddharma Pundarika*.

[2] Meaning that one most reveres the hotoké — the spirits of the dead regarded as Buddhas — in one's own household-shrine. There is an ironical play upon the word hotoké, which may mean either a dead person simply, or a Buddha. Perhaps the spirit of this proverb may be better explained by the help of another: "Nigéta sakana ni chisai wa nai; shinda kodomo ni warui ko wa nai": "Fish that escaped was never small; child that died was never bad."

[3] This curious saying is the only one in my collection containing the word "Nehan" (Nirvâna), and is here inserted chiefly for that reason. The common people seldom speak of Nehan, and have little knowledge of those profound doctrines to which the term is related. The above phrase, as might be inferred, is not a popular expression: it is rather an artistic and poetical reference to the aspect of a landscape covered with snow to the horizon-line — so that beyond the snow-circle there is only the great void of the sky.

[4] Not so commonplace a proverb as might appear at first sight; for it refers especially to the Buddhist belief that every kindness shown to us in this life is a return of kindness done to others in a former life, and that every wrong inflicted upon us is the reflex of some injustice which we committed in a previous birth.

Japanese Buddhist Proverbs

100. Zensé no yakusoku-goto.
Promised [or, destined] from a former birth.[1]

[1] A very common saying — often uttered as a comment upon the unhappiness of separation, upon sudden misfortune, upon sudden death, etc. It is used especially in relation to shinjū, or lovers' suicide. Such suicide is popularly thought to be a result of cruelty in some previous state of being, or the consequence of having broken, in a former life, the mutual promise to become husband and wife.

A Legend of Fugen-Bosatsu

THERE was once a very pious and learned priest, called Shōku Shōnin, who lived in the province of Harima. For many years he meditated daily upon the chapter of Fugen-Bosatsu [the Bodhisattva Samantabhadra] in the Sutra of the Lotus of the Good Law; and he used to pray, every morning and evening, that he might at some time be permitted to behold Fugen-Bosatsu as a living presence, and in the form described in the holy text.[2]

One evening, while he was reciting the Sutra, drowsiness overcame him; and he fell asleep leaning upon his kyōsoku.[3] Then he dreamed; and in his dream a voice told him that, in order to see Fugen-Bosatsu, he must go to the house of a certain courte-

---

[1] From the old story-book, *Jikkun-shō*.

[2] The priest's desire was probably inspired by the promises recorded in the chapter entitled "The Encouragement of Samantabhadra" (see Kern's translation of the Saddharma Pundarîka in the *Sacred Books of the East*, pp. 433-34): "Then the Bodhisattva Mahâsattva Samantabhadra said to the Lord: ... 'When a preacher who applies himself to this Dharmaparyâya shall take a walk, then, O Lord, will I mount a white elephant with six tusks, and betake myself to the place where that preacher is walking, in order to protect this Dharmaparyâya. And when that preacher, applying himself to this Dharmaparyâya, forgets, be it but a single word or syllable, then will I mount the white elephant with six tusks, and show my face to that preacher, and repeat this entire Dharmaparyâya.'" But these promises refer to "the end of time."

[3] The kyōsoku is a kind of padded arm-rest, or arm-stool, upon which the priest leans one arm while reading. The use of such an arm-rest is not confined, however, to the Buddhist clergy.

san, known as the "Yujō-no-Chōja,"[1] who lived in the town of Kanzaki. Immediately upon awakening he resolved to go to Kanzaki; — and, making all possible haste, he reached the town by the evening of the next day.

When he entered the house of the yujō, he found many persons already there assembled — mostly young men of the capital, who had been attracted to Kanzaki by the fame of the woman's beauty. They were feasting and drinking; and the yujō was playing a small hand-drum (tsuzumi), which she used very skillfully, and singing a song. The song which she sang was an old Japanese song about a famous shrine in the town of Murozumi; and the words were these:

> Within the sacred water-tank[2] of Murozumi in Suwō,
> Even though no wind be blowing,
> The surface of the water is always rippling.

The sweetness of the voice filled everybody with surprise and delight. As the priest, who had taken a place apart, listened and wondered, the girl suddenly fixed her eyes upon him; and in the same instant he saw her form change into the form of Fugen-Bosatsu, emitting from her brow a beam of light that seemed to pierce beyond the limits of the universe, and riding

---

[1] A yujō, in old days, was a singing-girl as well as a courtesan. The term "Yujō-no-Chōja," in this case, would mean simply "the first (or best) of yujō."

[2] Mitarai (or mitarashi) is the name especially given to the water-tanks, or water-fonts — of stone or bronze — placed before Shintō shrines in order that the worshiper may purify his lips and hands before making prayer. Buddhist tanks are not so named.

A Legend of Fugen-Bosatsu

a snow-white elephant with six tusks. And still she sang — but the song also was now transformed; and the words came thus to the ears of the priest:

On the Vast Sea of Cessation,
Though the Winds of the Six Desires and of the Five Corruptions
    never blow,
Yet the surface of that deep is always covered
With the billowings of Attainment to the Reality-in-Itself.

Dazzled by the divine ray, the priest closed his eyes: but through their lids he still distinctly saw the vision. When he opened them again, it was gone: he saw only the girl with her hand-drum, and heard only the song about the water of Murozumi. But he found that as often as he shut his eyes he could see Fugen-Bosatsu on the six-tusked elephant, and could hear the mystic Song of the Sea of Cessation. The other persons present saw only the yujō: they had not beheld the manifestation.

Then the singer suddenly disappeared from the banquet-room — none could say when or how. From that moment the revelry ceased; and gloom took the place of joy. After having waited and sought for the girl to no purpose, the company dispersed in great sorrow. Last of all, the priest departed, bewildered by the emotions of the evening. But scarcely had he passed beyond the gate, when the yujō appeared before him, and said: "Friend, do not speak yet to any one of what you have seen this night." And with these words she vanished away — leaving the air filled with a delicious fragrance.

The monk by whom the foregoing legend was recorded, comments upon it thus: The condition of a yujō is low and miserable, since she is condemned to serve the lusts of men. Who therefore could imagine that such a woman might be the nirmaṇakaya, or incarnation, of a Bodhisattva. But we must remember that the Buddhas and Bodhisattvas may appear in this world in countless different forms; choosing, for the purpose of their divine compassion, even the most humble or contemptible shapes when such shapes can serve them to lead men into the true path, and to save them from the perils of illusion.

The Sympathy of Benten

In Kyōto there is a famous temple called Amadera. Sadazumi Shinnō, the fifth son of the Emperor Seiwa, passed the greater part of his life there as a priest; and the graves of many celebrated persons are to be seen in the temple-grounds.

But the present edifice is not the ancient Amadera. The original temple, after the lapse of ten centuries, fell into such decay that it had to be entirely rebuilt in the fourteenth year of Genroku (1701 A.D.).

A great festival was held to celebrate the rebuilding of the Amadera; and among the thousands of persons who attended that festival there was a young scholar and poet named Hanagaki Baishū. He wandered about the newly laid-out grounds and gardens, delighted by all that he saw, until he reached the place of a spring at which he had often drunk in former times. He was then surprised to find that the soil about the spring had been dug away, so as to form a square pond, and that at one corner of this pond there had been set up a wooden tablet bearing the words "Tanjō-Sui" (Birth-Water).[2] He also saw that a small, but very handsome temple of the

[1] The original story is in the *Otogi-Hyaku-Monogatari*.
[2] The word "tanjō" (birth) should here be understood in its mystical Buddhist meaning of new life or rebirth, rather than in the Western signification of birth.

Goddess Benten had been erected beside the pond. While he was looking at this new temple, a sudden gust of wind blew to his feet a tanzaku,[1] on which the following poem had been written:

> Shirushi aréto
> Iwai zo somuru
> Tama hōki,
> Toruté bakari no
> Chigiri narétomo.

This poem — a poem on first love (hatsu koi), composed by the famous Shunrei Kyō — was not unfamiliar to him; but it had been written upon the tanzaku by a female hand, and so exquisitely that he could scarcely believe his eyes. Something in the form of the characters — an indefinite grace — suggested that period of youth between childhood and womanhood; and the pure rich color of the ink seemed to bespeak the purity and goodness of the writer's heart.[2]

Baishū carefully folded up the tanzaku, and took it home with him. When he looked at it again the

[1] Tanzaku is the name given to the long strips or ribbons of paper, usually colored, upon which poems are written perpendicularly. Poems written upon tanzaku are suspended to trees in flower, to wind-bells, to any beautiful object in which the poet has found an inspiration.

[2] It is difficult for the inexperienced European eye to distinguish in Chinese or Japanese writing those characteristics implied by our term "hand" — in the sense of individual style. But the Japanese scholar never forgets the peculiarities of a handwriting once seen; and he can even guess at the approximate age of the writer. Chinese and Japanese authors claim that the color (quality) of the ink used tells something of the character of the writer. As every person grounds or prepares his or her own ink, the deeper and clearer black would at least indicate something of personal carefulness and of the sense of beauty.

The Sympathy of Benten

writing appeared to him even more wonderful than at first. His knowledge in calligraphy assured him only that the poem had been written by some girl who was very young, very intelligent, and probably very gentle-hearted. But this assurance sufficed to shape within his mind the image of a very charming person; and he soon found himself in love with the unknown. Then his first resolve was to seek out the writer of the verses, and, if possible, make her his wife.... Yet how was he to find her? Who was she? Where did she live Certainly he could hope to find her only through the favor of the gods.

But presently it occurred to him that the gods might be very willing to lend their aid. The tanzaku had come to him while he was standing in front of the temple of Benten-Sama; and it was to this divinity in particular that lovers were wont to pray for happy union. This reflection impelled him to beseech the goddess for assistance. He went at once to the temple of Benten-of-the-Birth-Water (Tanjō-sui-no-Benten) in the grounds of the Amadera; and there, with all the fervor of his heart, he made his petition: "O Goddess, pity me! — help me to find where the young person lives who wrote the tanzaku! — vouchsafe me but one chance to meet her — even if only for a moment!" And after having made this prayer, he began to perform a seven days' religious service (nanuka-mairi)[1] in honor of the goddess;

[1] There are many kinds of religious exercises called "mairi." The

vowing at the same time to pass the seventh night in ceaseless worship before her shrine.

Now on the seventh night — the night of his vigil — during the hour when the silence is most deep, he heard at the main gateway of the temple-grounds a voice calling for admittance. Another voice from within answered; the gate was opened; and Baishū saw an old man of majestic appearance approaching with slow steps. This venerable person was clad in robes of ceremony; and he wore upon his snow-white head a black cap (eboshi) of the form indicating high rank. Reaching the little temple of Benten, he knelt down in front of it, as if respectfully awaiting some order. Then the outer door of the temple was opened; the hanging curtain of bamboo behind it, concealing the inner sanctuary, was rolled half-way up; and a chigo[1] came forward — a beautiful boy, with long hair tied back in the ancient manner. He stood at the threshold, and said to the old man in a clear loud voice:

"There is a person here who has been praying for a love-union not suitable to his present condition, and otherwise difficult to bring about. But as the young man is worthy of Our pity, you have been

performer of a nanuka-mairi pledges himself to pray at a certain temple every day for seven days in succession.

[1] The term "chigo" usually means the page of a noble household, especially an Imperial page. The chigo who appears in this story is of course a supernatural being — the court-messenger of the goddess, and her mouthpiece.

The Sympathy of Benten

called to see whether something can be done for him. If there should prove to be any relation between the parties from the period of a former birth, you will introduce them to each other."

On receiving this command, the old man bowed respectfully to the chigo: then, rising, he drew from the pocket of his long left sleeve a crimson cord. One end of this cord he passed round Baishū's body, as if to bind him with it. The other end he put into the flame of one of the temple-lamps; and while the cord was there burning, he waved his hand three times, as if to summon somebody out of the dark.

Immediately, in the direction of the Amadera, a sound of coming steps was heard; and in another moment a girl appeared — a charming girl, fifteen or sixteen years old. She approached gracefully, but very shyly — hiding the lower part of her face with a fan; and she knelt down beside Baishū. The chigo then said to Baishū:

"Recently you have been suffering much heart-pain; and this desperate love of yours has even impaired your health. We could not allow you to remain in so unhappy a condition; and We therefore summoned the Old-Man-under-the-Moon [1] to make you acquainted with the writer of that tanzaku. She is now beside you."

With these words, the chigo retired behind the

---

[1] Gekkawō. This is a poetical appellation for the God of Marriage, more usually known as "Musubi-no-kami." Throughout this story there is an interesting mingling of Shintō and Buddhist ideas.

bamboo curtain. Then the old man went away as he had come; and the young girl followed him. Simultaneously Baishū heard the great bell of the Amadera sounding the hour of dawn. He prostrated himself in thanksgiving before the shrine of Benten-of-the-Birth-Water, and proceeded homeward — feeling as if awakened from some delightful dream — happy at having seen the charming person whom he had so fervently prayed to meet — unhappy also because of the fear that he might never meet her again.

But scarcely had he passed from the gateway into the street, when he saw a young girl walking alone in the same direction that he was going; and, even in the dusk of the dawn, he recognized her at once as the person to whom he had been introduced before the temple of Benten. As he quickened his pace to overtake her, she turned and saluted him with a graceful bow. Then for the first time he ventured to speak to her; and she answered him in a voice of which the sweetness filled his heart with joy. Through the yet silent streets they walked on, chatting happily, till they found themselves before the house where Baishū lived. There he paused — spoke to the girl of his hopes and fears. Smiling, she asked: "Do you not know that I was sent for to become your wife?" And she entered with him.

Becoming his wife, she delighted him beyond expectation by the charm of her mind and heart.

The Sympathy of Benten

Moreover, he found her to be much more accomplished than he had supposed. Besides being able to write so wonderfully, she could paint beautiful pictures; she knew the art of arranging flowers, the art of embroidery, the art of music; she could weave and sew; and she knew everything in regard to the management of a house.

It was in the early autumn that the young people had met; and they lived together in perfect accord until the winter season began. Nothing, during those months, occurred to disturb their peace. Baishū's love for his gentle wife only strengthened with the passing of time. Yet, strangely enough, he remained ignorant of her history — knew nothing about her family. Of such matters she had never spoken; and, as the gods had given her to him, he imagined that it would not be proper to question her. But neither the Old-Man-under-the-Moon nor any one else came — as he had feared — to take her away. Nobody even made any inquiries about her. And the neighbors, for some undiscoverable reason, acted as if totally unaware of her presence.

Baishū wondered at all this. But stranger experiences were awaiting him.

One winter morning he happened to be passing through a somewhat remote quarter of the city, when he heard himself loudly called by name, and saw a man-servant making signs to him from the gateway of a private residence. As Baishū did not know the man's face, and did not have a single acquaintance in that part of Kyōto, he was more than startled by so abrupt a summons. But the servant, coming forward, saluted him with the utmost respect, and said, "My master greatly desires the honor of speaking with you: deign to enter for a moment." After an instant of hesitation, Baishū allowed himself to be conducted to the house. A dignified and richly dressed person, who seemed to be the master, welcomed him at the entrance, and led him to the guest-room. When the courtesies due upon a first meeting had been fully exchanged, the host apologized for the informal manner of his invitation, and said:

"It must have seemed to you very rude of us to call you in such a way. But perhaps you will pardon our impoliteness when I tell you that we acted thus upon what I firmly believe to have been an inspiration from the Goddess Benten. Now permit me to explain.

"I have a daughter, about sixteen years old, who can write rather well,[1] and do other things in the common way: she has the ordinary nature of woman. As we were anxious to make her happy by finding a good husband for her, we prayed the Goddess

[1] As it is the old Japanese rule that parents should speak depreciatingly of their children's accomplishments the phrase "rather well" in this connection would mean, for the visitor, "wonderfully well." For the same reason the expressions "common way" and "ordinary nature," as subsequently used, would imply almost the reverse of the literal meaning.

The Sympathy of Benten

Benten to help us; and we sent to every temple of Benten in the city a tanzaku written by the girl. Some nights later, the goddess appeared to me in a dream, and said: 'We have heard your prayer, and have already introduced your daughter to the person who is to become her husband. During the coming winter he will visit you.' As I did not understand this assurance that a presentation had been made, I felt some doubt; I thought that the dream might have been only a common dream, signifying nothing. But last night again I saw Benten-Sama in a dream; and she said to me: 'To-morrow the young man, of whom I once spoke to you, will come to this street: then you can call him into your house, and ask him to become the husband of your daughter. He is a good young man; and later in life he will obtain a much higher rank than he now holds.' Then Benten-Sama told me your name, your age, your birthplace, and described your features and dress so exactly that my servant found no difficulty in recognizing you by the indications which I was able to give him."

This explanation bewildered Baishū instead of reassuring him; and his only reply was a formal return of thanks for the honor which the master of the house had spoken of doing him. But when the host invited him to another room, for the purpose of presenting him to the young lady, his embarrassment became extreme. Yet he could not reasonably decline the introduction. He could not bring himself, under such extraordinary circumstances, to announce that he already had a wife — a wife given to him by the Goddess Benten herself; a wife from whom he could not even think of separating. So, in silence and trepidation, he followed his host to the apartment indicated.

Then what was his amazement to discover, when presented to the daughter of the house, that she was the very same person whom he had already taken to wife!

The same — yet not the same.
She to whom he had been introduced by the Old-Man-under-the-Moon, was only the soul of the beloved.

She to whom he was now to be wedded, in her father's house, was the body.

Benten had wrought this miracle for the sake of her worshipers.

The original story breaks off suddenly at this point, leaving several matters unexplained. The ending is rather unsatisfactory. One would like to know something about the mental experiences of the real maiden during the married life of her phantom. One would also like to know what became of the phantom — whether it continued to lead an independent existence; whether it waited patiently for the return of its husband; whether it paid a visit to the real bride. And the book says nothing about these things. But a Japanese friend explains the miracle thus:

"The spirit-bride was really formed out of the tanzaku. So it is possible that the real girl did not know anything about the meeting at the temple of Benten. When she wrote those beautiful characters upon the tanzaku, something of her spirit passed into them. Therefore it was possible to evoke from the writing the double of the writer."

Buddhist Names of Plants and Animals

At one time I hoped to compile a glossary of the Buddhist names given to Japanese animals and plants; and I began to collect material for the work. But I then knew very little about the real difficulties of such an undertaking. To mention only one, I may observe that in almost every province of Japan the folk-speech is different; and the difference appears even in the names given to certain plants, insects, reptiles, fishes, and birds. Such names must be learned, of course, from the lips of peasants and of fishermen; and that which I wished to do could never be well done except through the patient labors of a folk-lore society. And now I find that, instead of being able to prepare the glossary intended, I must content myself with a few general notes upon the subject.

But perhaps these notes — relics of an undertaking for which I possessed neither the requisite scholarship nor the means — will have at least a suggestive worth to future explorers in this unfamiliar region of Far-Eastern folk-lore.

The name Buddha appears in the appellations of several trees and plants. Marubushukan (round-fingers-of-Buddha) is the name of a kind of lemon-

Buddhist Names of Plants and Animals

tree — so called from the very remarkable shape of its fruit. The Chinese hibiscus is called Bussōgé (Buddha's mulberry); and a variety of rock-moss is popularly known by the picturesque names of Hotoké-no-tsumé and Bukkōsō — both signifying "finger-nails of Buddha." A kind of yam is called Tsukuné-imo — which appellation, as written with the proper Chinese characters, signifies "Buddha's-hand potato"; and a variety of clover is honored by the name Hotoké-no-za (Buddha's Throne).

Names of Bodhisattvas and of other Buddhist divinities are also to be found in the appellations of plants and animals. The name of Kwannon (Âvalokitesvara) appears in the term Kwannon-chiku (bamboo of Kwannon); and several different plants are known, in different provinces, by the name Kwannon-sō (herb of Kwannon). The name of Fugen (Samantabhadra) has been given to a variety of cherry-tree — the Fugen-zakura (Fugen's cherry-tree). The name of Dai-Mokukenren (Mahamaudgalyâyana) — shortened by popular usage into Mokuren — figures both in the common appellation of the *Ficus pumila*, known as Mokuren, and in that of the *Magnolia conspicua*, usually called Haku-mokuren (white Mokuren). The name of Brahma — known to Japanese Buddhism as Bonten — appears in the designation of a kind of upland rice, Bonten-mai. The memory of Bōdai-Daruma (Bôdhidharma) is preserved in the popular appellation of the *Aster spatufolium*, called Daruma-giku (Daruma's chrysanthemum) — as well as in the name of the swamp-cabbage, Daruma-sō (Daruma's plant). Two fishes also have been named after this patriarch: the *Priacanthus niphonius*, which is called Daruma-dai (Daruma's sea-bream); and the *Synanceia erosa*, popularly known as Daruma-kasago — "kasago" being properly the name of the fish scientifically called *Sebastes inermis*. More curious than any of the above terms, however, is the popular name for a species of grain weevil, Kokuzō — "Kokuzō" being the Japanese appellation of the great Bodhisattva Âkâsapratishthita.

The term Bosatsu (Bodhisattva) also appears in some plant-names. A variety of rose is known as the Bosatsu-ibara (thorny-rose of the Bodhisattva); and a kind of rice is called Bosatsu.

The term Rakan (Arhat) forms a prefix to several plant-names. Rakan-haku (Arhat's oak) is the popular name of the *Thuya dolobrata*. Rakan-shō (Arhat's pine) is the common appellation of the *Podocarpus macrophylla;* and the name Rakan-maki (Arhat's maki, "maki" being the Japanese name for the *Podocarpus chinensis*) has been given to the umbrella-pine. And the fruit of a tree, of which I cannot find the scientific name, is called in several provinces Rakan, or "the Arhat," because it curiously resembles in shape the rude stone images of Arhats set up in temple-gardens.

Kukai, or Kōbōdaishi, the great Japanese patriarch of the Shingon sect, also has a place in this no-

Buddhist Names of Plants and Animals

menclature. Kōbō-mugi (wheat of Kōbōdaishi) is a common name for the *Carex macrocephala;* and a variety of chestnut is called Kōbōdaishi-kawazu-no-kuri (the chestnut that Kōbōdaishi did not eat).

Many names of plants or living creatures refer to Buddhist customs, legends, rites, or beliefs. The word "bōzu," "priest" (the origin of our word "bonze") has been attached to several plant-names. No less than three different herbs are known, in different parts of the country, by the name of Bōzugusa (priest-grass). In the dialect of Chikuzen a kind of turtle is called Umi-bōzu (priest of the sea) — a name, by the way, also given to a mythical marine-monster, often represented in Japanese picture-books. The name of the famous Bo-tree of Buddhist tradition has been given in Japan, not only to the *Ficus religiosa,* but also to the *Tilia miqueliana,* popularly called Bōdaijū (Bodhidruma). The great Buddhist festival of the spring equinox, the festival of the Higan (farther shore) has furnished names for two plants which blossom about that time — the Higan-zakura (Higan cherry-tree) (*Prunus miqueliana*), and the Higan-bana, or "Flower of Higan" (*Lycoris radiata*). What we term "Job's Tears" are in Japan called Zuzudama, or Buddhist rosary-beads; and a kind of dove is known — probably because of its markings — as the Zuzukaké-bato (rosary-bearing dove). The *Allium victoriale* is called Gyoja-ninniku (hermit's garlic — "gyōja" being the Buddhist term for hermit); and the popular Japanese name for the bleeding-heart is Keman-sō, or "Keman-herb" — an appellation probably due to the resemblance of the flower to the Keman, or decoration, placed upon the head of the statue of Buddha. Perhaps the water-arum has the most curious of all such Buddhist appellations: its Japanese name, Kokuzen-sō literally signifies the "small-sitting-in-Dhyâna-meditation-plant."

The word sennin (commonly translated as "genius" or "fairy," but originally meaning Rishi — a being who has acquired supernatural power and unlimited life by force of ascetic practices) occasionally appears in plant-names. A variety of clematis is known as Sennin-sō (fairy-weed); and a kind of cactus has received the grotesque appellation of Sennin-shō (Sennin's palm) — the palm of the hand being referred to.

The Sanscrit term Yaksha, signifying a man-devouring demon, appears in several plant-names under its Japanese form — Yasha. The cone of the *Aldus firma* is picturesquely called Yasha-bushi (Yaksha's joint); and a water-plant is known by the curious name of Yasha-bishaku (Yaksha's ladle).

Very many Japanese names of vegetables, birds, fishes, and insects, have attached to them as a prefix the word "Oni," a Buddhist term for "demon" or

Buddhist Names of Plants and Animals

"devil" — just as in English folk-speech we have such names for plants and insects as devil's-apron, devil-wood, devil's-fingers, devil's-horse, and devil's-darning-needle. The tiger-lily is known in Japan by the equally fantastic name of Oni-yuri (devil-lily). A species of coix is called Oni-zuzudama (devil's rosary-beads). The bur-marigold is called Oni-bari (devil's needle); and a water-weed, injurious to lotus-cultivation, is popularly termed the Oni-basu (demon-lotus). This prefix of Oni is probably attached to hundreds of folk-names of flora and fauna: I have myself collected no less than seventy-one examples. Nevertheless, few of them are interesting.

The word Kijin, or Kishin, signifying a kind of goblin recognized by Japanese Buddhism, is similarly used as a prefix; — for example, a sort of needle-grass is known as Kishin-sō (goblin-weed). Kijo, another Buddhist word signifying a kind of female goblin, appears in the common name of an orchid — Kijoran (goblin-orchid). Also there is a prefix, Ki — abbreviation of a term for demon or goblin — which sometimes figures in plant-names: the *Pardanthus chinensis*, for instance, is called in Japan Kisen, meaning "goblin-fan." It is worthy of remark that these devilish names are given to vegetables or to animals, not merely because of some ugly or extraordinary shape, but even because of remarkable size. Thus a species of lark is called Oni-hibari (demon-lark) because it happens to be a much larger bird than the common field-lark; and a very large kind of dragon-fly is designated for the same reason Oni-yamma (demon-dragon-fly).

Many Buddhist names, both of creatures and of plants, are ghostly. A pretty green grasshopper is called Hotoké-uma (Buddha-horse); — the head of the insect curiously resembling the head of a horse in shape. But the word "hotoké" also means the spirit of a dead person — all good persons being supposed by popular faith to become Buddhas; — and the real meaning of the name Hotoké-uma is "the horse of the dead." Now during the great three-days' Festival of the Dead in the seventh month, it is believed that many spirits revisit their homes, or their former friends, either with the help of insects or actually in the form of insects. The name of this grasshopper really implies that it is used as a horse by the shadowy visitors. . . . Again, we find the word "shōryō" — a general term for the spirits of ancestors worshiped according to Buddhist rite — coupled with the name of a dragon-fly: Shōryō-yamma (the dragon-fly of the ancestral spirits). Shōrai-tombō (ghost dragon-fly), and Ki-yamma, a term of similar meaning, are names likewise intended to suggest the relation of the insect to the invisible world. Equally weird is the name by which the mole-cricket is known in the dialect of Kyōto — a name probably suggested by the creature's underground life — Shōrai-mushi (ghost-insect). Among appellations

Buddhist Names of Plants and Animals

of plants one finds also such terms as Yurei-daké (ghost-bamboo), and Yurei-bana (ghost-flower) — the latter name being not inappropriately given to a species of delicate mushroom.

Some of the Buddhist names, although highly interesting in themselves, could not be understood by the Western reader without the help of pictorial illustration, because they have reference to the furniture of temples, or to particular articles used in Buddhist religious service. Such, for example, is the name of a tree popularly known as sankō-matsu (sankō-pine); — the term "sankō" (Sanscrit, vadjra) signifying a brass object — shaped much like the classic representation of a thunderbolt, with prongs at either end — which priests use in certain rites as a symbol of supernatural power. Such also is the name hossugai (hossu-shell), given to the beautiful glass-sponge, *Hyalonema sieboldii*, because of its resemblance to the hossu — a brush or duster of long white hair used in Buddhist religious service. And such, again, is the excellent name of a little insect called the koromo-sémi (priest's robe cicada), because the general form and color of the creature, when resting with closed wings, really suggest the figure of a priest in his "koromo." But unless you had seen the insect, and the kind of "koromo" thus referred to, you could not appreciate the graphic worth of the appellation.

The Buddhist Writings of Lafcadio Hearn

Very remarkable Buddhist names have been given to some species of birds. There is a bird, known to ornithologists as *Eurysotmus orientalis*, which is called "buppōsō," because its cry resembles the sound of the word "buppōsō." This word is a Japanese equivalent for the Sanscrit term "triratna" or "ratnatraya" (three jewels); — the syllable "bu" standing for Butsu (the Buddha); "pō," for hō (the Law); and "sō" for the priesthood. The bird is also called sambōchō (the sambō-bird); — the word "sambō" being a literal translation of triratna. Another bird, of which I do not know the scientific appellation, is called the Jihishinchō (Compassionate-Mind-Bird) — because its call resembles the utterance of the phrase Jihi-shin (Compassionate Mind) which forms one of the epithets of the Buddha. "This bird," my informant writes, "lives only in the neighborhood of Nikkō, where in the summer it may be heard continually crying out, 'O thou Compassionate Mind! — O thou Compassionate Mind!'" ... Almost equally interesting is the common Buddhist name for the hototogisu (*Cuculus poliocephalus*), a species of cuckoo much celebrated by Japanese poets. It is called mujō-dori (the bird of impermanency). This name would not appear to be derived from the bird's note, which is popularly interpreted as "Honzon kakétaka?" — meaning, "Has the honzon yet been suspended?" (The "honzon" is the sacred picture displayed in temples upon the eighth day of the fourth month — a little before the time at which the bird makes its annual appearance.) It seems to me more probable that the name was given in the signification, "bird of death"; — for the word "mujō" has also the meaning of death as change; and this meaning is strongly suggested by the strange fact that the hototogisu is supposed to come from the spirit-world. It is also called Tama-mukaë-dori (the ghost-welcoming bird) because it is said to meet and to greet the spirits of the dead on their journey over the Mountain of Shidé to the River of Souls. There are many ghostly legends and fancies about the hototogisu; and this weird folk-lore sufficiently explains why the bird is known in the provinces by no less than fifty-two different names!

The uguisu, a variety of nightingale, and the sweetest-voiced of all Japanese singers, does not appear to have any popular Buddhist name; but its flute-like call is said to be an utterance of the word "Hokkékyō," which is the popular name for the Saddharma-Pundarîka-Sutra — the grand scripture of the Nichiren or Hokké sect. And Buddhist piety asserts that the bird passes its life in chanting the praise of the Sutra of the Lotus of the Good Law. So that the uguisu is really regarded as a Buddhist bird. Another bird which seems to have some relation to Buddhism is the snowy heron, to which the extraordinary appellation of bonnō-sagi (Bonnō-heron) has been given. "Bonnō" is a Buddhist term for worldly desire, lust, passion; and I am not able to say why it appears in the name of the bird.

The difficulty of guessing at the origin of these Buddhist names cannot even be imagined without the help of examples. The literal meaning, in many cases, serves only to mislead investigation. For instance, the hammer-headed shark is known on parts of the Kyūshū coast by the extraordinary appellation, Nembutsu-bō (Nembutsu-priest). The word "Nembutsu" is the name of the invocation, "Namu Amida Butsu!" (Salutation to the Buddha Amitâbha!) uttered by the pious of many sects as a prayer, and *especially as a prayer for the dead.* The grim suggestiveness of the name Nembutsu-bō reminded me that the modern French word for shark is, according to Littré, only a corruption of "requiem" — the appellation originally implying (as stated by Père Dutertre in 1667) that for the man caught by a shark there was nothing to be done except to chant his requiem. But I was wrong in imagining that the Buddhist name Nembutsu-bō implied something of the same kind. The real meaning of the term is proved by another Buddhist name for the same monster — shumoku-zamé (shumoku-shark). The word "shumoku" signifies a peculiar "T"-shaped mallet with which the priest strikes a gong during the repetition of the Nembutsu and of other prayers. (I may observe that the same kind of mallet is used to sound a gong during the chanting

Buddhist Names of Plants and Animals

of the Nembutsu, in some pious households, before the family shrine.) It was this use of the mallet and gong, during the repetition of the invocation, that suggested the term Nembutsu-bō as an alternate name for the shumoku-zamé (mallet-shark); — and the true signification of Nembutsu-bō is not "the Nembutsu-priest," but "the priest with the mallet."

Beside the Sea

I

THE Buddhist priests had announced that a ségaki-service, in behalf of all the drowned folk of Yaidzu, would be held on the shore at two o'clock in the afternoon. Yaidzu is an ancient place (it is mentioned, under the name of "Yakidzu," in the oldest chronicles of Japan); — and for thousands of years the fishers of Yaidzu have been regularly paying their toll of life to the great deep. And the announcement of the priests reminded me of something very much older than Buddhism — the fancy that the spirits of the drowned move with the waters forever. According to this belief, the sea off Yaidzu must be thick with souls. . . .

Early in the afternoon I went to the shore to observe preparations; and I found a multitude of people already there assembled. It was a burning July day — not a speck of cloud visible; and the coarse shingle of the slope, under the blaze of sun, was radiating heat like slag just raked from a furnace. But those fisher-folk, tanned to all tints of bronze, did not mind the sun: they sat on the scorching stones, and waited. The sea was at ebb, and gentle — moving in slow, long, lazy ripples.

Upon the beach there had been erected a kind of

rude altar, about four feet high; and on this had been placed an immense ihai, or mortuary tablet, of unpainted wood — the back of the tablet being turned to the sea. The ihai bore, in large Chinese characters, the inscription, "Sangai-Ban-Rei-I — signifying, "Resting-place [or, seat] of the myriad [innumerable] spirits of the Three States of Existence." Various food-offerings had been set before this tablet — including a bowl of cooked rice; rice-cakes; eggplants; pears; and, piled upon a fresh lotus leaf, a quantity of what is called "hyaku-mi-no-onjiki." It is really a mixture of rice and sliced eggplant, though the name implies one hundred different kinds of nourishment. In the bowl of boiled rice tiny sticks were fixed, with cuttings of colored paper attached to them. I also observed candles, a censer, some bundles of incense-rods, a vessel of water, and a pair of bamboo cups containing sprays of the sacred plant shikimi.[1] Beside the water-vessel there had been laid a bunch of miso-hagi,[2] with which to sprinkle water upon the food-offerings, according to the prescriptions of the rite.

To each of the four posts supporting the altar a freshly cut bamboo had been attached; and other bamboos had been planted in the beach, to right and left of the structure; and to every bamboo was fastened a little banner inscribed with Chinese characters. The banners of the bamboos at the four corners of the altar bore the names and attributes

[1] *Illicium religiosum.*   [2] A kind of bush-clover.

of the Four Deva Kings — Zōchō Tennō, guardian of the West; Jikoku Tennō, guardian of the East; Tamon Tennō, guardian of the North; and Kōmoku Tennō, guardian of the South.

In front of the altar straw-mattings had been laid, so as to cover a space of beach about thirty feet long by fifteen wide; and above this matted space awnings of blue cotton had been rigged up, to shelter the priests from the sun. I squatted down awhile under the awnings to make a rough drawing (afterwards corrected and elaborated by a Japanese friend) of the altar and the offerings.

The service was not held at the appointed time: it must have been nearly three o'clock when the priests made their appearance. There were seven of them, in vestments of great ceremony; and they were accompanied by acolytes carrying bells, books, stools, reading-stands, and other necessary furniture. Priests and acolytes took their places under the blue awning; the spectators standing outside, in the sun. Only one of the priests — the chief officiant — sat facing the altar; the others, with their acolytes, seated themselves to right and left of him — so as to form two ranks, facing each other.

II

AFTER some preliminary rearrangment of the offerings upon the altar, and the kindling of some incense-rods, the ceremony proper began with a Buddhist

Beside the Sea

hymn, or gâthâ, which was chanted to the accompaniment of hyōshigi[1] and of bells. There were two bells — a large deep-sounding bell; and a small bell of very sweet tone — in charge of a little boy. The big bell was tapped slowly; the little bell was sounded rapidly; and the hyōshigi rattled almost like a pair of castanets. And the effect of the gâthâ as chanted by all the officiants in unison, with this extraordinary instrumentation, was not less impressive than strange:

> Biku Bikuni
> Hosshin hōji
> Ikki jō-jiki,
> Fusé jippō,
> Kyū-jin kokū,
> Shūhen hōkai,
> Mijin setchū
> Sho-u kokudo,
> Issai gaki;
> Senbō kyūmétsu,
> Sansen chishu,
> Naishi koya,
> Shō-kijin to,
> Shōrai shushi....

This brief sonorous metre seemed to me particularly well adapted for invocatory or incantatory chanting; and the gâthâ of the ségaki-service was indeed a veritable incantation — as the following free translation will make manifest:

[1] Hyōshigi are small blocks of hard wood, which are used, either for signalling or for musical purposes, by striking them quickly together so as to produce a succession of sharp dry sounds.

We, Bhikshus and Bhikunis, devoutly presenting this vessel of pure food, do offer the same to all, without exception, of the Pretas dwelling in the Ten Directions of Space, in the surrounding Dharma-worlds, and in every part of the Earth — not excepting the smallest atom of dust within a temple. And also to the spirits of those long dead and passed away — and likewise unto the Lord-Spirits of mountain and river and soil, and of waste places. Hither deign therefore to approach and to gather, all ye goblins! — we now, out of our pity and compassion, desire to give you food. We wish that each and all of you may enjoy this our food-gift. And moreover we shall pray, doing homage to all the Buddhas and to all the Heavenly Ones who dwell within the Zones of Formlessness, that you, and that all beings having desire, may be enabled to obtain contentment. We shall pray that all of you, by virtue of the utterance of the dhâranîs, and by the enjoyment of this food-offering, may find the higher knowledge, and be freed from every pain, and soon obtain rebirth in the Zone Celestial — there to know every bliss, moving freely in all the Ten Directions, and finding everywhere delight. Awaken within yourselves the Bodhi-Mind! — follow the Way of Enlightenment! Rise to Buddhahood! Turn ye no more backward! — neither linger on the path! Let such among you as first obtain the Way vow each to lead up the rest, and so become free! — Also we beseech you now to watch over us and to guard us, by night and by day. And help us even now to obtain our desire in bestowing this food upon you — that the merit produced by this action may be extended to all beings dwelling within the Dharma-worlds, and that the power of this merit may help to spread the Truth through all those Dharma-worlds, and help all beings therein to find the Supreme Enlightenment, and to obtain all wisdom. And we now pray that all your acts hereafter may serve to gain for you the merit that will help you to Buddhahood. And thus we desire that you quickly become Buddhas."

Then began the most curious part of the service — namely, the sprinkling and the presentation of the food-offerings, with recitation of certain dhâranîs, or magical verses, composed of talismanic Sanscrit words. This portion of the rite was brief; but to recount all its details would require much space — every utterance or gesture of the officiant being made according to rule. For example, the hands and fingers of the priest, during the recital of any dhâranî, must be held in a position prescribed for that particular dhâranî. But the principal incidents of this complicated ritual are about as follows:

First of all is recited, seven times, the Dhâranî of Invitation, to summon the spirits from the Ten Directions of Space. During its recitation the officiant must hold out his right hand, with the tip of the middle finger touching the tip of the thumb, and the rest of the fingers extended. Then is recited, with a different, but equally weird gesture, the Dhâranî of the Breaking of the Gates of Hell. Next is repeated the Se-Kanrō verse, or Dhâranî of the Bestowal of the Amrita, — by virtue of which it is supposed that the food-offerings are transformed, for the sake of the ghosts, into heavenly nectar and ambrosia. And thereafter is chanted, three times, an invocation to the Five Tathâgatas:

Salutation to Hōshō Nyōrai — hereby besought to

relieve [the Pretas] from the karma of all desire, and to fill them with bliss!

Salutation to Myō-Shikishin-Nyōrai — besought to take away from them every imperfection of form!

Salutation to Kanrō-Ō-Nyōrai — besought to purify their bodies and their minds, and to give them peace of heart!

Salutation to Kobaku-Shin-Nyōrai — besought to favor them with the delight of excellent taste!

Salutation to Rifui-Nyōrai — besought to free them from all their fears, and to deliver them out of the World of Hungry Spirits!

The book "Bongyō Ségaki-Monben" says:

When the officiants have thus recited the names of the Five Tathâgatas, then, by the grace of the power of those Buddhas, all the Pretas shall be liberated from the karma of their former errors — shall experience immeasurable bliss — shall receive excellent features and complete bodies — shall be rid of all their terrors — and, after having partaken of the food-offerings which have been changed for them into amrita of delightful taste, shall soon be reborn into the Pure Land [Jōdo].

After the invocation of the Five Tathâgatas, other verses are recited; and during this recitation the food-offerings are removed, one by one. (There is a mysterious regulation that, after having been taken from the altar, they must not be placed under a willow-tree, a peach-tree, or a pomegranate-tree.) Last of all is recited the Dhâranî of Dismissal, seven times — the priest each time snapping his fingers as a signal to the ghosts that they are free to return. This is called the "Hakken," or Sending-Away.

Beside the Sea

III

THE sea never ebbs far on this steep coast — though it often rises tremendously, breaking into the town; and its gentler moods are not to be trusted. By way of precaution the posts of the ihai-stand had been driven deeply into the beach. The event proved that this precaution had not been taken in vain; for the rite began, owing to the delay of the priests, only with the turn of the tide. Even while the gâthâ was being chanted, the sea roughened and darkened; and then — as if the outer deep responded — the thunder-roll of a great breaker suddenly smothered the voices of the singers and the clanging of the bells. Soon another heavy surge boomed along the shore — then another; and during the reciting of the dhâranîs the service could be heard only in the intervals of wave-bursts — while the foam sheeted up the slope, whirling and hissing even to within a few paces of the altar....

And again I found myself thinking of the old belief in some dim relation between the dead and the sea. In that moment the primitive fancy appeared to me much more reasonable and more humane than the ghastly doctrine of a Preta-world, with its thirty-six orders of hideous misery, — its swarms of goblins hungering and burning!... Nay, the poor dead! — why should they be thus deformed and doomed by human judgment? Wiser and kindlier to dream of them as mingling with flood and wind and cloud — or quickening the heart of the flower — or flushing the cheek of the fruit — or shrilling with the cicadæ in forest-solitudes, — or thinly humming in summer-dusk with the gathering of the gnats. . . . I do not believe — I do not wish to believe in hungry ghosts. . . . Ghosts break up, I suppose, into soul-dust at the touch of death — though their atoms, doubtless, thereafter recombine with other dust for the making of other ghosts. . . . Still, I cannot convince myself that even the grosser substance of vanished being ever completely dies, however dissolved or scattered — fleeting in the gale — floating in the mists — shuddering in the leaf — flickering in the light of waters — or tossed on some desolate coast in a thunder of surf, to whiten and writhe in the clatter of shingle. . . .

As the ceremony ended, a fisherman mounted lightly to the top of one of the awning-posts: and there, gymnastically poised, he began to shower down upon the crowd a quantity of very small rice-cakes, which the young folks scrambled for, with shouts of laughter. After the uncanny solemnity of that rite, the outburst of merriment was almost startling; but I found it also very natural, and pleasant, and human. Meanwhile the seven priests departed in many-colored procession — their acolytes trudging wearily behind them, under much weight of stands and stools and bells. Soon the assembly scattered — all the rice-cakes having been distributed and appropriated; — then the altar, the awnings, the mattings were removed; — and in a surprisingly short time every trace of the strange ceremony had disappeared. . . . I looked about me; — I was alone upon the beach. . . . There was no sound but the sound of the returning tide: a muttering enormous, appalling — as of some Life innominable, that had been at peace, awakened to immeasurable pain. . . .

Otokichi's Daruma

I

The young folks are delighted, because last night a heavy fall of snow made for us what the Japanese poets so prettily call "a silver world." . . . Really these poets have been guilty of no extravagance in their charming praises of winter. For in Japan winter is beautiful — fantastically beautiful. It bestirs no melancholy imaginings about "the death of Nature" — inasmuch as Nature remains most visibly alive during even the Period of Greatest Cold.

It does not afflict the æsthetic eye with the spectacle of "skeleton-woods" — for the woods largely consist of evergreens. And the snow — heaping softly upon the needles of the pines, or forcing the bamboos to display their bending grace under its momentary weight — never suggests to Far-Eastern poet the dismal fancy of a winding-sheet. Indeed the singular charm of Japanese winter is made by this snow — lumping itself into grostesqueries unimaginable above the constant verdure of woods and gardens.

This morning my two students, Aki and Niimi, have been amusing themselves and the children by

Otokichi's Daruma

making a Yuki-Daruma; and I have been amusing myself by watching them. The rules for making a Yuki-Daruma are ancient and simple. You first compose a huge snowball — between three and four feet in diameter, if possible — which is to represent the squatting body of Daruma. Then you make a smaller snowball, about two feet in diameter, to represent his head; and you put this smaller ball on top of the other — packing snow around the underparts of both, so as to fix them in place. Two round lumps of charcoal serve to make eyes for Daruma; and some irregular fragments of the same material will suffice to indicate his nose and mouth. Finally, you must scoop out a hollow in the great belly of him, to represent a navel, and stick a lighted candle inside. The warmth of the candle gradually enlarges the opening. . . .

But I forgot to explain the term Yuki-Daruma, or Snow-Daruma. "Daruma" is an abbreviation of the name Bodai-Daruma — Japanese rendering of the Sanscrit "Bodhidharma." And who was Bodhidharma?

Bodhidharma, or Bodhitara, was the twenty-eighth patriarch of Buddhism, by succession from the great Kâsyapa. He went to China as a Buddhist missionary in the first year of the Ryō dynasty [520 A.D.]; and in China he founded the great Zen (Dhyâna) sect — whose doctrine is called "The Doctrine of Thought transmitted by Thought":

that is to say, transmitted without words, either written or spoken. Says Professor Bunyiu Nanjio, in his "History of the Twelve Buddhist Sects": "Besides all the doctrines of the Mahâyâna and Hînayâna, there is one distinct line of transmission of a secret doctrine, which is not subject to any utterance at all. According to this doctrine, one is to see the so-called key to the thought of Buddha, or the nature of Buddha, directly by his own thought."

The tradition of the Zen doctrine is curious. When the Buddha was preaching upon the Vulture Peak, there suddenly appeared before him the great Brahma, who presented a gold-colored flower to the Blessed One, and therewith besought him to preach the Law. The Blessed One accepted the heavenly flower, and held it in his hand, but spoke no word. Then the great assembly wondered at the silence of the Blessed One. But the venerable Kâsyapa smiled. And the Blessed One said to the venerable Kâsyapa: "I have the wonderful thought of Nirvâna, the Eye of the True Law, which I now shall give you." ... So by thought alone the doctrine was transmitted to Kâsyapa; and by thought alone Kâsyapa transmitted it to Ananda; and thereafter by thought alone it was transmitted from patriarch to patriarch even to the time of Bodhidharma, who communicated it to his successor, the second Chinese patriarch of the sect. By some writers it is said that Bodhidharma visited Japan;

but this statement appears to have little foundation. At all events, the Zen doctrine was not introduced into Japan before the eighth century.

Now of the many legends about Daruma, the most famous is the story that he once remained for nine years in uninterrupted meditation, during which time his legs fell off. Wherefore images of him are made without legs.

Certainly Daruma has large claims to respect. But the artists and the toymakers of the Far East have never allowed these claims to interfere with the indulgence of their sense of humor — originally bestirred, no doubt, by the story of the loss of his legs. For centuries this legendary mishap has been made the subject of comical drawings and comical carvings; and generations of Japanese children have amused themselves with a certain toy-image of Daruma so contrived that, however the little figure be thrown down, it will always bob up again into a squatting posture. This still popular toy, called "Okiagari-koboshi" (The Getting-up Little Priest) may have been originally modeled, or remodeled, after a Chinese toy made upon the same principle, and called "Puh-Tau-Ung" (The Not-falling-down Old Man). Mention is made of the Okiagari-Koboshi in a Japanese play called "Manjū-Kui," known to have been composed in the fourteenth century. But the earlier forms of the toy do not seem to have been representations of Daruma.

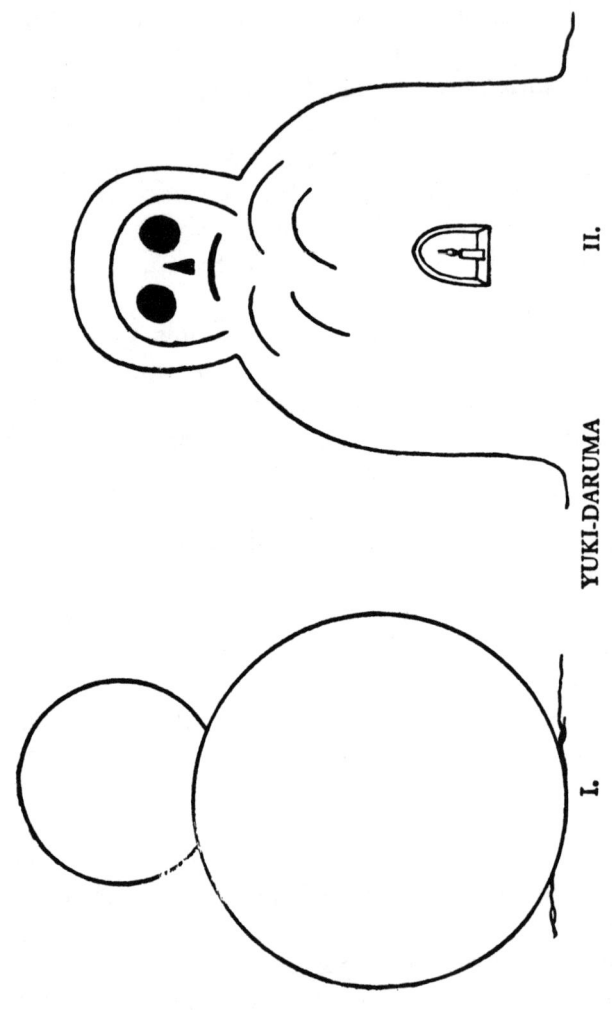

YUKI-DARUMA

Otokichi's Daruma

Thereis, however, a children's-song, dating from the seventeenth century, which proves that the Daruma-toy was popular more than two hundred years ago:

>Hi ni! fu ni!
>Fundan Daruma ga
>Akai zukin kaburi sunmaita!

[Once! twice!... Ever the red-hooded Daruma heedlessly sits up again!]

From this little song it would seem that the form of the toy has not been much changed since the seventeenth century; Daruma still wears his hood, and is still painted red — all of him except his face.

Besides the Snow-Daruma already described, and the toy-Daruma (usually made of papier-mâché), there are countless comical varieties of Daruma: figures moulded or carved in almost every kind of material, and ranging in size from the tiny metal Daruma, half-an-inch long, designed for a pouch-clasp, to the big wooden Daruma, two or three feet high, which the Japanese tobacconist has adopted for a shop-sign.... Thus profanely does popular art deride the holy legend of the nine years' meditation.

Toy-Daruma

II

Now that Yuki-Daruma in my garden reminds me of a very peculiar Daruma which I discovered several years ago, at a certain fishing-village on the eastern coast where I passed a happy summer. There was no hotel in the place; but a good man called Otokichi, who kept a fish-shop, used to let me

occupy the upper part of his house, and fed me with fish cooked in a wonderful variety of ways.

One morning he called me into his shop to show me a very fine hōbō.... I wonder if you ever saw anything resembling a hōbō. It looks so much like a gigantic butterfly or moth, that you must examine it closely to make sure that it is not an insect, but a fish — a sort of gurnard. It has four fins arranged like pairs of wings — the upper pair dark, with bright spots of sky-blue; the lower pair deep red. It seems also to have legs like a butterfly — slender legs upon which it runs about quickly. . . .

"Is it good to eat?" I asked.

"Hé!" answered Otokichi: "this shall be prepared for the Honorable Dinner."

[To any question asked of him — even a question requiring answer in the negative — Otokichi would begin his reply with the exclamation "Hé" (Yes) — uttered in such a tone of sympathy and good-will as to make the hearer immediately forget all the tribulations of existence.]

Then I wandered back into the shop, looking at things. On one side were rows of shelves supporting boxes of dried fish, and packages of edible seaweed, and bundles of straw sandals, and gourds for holding saké, and bottles of lemonade! On the opposite side, high up, I perceived the kamidana — the Shelf of the Gods; and I noticed, under the kamidana, a smaller shelf occupied by a red image of Daruma. Evidently the image was not a toy: there were offerings in front of it. I was not surprised to find Daruma accepted as a household divinity — because I knew that in many parts of Japan prayers were addressed to him on behalf of children attacked by smallpox. But I was rather startled by the peculiar aspect of Otokichi's Daruma, which had only one eye — a large and formidable eye that seemed to glare through the dusk of the shop like the eye of a great owl. It was the right eye, and was made of glazed paper. The socket of the left eye was a white void.

Therefore I called to Otokichi:

"Otokichi San! — did the children knock out the left eye of Daruma Sama?"

"Hé, hé!" sympathetically chuckled Otokichi —

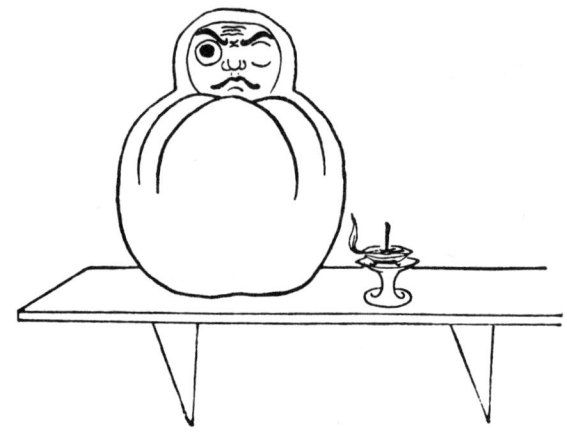

lifting a superb katsuo to the cutting-bench — "he never had a left eye."

"Was he made that way?" I asked.

"Hé!" responded Otokichi — as he swept his long knife soundlessly through the argent body — "the folk here make only blind Darumas. When I got that Daruma, he had no eyes at all. I made the right eye for him last year — after a day of great fishing."

"But why not have given him both eyes?" I queried; "he looks so unhappy with only one eye!"

Otokichi's Daruma

"Hé, hé!" replied Otokichi — skillfully ranging the slices of pink-and-silver flesh upon a little mat of glass rods [1] — "when we have another day of great good fortune, then he shall be given the other eye."

Then I walked about the streets of the village, peeping into the houses and shops; and I discovered various other Darumas in different stages of development — some without eyes, some with only one, and some with two. I remembered that in Izumo it was especially Hotei — the big-bellied God of Comfort — who used to be practically rewarded for his favors. As soon as the worshiper found reason for gratitude, Hotei's recumbent image was put upon a soft cushion; and for each additional grace bestowed the god would be given an additional cushion. But it occurred to me that Daruma could not be given more than two eyes: three would change him into the sort of goblin called "Mitsumé-Kozō." . . . I learned, upon inquiry, that when a Daruma has been presented with a pair of eyes, and with sundry small offerings, he is put away to make room for an eyeless successor. The blind Daruma can be expected to do wonderful things, because he has to work for his eyes.

There are many such funny little deities in Japan — so many that it would need a very big book to describe them; and I have found that the people

[1] Such a little glass mat is called sudaré.

who worship these queer little gods are, for the most part, pathetically honest. Indeed my own experience would almost justify the belief that the more artless the god, the more honest the man — though I do not want my reader to make any hasty deductions. I do not wish to imply, for example, that the superlative point of honesty might begin at the vanishing point of the god. Only this much I would venture: Faith in very small gods — toy-gods — belongs to that simplicity of heart which, in this wicked world, makes the nearest possible approach to pure goodness.

On the evening before I left the village, Otokichi brought me his bill — representing the cost of two months' good cheer; — and the amount proved to be unreasonably small. Of course a present was expected, according to the kindly Japanese custom; but, even taking that fact into consideration, the bill was absurdly honest. The least that I could do to show my appreciation of many things was to double the payment requested; and Otokichi's satisfaction, because perfectly natural and at the same time properly dignified, was something beautiful to see.

I was up and dressed by half-past three the next morning, in order to take an early express-train; but even at that ghostly hour I found a warm breakfast awaiting me downstairs, and Otokichi's little brown daughter ready to serve me.... As I swallowed the final bowl of warm tea, my gaze involuntarily wandered in the direction of the household gods, whose tiny lamps were still glowing. Then I noticed that a light was burning also in front of Daruma; and almost in the same instant I perceived that Daruma was looking straight at me — WITH TWO EYES! . . .

A Drop of Dew

To the bamboo lattice of my study-window a single dewdrop hangs quivering.

Its tiny sphere repeats the colors of the morning — colors of sky and field and far-off trees. Inverted images of these can be discerned in it — also the microscopic picture of a cottage, upside down, with children at play before the door.

Much more than the visible world is imaged by that dewdrop: the world invisible, of infinite mystery, is likewise therein repeated. And without as within the drop there is motion unceasing — motion forever incomprehensible of atoms and forces — faint shiverings also, making prismatic reply to touches of air and sun.

Buddhism finds in such a dewdrop the symbol of that other microcosm which has been called the Soul. . . . What more, indeed, is man than just such a temporary orbing of viewless ultimates — imaging sky and land and life — filled with perpetual mysterious shudderings — and responding in some wise to every stir of the ghostly forces that environ him? . . .

Soon that tiny globe of light, with all its fairy tints and topsy-turvy picturings, will have vanished

A Drop of Dew

away. Even so, within another little while, you and I must likewise dissolve and disappear.

Between the vanishing of the drop and the vanishing of the man, what difference? A difference of words. . . . But ask yourself what becomes of the dewdrop?

By the great sun its atoms are separated and lifted and scattered. To cloud and earth, to river and sea they go; and out of land and stream and sea again they will be updrawn, only to fall and to scatter anew. They will creep in opalescent mists; — they will whiten in frost and hail and snow; — they will reflect again the forms and the colors of the macrocosm; they will throb to the ruby pulsing of hearts that are yet unborn. For each one of them must combine again with countless kindred atoms for the making of other drops — drops of dew and rain and sap, of blood and sweat and tears. . . .

How many times? Billions of ages before our sun began to burn, those atoms probably moved in other drops, reflecting the sky-tints and the earth-colors of worlds in some past universe. And after this present universe shall have vanished out of Space, those very same atoms — by virtue of the forces incomprehensible that made them — will probably continue to sphere in dews that will shadow the morning beauty of planets yet to be.

Even so with the particles of that composite which you term your very Self. Before the hosts of heaven the atoms of you were — and thrilled — and quickened — and reflected appearances of things. And when all the stars of the visible Night shall have burnt themselves out, those atoms will doubtless again take part in the orbing of Mind — will tremble again in thoughts, emotions, memories — in all the joys and pains of lives still to be lived in worlds still to be evolved. . . .

Your personality? — your peculiarity? That is to say, your ideas, sentiments, recollections? — your very particular hopes and fears and loves and hates? Why, in each of a trillion of dewdrops there must be differences infinitesimal of atom-thrilling and of reflection. And in every one of the countless pearls of ghostly vapor updrawn from the Sea of Birth and Death there are like infinitesimal peculiarities. Your personality signifies, in the eternal order, just as much as the especial motion of molecules in the shivering of any single drop. Perhaps in no other drop will the thrilling and the picturing be ever exactly the same; but the dews will continue to gather and to fall, and there will always be quivering pictures. . . . The very delusion of delusions is the idea of death as loss.

There is no loss — because there is not any Self that can be lost. Whatsoever was, that you have been; — whatsoever is, that you are; — whatsoever will be, that you must become. Personality! — individuality! — the ghosts of a dream in a dream!

A Drop of Dew

Life infinite only there is; and all that appears to be is but the thrilling of it — sun, moon, and stars — earth, sky, and sea — and Mind and Man, and Space and Time. All of them are shadows. The shadows come and go; — the Shadow-Maker shapes forever.

Gaki

"Venerable Nagasena, are there such things as demons in the world?"
"Yes, O King."
"Do they ever leave that condition of existence?"
"Yes, they do."
"But, if so, why is it that the remains of those demons are never found?"
"Their remains are found, O King.... The remains of bad demons can be found in the form of worms and beetles and ants and snakes and scorpions and centipedes." ...

The Questions of King Milinda

I

THERE are moments in life when truths but dimly known before — beliefs first vaguely reached through multiple processes of reasoning — suddenly assume the vivid character of emotional convictions. Such an experience came to me the other day, on the Suruga coast. While resting under the pines that fringed the beach, something in the vital warmth and luminous peace of the hour — some quivering rapture of wind and light — very strangely bestirred an old belief of mine: the belief that all being is One. One I felt myself to be with the thrilling of breeze and the racing of wave — with every flutter of shadow and flicker of sun — with the azure of sky and sea — with the great green hush of the land. In some new and wonderful way I found myself assured that there never could have been a beginning — that there never could be an end. Nevertheless, the ideas of the moment were not new: the novelty of the experience was altogether

Gaki

in the peculiar intensity with which they presented themselves; making me feel that the flashing dragon-flies, and the long gray sand-crickets, and the shrilling sémi overhead, and the little red crabs astir under the roots of the pines, were all of them brothers and sisters. I seemed to understand, as never before, how the mystery that is called the Soul of me must have quickened in every form of past existence, and must as certainly continue to behold the sun, for other millions of summers, through eyes of other countless shapes of future being. And I tried to think the long slow thoughts of the long gray crickets — and the thoughts of the darting, shimmering dragon-flies — and the thoughts of the basking, trilling cicadæ — and the thoughts of the wicked little crabs that lifted up their claws from between the roots of the pines.

Presently I discovered myself wondering whether the consequence of such thoughts could have anything to do with the recombination of my soul-dust in future spheres of existence. For thousands of years the East has been teaching that what we think or do in this life really decides — through some inevitable formation of atom-tendencies, or polarities — the future place of our substance, and the future state of our sentiency. And the belief is worth thinking about — though no amount of thinking can enable us either to confirm or to disprove it. Very possibly, like other Buddhist doctrines, it may adumbrate some cosmic truth; but its literal assertions I doubt, because I must doubt the power ascribed to thought. By the whole infinite past I have been moulded, within and without: how should the impulse of a moment reshape me against the weight of the eternities? ... Buddhism indeed answers how, and that astounding answer is irrefutable — but I doubt. ...

Anyhow, acts and thoughts, according to Buddhist doctrine, are creative. Visible matter is made by acts and thoughts — even the universe of stars, and all that has form and name, and all the conditions of existence. What we think or do is never for the moment only, but for measureless time: it signifies some force directed to the shaping of worlds — to the making of future bliss or pain. Remembering this, we may raise ourselves to the zones of the Gods. Ignoring it, we may deprive ourselves even of the right to be reborn among men, and may doom ourselves, though innocent of the crimes that cause rebirth in hell, to reënter existence in the form of animals, or of insects, or of goblins — gaki.[1]

So it depends upon ourselves whether we are to become insects or goblins hereafter; and in the Buddhist system the difference between insects and goblins is not so well defined as might be supposed. The belief in a mysterious relation between ghosts and insects, or rather between spirits and insects, is

---

[1] The word "gaki" is the Japanese Buddhist rendering of the Sanscrit term "preta," signifying a spirit in that circle or state of torment called the World of Hungry Ghosts.

a very ancient belief in the East, where it now assumes innumerable forms — some unspeakably horrible, others full of weird beauty. "The White Moth" of Mr. Quiller-Couch would not impress a Japanese reader as novel; for the night-moth or the butterfly figures in many a Japanese poem and legend as the soul of a lost wife. The night-cricket's thin lament is perhaps the sorrowing of a voice once human; — the strange red marks upon the heads of cicadæ are characters of spirit-names; — dragon-flies and grasshoppers are the horses of the dead. All these are to be pitied with the pity that is kin to love. But the noxious and dangerous insects represent the results of another quality of karma — that which produces goblins and demons. Grisly names have been given to some of these insects — as, for example, "Jigokumushi," or "Hell-Insect," to the ant-lion; and "Kappa-mushi," to a gigantic water-beetle which seizes frogs and fish, and devours them alive, thus realizing, in a microcosmic way, the hideous myth of the Kappa, or River-Goblin. Flies, on the other hand, are especially identified with the world of hungry ghosts. How often, in the season of flies, have I heard some persecuted toiler exclaim, "Kyō no hai wa, gaki no yo da né?" (The flies to-day, how like gaki they are!)

II

IN the old Japanese, or, more correctly speaking, Chinese, Buddhist literature relating to the gaki, the Sanscrit names of the gaki are given in a majority of cases; but some classes of gaki described have only Chinese names. As the Indian belief reached Japan by way of China and Korea, it is likely to have received a peculiar coloring in the course of its journey. But, in a general way, the Japanese classification of gaki corresponds closely to the Indian classification of the pretas.

The place of gaki in the Buddhist system is but one degree removed from the region of the hells, or Jigokudō — the lowest of all the States of Existence. Above the Jigokudō is the Gakidō, or World of Hungry Spirits; above the Gakidō is the Chikushōdō, or World of Animals; and above this, again, is the Shuradō, a region of perpetual fighting and slaughter. Higher than these is placed the Ningendō, or World of Mankind.

Now a person released from hell, by exhaustion of the karma that sent him there, is seldom reborn at once into the zone of human existence, but must patiently work his way upward thither, through all the intermediate states of being. Many of the gaki have been in hell.

But there are gaki also who have not been in hell. Certain kinds or degrees of sin may cause a person to be reborn as a gaki immediately after having died in this world. Only the greatest degree of sin condemns the sinner directly to hell. The second degree degrades him to the Gakidō. The third causes him to be reborn as an animal.

Gaki

Japanese Buddhism recognizes thirty-six principal classes of gaki. "Roughly counting," says the "Shōbō-nen-jō-kyō, "we find thirty-six classes of gaki; but should we attempt to distinguish all the different varieties, we should find them to be innumerable." The thirty-six classes form two great divisions, or orders. One comprises all "Gaki-World-Dwellers" (Gaki-Sekai-Jū); — that is to say, all Hungry Spirits who remain in the Gakidō proper, and are, therefore, never seen by mankind. The other division is called "Nin-chū-Jū," or "Dwellers among men": these gaki remain always in this world, and are sometimes seen.

There is yet another classification of gaki, according to the character of their penitential torment. All gaki suffer hunger and thirst; but there are three degrees of this suffering. The Muzai-gaki represent the first degree: they must hunger and thirst uninterruptedly, without obtaining any nourishment whatever. The Shōzai-gaki suffer only in the second degree: they are able to feed occasionally upon impure substances. The Usai-gaki are more fortunate: they can eat such remains of food as are thrown away by men, and also the offerings of food set before the images of the gods, or before the tablets of the ancestors. The last two classes of gaki are especially interesting, because they are supposed to meddle with human affairs.

Before modern science introduced exact knowledge of the nature and cause of certain diseases, Buddhists explained the symptoms of such diseases by the hypothesis of gaki. Certain kinds of intermittent fever, for example, were said to be caused by a gaki entering the human body for the sake of nourishment and warmth. At first the patient would shiver with cold, because the gaki was cold. Then, as the gaki gradually became warm, the chill would pass, to be succeeded by a burning heat. At last the satiated haunter would go away, and the fever disappear; but upon another day, and usually at an hour corresponding to that of the first attack, a second fit of ague would announce the return of the gaki. Other zymotic disorders could be equally well explained as due to the action of gaki.

In the "Shōbō-nen-jō-kyō a majority of the thirty-six kinds of gaki are associated with putrescence, disease, and death. Others are plainly identified with insects. No particular kind of gaki is identified by name with any particular kind of insect; but the descriptions suggest conditions of insect-life; and such suggestions are reënforced by a knowledge of popular superstitions. Perhaps the descriptions are vague in the case of such spirits as the Jiki-ketsu-gaki, or blood-suckers; the Jiki-niku-gaki, or flesh-eaters; the Jiki-da-gaki, or . . . -eaters; the Jiki-fun-gaki, or . . . -eaters; the Jiki-doku-gaki, or poison-eaters; the Jiki-fu-gaki, or wind-eaters; the Jiki-ké-gaki, or smell-eaters; the

Gaki

Jiki-kwa-gaki, or fire-eaters (perhaps they fly into lamps?); the Shikkō-gaki, who devour corpses and cause pestilence; the Shinen-gaki, who appear by night as wandering fires; the Shin-ko-gaki, or needle-mouthed; and the Kwaku-shin-gaki, or cauldron-bodied — each a living furnace, filled with flame that keeps the fluids of its body humming like a boiling pot. But the suggestion of the following excerpts[1] will not be found at all obscure:

Jiki-man-gaki. These gaki can live only by eating the wigs of false hair with which the statues of certain divinities are decorated. . . . Such will be the future condition of persons who steal objects of value from Buddhist temples.

Fujō-ko-hyaku-gaki. These gaki can eat only street filth and refuse. Such a condition is the consequence of having given putrid or unwholesome food to priests or nuns, or pilgrims in need of alms.

Cho-ken-jū-jiki-netsu-gaki. These are the eaters of the refuse of funeral-pyres and of the clay of graves. . . . They are the spirits of men who despoiled Buddhist temples for the sake of gain.

Ju-chū-gaki. These spirits are born within the wood of trees, and are tormented by the growing of the grain. . . . Their condition is the result of having cut down shade-trees for the purpose of selling the timber. Persons who cut down the trees in Buddhist cemeteries or temple-grounds are especially likely to become ju-chū-gaki.[2]

---

[1] Abridged from the *Shōbō-nen-jō-Kyō*. A full translation of the extraordinary chapter relating to the gaki would try the reader's nerves rather severely.

[2] The following story of a tree-spirit is typical:
In the garden of a Samurai named Satsuma Shichizaëmon, who lived

Moths, flies, beetles, grubs, worms, and other unpleasant creatures seem thus to be indicated. But some kinds of gaki cannot be identified with insects — for example, the species called Jiki-hō-gaki, or doctrine-eaters. These can exist only by hearing the preaching of the Law of the Buddha in some temple. While they hear such preaching, their torment is assuaged; but at all other times they suffer agonies unspeakable. To this condition are liable after death all Buddhist priests or nuns

in the village of Echigawa in the province of Ōmi, there was a very old énoki. (The énoki, or "Celtis chinensis," is commonly thought to be a goblin-tree.) From ancient times the ancestors of the family had been careful never to cut a branch of this tree or to remove any of its leaves. But Shichizaëmon, who was very self-willed, one day announced that he intended to have the tree cut down. During the following night a monstrous being appeared to the mother of Shichizaëmon, in a dream, and told her that if the énoki were cut down, every member of the household should die. But when this warning was communicated to Shichizaëmon, he only laughed; and he then sent a man to cut down the tree. No sooner had it been cut down than Shichizaëmon became violently insane. For several days he remained furiously mad, crying out at intervals, "The tree! the tree! the tree!" He said that the tree put out its branches, like hands, to tear him. In this condition he died. Soon afterward his wife went mad, crying out that the tree was killing her; and she died screaming with fear. One after another, all the people in that house, not excepting the servants, went mad and died. The dwelling long remained unoccupied thereafter, no one daring even to enter the garden. At last it was remembered that before these things happened a daughter of the Satsuma family had become a Buddhist nun, and that she was still living, under the name of Jikun, in a temple at Yamashirō. This nun was sent for; and by request of the villagers she took up her residence in the house, where she continued to live until the time of her death — daily reciting a special service on behalf of the spirit that had dwelt in the tree. From the time that she began to live in the house the tree-spirit ceased to give trouble. This story is related on the authority of the priest Shungyō, who said that he had heard it from the lips of the nun herself.

Gaki

who proclaim the law for the mere purpose of making money.... Also there are gaki who appear sometimes in beautiful human shapes. Such are the Yoku-shiki-gaki, spirits of lewdness — corresponding in some sort to the incubi and succubi of our own Middle Ages. They can change their sex at will, and can make their bodies as large or as small as they please. It is impossible to exclude them from any dwelling, except by the use of holy charms and spells, since they are able to pass through an orifice even smaller than the eye of a needle. To seduce young men, they assume beautiful feminine shapes — often appearing at wine-parties as waitresses or dancing-girls. To seduce women they take the form of handsome lads. This state of Yoku-shiki-gaki is a consequence of lust in some previous human existence; but the supernatural powers belonging to their condition are results of meritorious Karma which the evil Karma could not wholly counterbalance.

Even concerning the Yoku-shiki-gaki, however, it is plainly stated that they may take the form of insects. Though wont to appear in human shape, they can assume the shape of any animal or other creature, and "fly freely in all directions of space" — or keep their bodies "so small that mankind cannot see them." ... All insects are not necessarily gaki; but most gaki can assume the form of insects when it serves their purpose.

III

GROTESQUE as these beliefs now seem to us, it was not unnatural that ancient Eastern fancy should associate insects with ghosts and devils. In our visible world there are no other creatures so wonderful and so mysterious; and the true history of certain insects actually realizes the dreams of mythology. To the minds of primitive men, the mere facts of insect-metamorphosis must have seemed uncanny; and what but goblinry or magic could account for the monstrous existence of beings so similar to dead leaves, or to flowers, or to joints of grass, that the keenest human sight could detect their presence only when they began to walk or to fly? Even for the entomologist of to-day, insects remain the most incomprehensible of creatures. We have learned from him that they must be acknowledged "the most successful of organized beings" in the battle for existence; — that the delicacy and the complexity of their structures surpass anything ever imagined of marvelous before the age of the microscope; — that their senses so far exceed our own in refinement as to prove us deaf and blind by comparison. Nevertheless, the insect world remains a world of hopeless enigmas. Who can explain for us the mystery of the eyes of a myriad facets, or the secret of the ocular brains connected with them? Do those astounding eyes perceive the ultimate structure of matter? does their vision pierce opacity, after the manner of the Röntgen rays? (Or how interpret the deadly aim of that ichneumon-fly which plunges its ovipositor through solid wood to reach the grub embedded in the grain?) What, again, of those marvelous ears in breasts and thighs and knees and feet — ears that hear sounds beyond the limit of human audition? and what of the musical structures evolved to produce such fairy melody? What of the ghostly feet that walk upon flowing water? What of the chemistry that kindles the firefly's lamp — making the cold and beautiful light that all our electric science cannot imitate? And those newly discovered, incomparably delicate organs for which we have yet no name, because our wisest cannot decide the nature of them — do they really, as some would suggest, keep the insect-mind informed of things unknown to human sense — visibilities of magnetism, odors of light, tastes of sound? . . . Even the little that we have been able to learn about insects fills us with the wonder that is akin to fear. The lips that are hands, and the horns that are eyes, and the tongues that are drills; the multiple devilish mouths that move in four ways at once; the living scissors and saws and boring-pumps and brace-bits; the exquisite elfish weapons which no human skill can copy, even in the finest watch-spring steel — what superstition of old ever dreamed of sights like these? Indeed, all that nightmare ever conceived of faceless horror, and all that ecstasy ever imagined of phantasmal pulchritude, can appear but vapid and void by comparison with the stupefying facts of entomology. But there is something spectral, something alarming, in the very beauty of insects....

IV

WHETHER gaki do or do not exist, there is at least some shadowing of truth in the Eastern belief that the dead become insects. Undoubtedly our human dust must help, over and over again for millions of ages, to build up numberless weird shapes of life. But as to that question of my revery under the pine-trees — whether present acts and thoughts can have anything to do with the future distribution and requickening of that dust — whether human conduct can of itself predetermine the shapes into which human atoms will be recast — no reply is possible. I doubt — but I do not know. Neither does anybody else.

Supposing, however, that the order of the universe were really as Buddhists believe, and that I knew myself foredoomed, by reason of stupidities in this existence, to live hereafter the life of an insect, I am not sure that the prospect would frighten me. There are insects of which it is difficult to think with equanimity; but the state of an independent, highly organized, respectable insect could not be so very bad. I should even look forward, with some pleasurable curiosity, to any chance of viewing the world through the marvelous compound eyes of a beetle, an ephemera, or a dragon-fly. As an ephemera, indeed, I might enjoy the possession of three different kinds of eyes, and the power to see colors now totally unimaginable. Estimated in degrees of human time, my life would be short — a single summer day would include the best part of it; but to ephemeral consciousness a few minutes would appear a season; and my one day of winged existence — barring possible mishaps — would be one unwearied joy of dancing in golden air. And I could feel in my winged state neither hunger nor thirst — having no real mouth or stomach: I should be, in very truth, a wind-eater. . . . Nor should I fear to enter upon the much less ethereal condition of a dragon-fly. I should then have to bear carnivorous hunger, and to hunt a great deal; but even dragon-flies, after the fierce joy of the chase, can indulge themselves in solitary meditation. Besides, what wings would then be mine! — and what eyes! . . . I could pleasurably anticipate even the certainty of becoming an amembō,[1] and so being able to run and to slide upon water — though children might catch me, and bite off my long fine legs. But I think that I should better enjoy the existence of a sémi — a large and lazy cicada, basking on wind-rocked trees, sipping only dew, and singing from

---

[1] A water-insect, much resembling what we call a "skater." In some parts of the country it is said that the boy who wants to become a good swimmer must eat the legs of an amembō.

dawn till dusk. Of course there would be perils to encounter — danger from hawks and crows and sparrows — danger from insects of prey — danger from bamboos tipped with birdlime by naughty little boys. But in every condition of life there must be risks; and in spite of the risks, I imagine that Anacreon uttered little more than the truth, in his praise of the cicada: "O thou earth-born — song-loving — free from pain — having flesh without blood — thou art nearly equal to the Gods!" . . . In fact I have not been able to convince myself that it is really an inestimable privilege to be reborn a human being. And if the thinking of this thought, and the act of writing it down, must inevitably affect my next rebirth, then let me hope that the state to which I am destined will not be worse than that of a cicada or of a dragon-fly; — climbing the cryptomerias to clash my tiny cymbals in the sun — or haunting, with soundless flicker of amethyst and gold, some holy silence of lotus-pools.

The Introduction of Buddhism

THE nature of the opposition which the ancient religion of Japan could offer to the introduction of any hostile alien creed, should now be obvious. The family being founded upon ancestor-worship, the commune being regulated by ancestor-worship, the clan-group or tribe being governed by ancestor-worship, and the Supreme Ruler being at once the high-priest and deity of an ancestral cult which united all the other cults in one common tradition, it must be evident that the promulgation of any religion essentially opposed to Shintō would have signified nothing less than an attack upon the whole system of society. Considering these circumstances, it may well seem strange that Buddhism should have succeeded, after some preliminary struggles (which included one bloody battle), in getting itself accepted as a second national faith. But although the original Buddhist doctrine was essentially in disaccord with Shintō beliefs, Buddhism had learned in India, in China, in Korea, and in divers adjacent countries, how to meet the spiritual needs of peoples maintaining a persistent ancestor-worship. Intolerance of ancestor-worship would have long ago resulted in the extinction of Buddhism; for its vast conquests have all been made among ancestor-worshiping races. Neither in India nor in China nor in Korea — neither in Siam nor Burmah nor Annam — did it attempt to extinguish ancestor-worship. Everywhere it made itself accepted as an ally, nowhere as an enemy, of social custom. In Japan it adopted the same policy which had secured its progress on the continent; and in order to form any clear conception of Japanese religious conditions, this fact must be kept in mind.

As the oldest extant Japanese texts — with the probable exception of some Shintō rituals — date from the eighth century, it is only possible to surmise the social conditions of that earlier epoch in which there was no form of religion but ancestor-worship. Only by imagining the absence of all Chinese and Korean influences can we form some vague idea of the state of things which existed during the so-called Age of the Gods — and it is difficult to decide at what period these influences began to operate. Confucianism appears to have preceded Buddhism by a considerable interval; and its progress, as an organizing power, was much more rapid. Buddhism was first introduced from Korea, about 552 A.D.; but the mission accomplished little. By the end of the eighth century the whole fabric of Japanese administration had been reorganized upon the Chinese plan, under Confucian influence; but it was not until well into the ninth century that Buddhism really began to spread throughout the country. Eventually it overshadowed the national

The Introduction of Buddhism

life, and colored all the national thought. Yet the extraordinary conservatism of the ancient ancestor cult — its inherent power of resisting fusion — was exemplified by the readiness with which the two religions fell apart on the disestablishment of Buddhism in 1871. After having been literally overlaid by Buddhism for nearly a thousand years, Shintō immediately reassumed its archaic simplicity, and reëstablished the unaltered forms of its earliest rites.

But the attempt of Buddhism to absorb Shintō seemed at one period to have almost succeeded. The method of the absorption is said to have been devised, about the year 800, by the famous founder of the Shingon sect, Kūkai, or "Kōbōdaishi" (as he is popularly called), who first declared the higher Shintō gods to be incarnations of various Buddhas. But in this matter, of course, Kōbōdaishi was merely following precedents of Buddhist policy. Under the name of Ryōbu-Shintō,[1] the new compound of Shintō and Buddhism obtained Imperial approval and support. Thereafter, in hundreds of places, the two religions were domiciled within the same precinct — sometimes even within the same building: they seemed to have been veritably amalgamated. And nevertheless there was no real fusion; — after ten centuries of such contact they separated again, as lightly as if they had never touched. It was only in the domestic form of the ancestor cult that

[1] The term "Ryobu" signifies "two departments" or "two religions."

The Buddhist Writings of Lafcadio Hearn

Buddhism really affected permanent modifications; yet even these were neither fundamental nor universal. In certain provinces they were not made; and almost everywhere a considerable part of the population preferred to follow the Shintō form of the ancestor cult. Yet another large class of persons, converts to Buddhism, continued to profess the older creed as well; and, while practicing their ancestor-worship according to the Buddhist rite, maintained separately also the domestic worship of the elder gods. In most Japanese houses to-day, the "god-shelf" and the Buddhist shrine can both be found; both cults being maintained under the same roof.[1] . . . But I am mentioning these facts only as illustrating the conservative vitality of Shintō, not as indicating any weakness in the Buddhist propaganda. Unquestionably the influence which Buddhism exerted upon Japanese civilization was immense, profound, multiform, incalculable; and the only wonder is that it should not have been able to stifle Shintō forever. To state, as various writers have carelessly stated, that Buddhism became the popular religion, while Shintō remained the official religion, is altogether misleading. As a matter of fact Buddhism became as much an official religion as Shintō itself, and influenced the lives of the high-

---

[1] The ancestor-worship and the funeral rites are Buddhist, as a general rule, if the family be Buddhist; but the Shintō gods are also worshiped in most Buddhist households, except those attached to the Shin sect. Many followers of even the Shin sect, however, appear to follow the ancient religion likewise; and they have their Ujigami.

The Introduction of Buddhism

est classes not less than the lives of the poor. It made monks of Emperors, and nuns of their daughters; it decided the conduct of rulers, the nature of decrees, and the administration of laws. In every community the Buddhist parish-priest was a public official as well as a spiritual teacher: he kept the parish register, and made report to the authorities upon local matters of importance.

By introducing the love of learning, Confucianism had partly prepared the way for Buddhism. As early even as the first century there were some Chinese scholars in Japan; but it was toward the close of the third century that the study of Chinese literature first really became fashionable among the ruling classes. Confucianism, however, did not represent a new religion: it was a system of ethical teachings founded upon an ancestor-worship much like that of Japan. What it had to offer was a kind of social philosophy — an explanation of the eternal reason of things. It reënforced and expanded the doctrine of filial piety; it regulated and elaborated preëxisting ceremonial; and it systematized all the ethics of government. In the education of the ruling classes it became a great power, and has so remained down to the present day. Its doctrines were humane, in the best meaning of the word; and striking evidence of its humanizing effect on government policy may be found in the laws and the maxims of that wisest of Japanese rulers — Iyéyasu.

But the religion of the Buddha brought to Japan another and a wider humanizing influence — a new gospel of tenderness — together with a multitude of new beliefs that were able to accommodate themselves to the old, in spite of fundamental dissimilarity. In the highest meaning of the term, it was a civilizing power. Besides teaching new respect for life, the duty of kindness to animals as well as to all human beings, the consequence of present acts upon the conditions of a future existence, the duty of resignation to pain as the inevitable result of forgotten error, it actually gave to Japan the arts and the industries of China. Architecture, painting, sculpture, engraving, printing, gardening — in short, every art and industry that helped to make life beautiful — developed first in Japan under Buddhist teaching.

There are many forms of Buddhism; and in modern Japan there are twelve principal Buddhist sects; but, for present purposes, it will be enough to speak, in the most general way, of popular Buddhism only, as distinguished from philosophical Buddhism, which I shall touch upon in a subsequent chapter. The higher Buddhism could not, at any time or in any country, have had a large popular following; and it is a mistake to suppose that its particular doctrines — such as the doctrine of Nirvana — were taught to the common people. Only such forms of doctrine were preached as could be

The Introduction of Buddhism

made intelligible and attractive to very simple minds. There is a Buddhist proverb: "First observe the person; then preach the Law" — that is to say, Adapt your instruction to the capacity of the listener. In Japan, as in China, Buddhism had to adapt its instruction to the mental capacity of large classes of people yet unaccustomed to abstract ideas. Even to this day the masses do not know so much as the meaning of the word "Nirvana" (Néhan): they have been taught only the simpler forms of the religion; and in dwelling upon these, it will be needless to consider differences of sect and dogma.

To appreciate the direct influence of Buddhist teaching upon the minds of the common people, we must remember that in Shintō there was no doctrine of metempsychosis. As I have said before, the spirits of the dead, according to ancient Japanese thinking, continued to exist in the world: they mingled somehow with the viewless forces of nature, and acted through them. Everything happened by the agency of these spirits — evil or good. Those who had been wicked in life remained wicked after death; those who had been good in life became good gods after death; but all were to be propitiated. No idea of future reward or punishment existed before the coming of Buddhism: there was no notion of any heaven or hell. The happiness of ghosts and gods alike was supposed to depend upon the worship and the offerings of the living.

With these ancient beliefs Buddhism attempted

to interfere only by expanding and expounding them — by interpreting them in a totally new light. Modifications were effected, but no suppressions: we might even say that Buddhism accepted the whole body of the old beliefs. It was true, the new teaching declared, that the dead continued to exist invisibly; and it was not wrong to suppose that they became divinities, since all of them were destined, sooner or later, to enter upon the way to Buddhahood — the divine condition. Buddhism acknowledged likewise the greater gods of Shintō, with all their attributes and dignities — declaring them incarnations of Buddhas or Bodhisattvas: thus the Goddess of the Sun was identified with Dai-Nichi-Nyōrai (the Tathâgata Mahâvairokana); the deity Hachiman was identified with Amida (Amitâbha). Nor did Buddhism deny the existence of goblins and evil gods: these were identified with the pretas and the Marakâyikas; and the Japanese popular term for goblin, "ma," to-day reminds us of this identification. As for wicked ghosts, they were to be thought of as pretas only — gaki — self-doomed by the errors of former lives to the Circle of Perpetual Hunger. The ancient sacrifices to the various gods of disease and pestilence — gods of fever, small-pox, dysentery, consumption, coughs, and colds — were continued with Buddhist approval; but converts were bidden to consider such maleficent beings as pretas, and to present them with only such food-offerings as are bestowed upon

The Introduction of Buddhism

pretas — not for propitiation, but for the purpose of relieving ghostly pain. In this case, as in the case of the ancestral spirits, Buddhism prescribed that the prayers to be repeated were to be said *for* the sake of the haunters, rather than *to* them. . . . The reader may be reminded of the fact that Roman Catholicism, by making a similar provision, still practically tolerates a continuance of the ancient European ancestor-worship. And we cannot consider that worship extinct in any of those Western countries where the peasants still feast their dead upon the Night of All Souls.

Buddhism, however, did more than tolerate the old rites. It cultivated and elaborated them. Under its teaching a new and beautiful form of the domestic cult came into existence; and all the touching poetry of ancestor-worship in modern Japan can be traced to the teaching of the Buddhist missionaries. Though ceasing to regard their dead as gods in the ancient sense, the Japanese converts were encouraged to believe in their presence, and to address them in terms of reverence and affection. It is worthy of remark that the doctrine of pretas gave new force to the ancient fear of neglecting the domestic rites. Ghosts unloved might not become "evil gods" in the Shintō meaning of the term; but the malevolent gaki was even more to be dreaded than the malevolent kami — for Buddhism defined in appalling ways the nature of the gaki's power to harm. In various Buddhist funeral rites, the dead are actually addressed as gaki — beings to be pitied, but also to be feared — much needing human sympathy and succor, but able to recompense the food-giver by ghostly help.

One particular attraction of Buddhist teaching was its simple and ingenious interpretation of nature. Countless matters which Shintō had never attempted to explain, and could not have explained, Buddhism expounded in detail, with much apparent consistency. Its explanations of the mysteries of birth, life, and death were at once consoling to pure minds, and wholesomely discomforting to bad consciences. It taught that the dead were happy or unhappy not directly because of the attention or the neglect shown them by the living, but because of their past conduct while in the body.[1] It did not attempt to teach the higher doctrine of successive rebirths — which the people could not possibly have understood — but the merely symbolic doctrine of transmigration, which everybody could understand. To die was not to melt back into nature, but to be reincarnated; and the character of

[1] The reader will doubtless wonder how Buddhism could reconcile its doctrine of successive rebirths with the ideas of ancestor-worship. If one died only to be born again, what could be the use of offering food or addressing any kind of prayer to the reincarnated spirit? This difficulty was met by the teaching that the dead were not immediately reborn in most cases, but entered into a particular condition called "Chū-U." They might remain in this disembodied condition for the time of one hundred years, after which they were reincarnated. The Buddhist services for the dead are consequently limited to the time of one hundred years.

The Introduction of Buddhism

the new body, as well as the conditions of the new existence, would depend upon the quality of one's deeds and thoughts in the present body. All states and conditions of being were the consequence of past actions. Such a man was now rich and powerful, because in previous lives he had been generous and kindly; such another man was now sickly and poor, because in some previous existence he had been sensual and selfish. This woman was happy in her husband and her children, because in the time of a former birth she had proved herself a loving daughter and a faithful spouse; this other was wretched and childless, because in some anterior existence she had been a jealous wife and a cruel mother. "To hate your enemy," the Buddhist preacher would proclaim, "is foolish as well as wrong: he is now your enemy only because of some treachery that you practiced upon him in a previous life, when he desired to be your friend. Resign yourself to the injury which he now does you: accept it as the expiation of your forgotten fault. . . . The girl whom you hoped to marry has been refused you by her parents — given away to another. But once, in another existence, she was yours by promise; and you broke the pledge then given. . . . Painful, indeed, the loss of your child; but this loss is the consequence of having, in some former life, refused affection where affection was due. . . . Maimed by mishap, you can no longer earn your living as before. Yet this mishap is really due to the fact that in some previous existence you wantonly inflicted bodily injury. Now the evil of your own act has returned upon you: repent of your crime, and pray that its Karma may be exhausted by this present suffering." . . . All the sorrows of men were thus explained and consoled. Life was expounded as representing but one stage of a measureless journey, whose way stretched back through all the night of the past, and forward through all the mystery of the future — out of eternities forgotten into the eternities to be; and the world itself was to be thought of only as a traveler's resting-place, an inn by the roadside.

Instead of preaching to the people about Nirvana, Buddhism discoursed to them of blisses to be won and pains to be avoided: the Paradise of Amida, Lord of Immeasurable Light; the eight hot hells called To-kwatsu, and the eight icy hells called Abuda. On the subject of future punishment the teaching was very horrible: I should advise no one of delicate nerves to read the Japanese, or rather the Chinese accounts of hell. But hell was the penalty for supreme wickedness only: it was not eternal; and the demons themselves would at last be saved. . . . Heaven was to be the reward of good deeds: the reward might indeed be delayed, through many successive rebirths, by reason of lingering Karma; but, on the other hand, it might be attained by virtue of a single holy act in this present life. Besides, prior to the period of supreme reward, each

The Introduction of Buddhism

succeeding rebirth could be made happier than the preceding one by persistent effort in the holy Way. Even as regarded conditions in this transitory world, the results of virtuous conduct were not to be despised. The beggar of to-day might to-morrow be reborn in the palace of a daimyō; the blind shampooer might become, in his very next life, an Imperial minister. Always the recompense would be proportionate to the sum of merit. In this lower world to practice the highest virtue was difficult; and the great rewards were hard to win. But for all good deeds a recompense was sure; and there was no one who could not acquire merit.

Even the Shintō doctrine of conscience — the god-given sense of right and wrong — was not denied by Buddhism. But this conscience was interpreted as the essential wisdom of the Buddha dormant in every human creature — wisdom darkened by ignorance, clogged by desire, fettered by Karma, but destined sooner or later to fully awaken and to flood the mind with light.

It would seem that the Buddhist teaching of the duty of kindness to all living creatures, and of pity for all suffering, had a powerful effect upon national habit and custom, long before the new religion found general acceptance. As early as the year 675, a decree was issued by the Emperor Temmu forbidding the people to eat "the flesh of kine, horses, dogs, monkeys, or barn-door fowls," and prohibiting the use of traps or the making of pitfalls in catching game.[1] The fact that all kinds of flesh-meat were not forbidden is probably explained by this Emperor's zeal for the maintenance of both creeds; — an absolute prohibition might have interfered with Shintō usages, and would certainly have been incompatible with Shintō traditions. But, although fish never ceased to be an article of food for the laity, we may say that from about this time the mass of the nation abandoned its habits of diet, and forswore the eating of meat, in accordance with Buddhist teaching. . . . This teaching was based upon the doctrine of the unity of all sentient existence. Buddhism explained the whole visible world by its doctrine of Karma — simplifying that doctrine so as to adapt it to popular comprehension. The forms of all creatures — bird, reptile, or mammal; insect or fish — represented only different results of Karma: the ghostly life in each was one and the same; and, in even the lowest, some spark of the divine existed. The frog or the serpent, the bird or the bat, the ox or the horse — all had had, at some past time, the privilege of human (perhaps even superhuman) shape: their present conditions represented only the consequence of ancient faults. Any human being also, by reason of like faults, might hereafter be reduced to the same dumb state — might be reborn as a reptile, a fish, a bird, or a beast of burden. The consequence of wanton

[1] See Aston's translation of the *Nihongi*, vol. II, p. 328.

The Introduction of Buddhism

cruelty to any animal might cause the perpetrator of that cruelty to be reborn as an animal of the same kind, destined to suffer the same cruel treatment. Who could even be sure that the goaded ox, the overdriven horse, or the slaughtered bird, had not formerly been a human being of closest kin — ancestor, parent, brother, sister, or child? . . .

Not by words only were all these things taught. It should be remembered that Shintō had no art: its ghost-houses, silent and void, were not even decorated. But Buddhism brought in its train all the arts of carving, painting, and decoration. The images of its Bodhisattvas, smiling in gold — the figures of its heavenly guardians and infernal judges, its feminine angels and monstrous demons — must have startled and amazed imaginations yet unaccustomed to any kind of art. Great paintings hung in the temples, and frescoes limned upon their walls or ceilings, explained better than words the doctrine of the Six States of Existence, and the dogma of future rewards and punishments. In rows of kakemono, suspended side by side, were displayed the incidents of a Soul's journey to the realm of judgment, and all the horrors of the various hells. One pictured the ghosts of faithless wives, for ages doomed to pluck, with bleeding fingers, the rasping bamboo-grass that grows by the Springs of Death; another showed the torment of the slanderer, whose tongue was torn by demon-pincers; in a third appeared the spectres of lustful men, vainly seeking to flee the embraces of women of fire, or climbing, in frenzied terror, the slopes of the Mountain of Swords. Pictured also were the circles of the preta-world, and the pangs of the Hungry Ghosts, and likewise the pains of rebirth in the form of reptiles and of beasts. And the art of these early representations — many of which have been preserved — was an art of no mean order. We can hardly conceive the effect upon inexperienced imagination of the crimson frown of Emma (Yama), Judge of the dead — or the vision of that weird Mirror which reflected to every spirit the misdeeds of its life in the body — or the monstrous fancy of that double-faced Head before the judgment seat, representing the visage of the woman Mirumé, whose eyes behold all secret sin; and the vision of the man Kaguhana, who smells all odors of evil-doing. . . . Parental affection must have been deeply touched by the painted legend of the world of children's ghosts — the little ghosts that must toil, under demon-surveillance, in the Dry Bed of the River of Souls. . . . But pictured terrors were offset by pictured consolations — by the beautiful figure of Kwannon, white Goddess of Mercy — by the compassionate smile of Jizō, the playmate of infant ghosts — by the charm also of celestial nymphs, floating on iridescent wings in light of azure. The Buddhist painter opened to simple fancy the palaces of heaven, and guided hope, through gardens of jewel-trees, even to the shores

The Introduction of Buddhism

of that lake where the souls of the blessed are reborn in lotus-blossoms, and tended by angel nurses.

Moreover, for people accustomed only to such simple architecture as that of the Shintō *miya*, the new temples erected by the Buddhist priests must have been astonishments. The colossal Chinese gates, guarded by giant statues; the lions and lanterns of bronze and stone; the enormous suspended bells, sounded by swinging beams; the swarming of dragon-shapes under the eaves of the vast roofs; the glimmering splendor of the altars; the ceremonial likewise, with its chanting and its incense-burning and its weird Chinese music — cannot have failed to inspire the wonder-loving with delight and awe. It is a noteworthy fact that the earliest Buddhist temples in Japan still remain, even to Western eyes, the most impressive. The Temple of the Four Deva Kings at Ōsaka — which, though more than once rebuilt, preserves the original plan — dates from 600 A.D.; the yet more remarkable temple called Hōryūji, near Nara, dates from about the year 607.

Of course the famous paintings and the great statues could be seen at the temples only; but the Buddhist image-makers soon began to people even the most desolate places with stone images of Buddhas and of Bodhisattvas. Then first were made those icons of Jizō, which still smile upon the traveler from every roadside — and the images of Kōshin, protector of highways, with his three symbolic Apes — and the figure of that Batō-Kwannon, who protects the horses of the peasant — with other figures in whose rude but impressive art suggestions of Indian origin are yet recognizable. Gradually the graveyards became thronged with dreaming Buddhas or Bodhisattvas — holy guardians of the dead, throned upon lotus-flowers of stone, and smiling with closed eyes the smile of the Calm Supreme. In the cities everywhere Buddhist sculptors opened shops, to furnish pious households with images of the chief divinities worshiped by the various Buddhist sects; and the makers of ihai, or Buddhist mortuary tablets, as well as the makers of household shrines, multiplied and prospered.

Meanwhile the people were left free to worship their ancestors according to either creed; and if a majority eventually gave preference to the Buddhist rite, this preference was due in large measure to the peculiar emotional charm which Buddhism had infused into the cult. Except in minor details, the two rites differed scarcely at all; and there was no conflict whatever between the old ideas of filial piety and the Buddhist ideas attaching to the new ancestor-worship. Buddhism taught that the dead might be helped and made happier by prayer, and that much ghostly comfort could be given them by food-offerings. They were not to be offered flesh or wine; but it was proper to gratify them with fruits

The Introduction of Buddhism

and rice and cakes and flowers and the smoke of incense. Besides, even the simplest food-offerings might be transmuted, by force of prayer, into celestial nectar and ambrosia. But what especially helped the new ancestor cult to popular favor, was the fact that it included many beautiful and touching customs not known to the old. Everywhere the people soon learned to kindle the hundred and eight fires of welcome for the annual visit of their dead — to supply the spirits with little figures made of straw, or made out of vegetables, to serve for oxen or horses [1] — also to prepare the ghost-ships (shōryōbuné), in which the souls of the ancestors were to return, over the sea, to their under-world. Then too were instituted the Bon-odori, or Dances of the Festival of the Dead,[2] and the custom of suspending white lanterns at graves, and colored lanterns at house-gates, to light the coming and the going of the visiting dead.

[1] An eggplant, with four pegs of wood stuck into it, to represent legs, usually stands for an ox; and a cucumber, with four pegs, serves for a horse. . . . One is reminded of the fact that, at some of the ancient Greek sacrifices, similar substitutes for real animals were used. In the worship of Apollo, at Thebes, apples with wooden pegs stuck into them, to represent feet and horns, were offered as substitutes for sheep.

[2] The dances themselves — very curious and very attractive to witness — are much older than Buddhism; but Buddhism made them a feature of the festival referred to, which lasts for three days. No person who has not witnessed a Bon-odori can form the least idea of what Japanese dancing means: it is something utterly different from what usually goes by the name — something indescribably archaic, weird, and nevertheless fascinating. I have repeatedly sat up all night to watch the peasants dancing. Japanese dancing-girls, be it observed, do not dance; they pose. The peasants dance.

But perhaps the greatest value of Buddhism to the nation was educational. The Shintō priests were not teachers. In early times they were mostly aristocrats, religious representatives of the clans; and the idea of educating the common people could not even have occurred to them. Buddhism, on the other hand, offered the boon of education to all — not merely a religious education, but an education in the arts and the learning of China. The Buddhist temples eventually became common schools, or had schools attached to them; and at each parish-temple the children of the community were taught, at a merely nominal cost, the doctrines of the faith, the wisdom of the Chinese classics, calligraphy, drawing, and much besides. By degrees the education of almost the whole nation came under Buddhist control; and the moral effect was of the best. For the military class indeed there was another and special system of education; but samurai scholars sought to perfect their knowledge under Buddhist teachers of renown; and the Imperial household itself employed Buddhist instructors. For the common people everywhere the Buddhist priest was the schoolmaster; and by virtue of his occupation as teacher, not less than by reason of his religious office, he ranked with the samurai. Much of what remains most attractive in Japanese character — the winning and graceful aspects of it — seems to have been developed under Buddhist training.

The Introduction of Buddhism

It was natural enough that to his functions of public instructor, the Buddhist priest should have added those of a public registrar. Until the period of disendowment, the Buddhist clergy remained, throughout the country, public as well as religious officials. They kept the parish records, and furnished at need certificates of birth, death, or family descent.

To give any just conception of the immense civilizing influence which Buddhism exerted in Japan would require many volumes. Even to summarize the results of that influence by stating only the most general facts, is scarcely possible — for no general statement can embody the whole truth of the work accomplished. As a moral force, Buddhism strengthened authority and cultivated submission, by its capacity to inspire larger hopes and fears than the more ancient religion could create. As teacher, it educated the race, from the highest to the humblest, both in ethics and in æsthetics. All that can be classed under the name of art in Japan was either introduced or developed by Buddhism; and the same may be said regarding nearly all Japanese literature possessing real literary quality — excepting some Shintō rituals, and some fragments of archaic poetry. Buddhism introduced drama, the higher forms of poetical composition, and fiction, and history, and philosophy. All the refinements of Japanese life were of Buddhist introduction, and at least a majority of its diversions and pleasures. There is even to-day scarcely one interesting or beautiful thing, produced in the country, for which the nation is not in some sort indebted to Buddhism. Perhaps the best and briefest way of stating the range of such indebtedness is simply to say that Buddhism brought the whole of Chinese civilization into Japan, and thereafter patiently modified and reshaped it to Japanese requirements. The elder civilization was not merely superimposed upon the social structure, but fitted carefully into it, combined with it so perfectly that the marks of the welding, the lines of the juncture, almost totally disappeared.

The Higher Buddhism

PHILOSOPHICAL Buddhism requires some brief consideration in this place — for two reasons. The first is that misapprehension or ignorance of the subject has rendered possible the charge of atheism against the intellectual classes of Japan. The second reason is that some persons imagine the Japanese common people — that is to say, the greater part of the nation — believers in the doctrine of Nirvana as extinction (though, as a matter of fact, even the meaning of the word is unknown to the masses), and quite resigned to vanish from the face of the earth, because of that incapacity for struggle which the doctrine is supposed to create. A little serious thinking ought to convince any intelligent man that no such creed could ever have been the religion of either a savage or a civilized people. But myriads of Western minds are ready at all times to accept statements of impossibility without taking the trouble to think about them; and if I can show some of my readers how far beyond popular comprehension the doctrines of the higher Buddhism really are, something will have been accomplished for the cause of truth and common sense. And besides the reasons already given for dwelling upon the subject, there is this third and special reason — that it is one of extraordinary interest to the student of modern philosophy.

Before going further, I must remind you that the metaphysics of Buddhism can be studied anywhere else quite as well as in Japan, since the more important sutras have been translated into various European languages, and most of the untranslated texts edited and published. The texts of Japanese Buddhism are Chinese; and only Chinese scholars are competent to throw light upon the minor special phases of the subject. Even to read the Chinese Buddhist canon of seven thousand volumes is commonly regarded as an impossible feat — though it has certainly been accomplished in Japan. Then there are the commentaries, the varied interpretations of different sects, the multiplications of later doctrine, to heap confusion upon confusion. The complexities of Japanese Buddhism are incalculable; and those who try to unravel them soon become, as a general rule, hopelessly lost in the maze of detail. All this has nothing to do with my present purpose. I shall have very little to say about Japanese Buddhism as distinguished from other Buddhism, and nothing at all to say about sect differences. I shall keep to general facts as regards the higher doctrine — selecting from among such facts only those most suitable for the illustration of that doctrine. And I shall not take up the subject of Nirvana, in spite of its great importance — having treated it as fully as

The Higher Buddhism

I was able in my "Gleanings in Buddha-Fields" — but confine myself to the topic of certain analogies between the conclusions of Buddhist metaphysics and the conclusions of contemporary Western thought.

In the best single volume yet produced in English on the subject of Buddhism,[1] the late Mr. Henry Clarke Warren observed: "A large part of the pleasure that I have experienced in the study of Buddhism has arisen from what I may call the strangeness of the intellectual landscape. All the ideas, the modes of argument, even the postulates assumed and not argued about, have always seemed so strange, so different from anything to which I have been accustomed, that I felt all the time as though walking in Fairyland. Much of the charm that the Oriental thoughts and ideas have for me appears to be because they so seldom fit into Western categories." . . . The serious attraction of Buddhist philosophy could not be better suggested: it is indeed "the strangeness of the intellectual landscape," as of a world inside-out and upside-down, that has chiefly interested Western thinkers heretofore. Yet after all, there *is* a class of Buddhist concepts which can be fitted, or very nearly fitted, into Western categories. The higher Buddhism is a kind of Monism; and it includes doctrines that accord, in

[1] *Buddhism in Translations*, by Henry Clarke Warren (Cambridge, Massachusetts, 1896). Published by Harvard University.

the most surprising manner, with the scientific theories of the German and the English monists. To my thinking, the most curious part of the subject, and its main interest, is represented just by these accordances — particularly in view of the fact that the Buddhist conclusions have been reached through mental processes unknown to Western thinking, and unaided by any knowledge of science. . . . I venture to call myself a student of Herbert Spencer; and it was because of my acquaintance with the Synthetic Philosophy that I came to find in Buddhist philosophy a more than romantic interest. For Buddhism is also a theory of evolution, though the great central idea of our scientific evolution (the law of progress from homogeneity to heterogeneity) is not correspondingly implied by Buddhist doctrine as regards the life of this world. The course of evolution as we conceive it, according to Professor Huxley, "must describe a trajectory like that of a ball fired from a mortar; and the sinking half of that course is as much a part of the general process of evolution as the rising." The highest point of the trajectory would represent what Mr. Spencer calls Equilibration — the supreme point of development preceding the period of decline; but, in Buddhist evolution, this supreme point vanishes into Nirvana. I can best illustrate the Buddhist position by asking you to imagine the trajectory line upside-down — a course descending out of the infinite, touching ground, and ascending again to

The Higher Buddhism

mystery.... Nevertheless, some Buddhist ideas do offer the most startling analogy with the evolutional ideas of our own time; and even those Buddhist concepts most remote from Western thought can be best interpreted by the help of illustrations and of language borrowed from modern science.

I think that we may consider the most remarkable teachings of the higher Buddhism — excluding the doctrine of Nirvana, for the reason already given — to be the following:

That there is but one Reality;
That the consciousness is not the real Self;
That Matter is an aggregate of phenomena created by the force of acts and thoughts;
That all objective and subjective existence is made by Karma — the present being the creation of the past, and the actions of the present and the past, in combination, determining the conditions of the future....

(Or, in other words, that the universe of Matter, and the universe of [conditioned] Mind, represent in their evolution a strictly moral order.)

It will be worth while now to briefly consider these doctrines in their relation to modern thought — beginning with the first, which is Monism.

All things having form or name — Buddhas, gods, men, and all living creatures — suns, worlds, moons, the whole visible cosmos — are transitory phenomena.... Assuming, with Herbert Spencer, that the test of reality is permanence, one can scarcely question this position; it differs little from the statement with which the closing chapter of the "First Principles" concludes:

> Though the relation of subject and object renders necessary to us these antithetical conceptions of Spirit and Matter, the one is no less than the other to be regarded as but a sign of the Unknown Reality which underlies both.[1]

For Buddhism the sole reality is the Absolute — Buddha as unconditioned and Infinite Being. There is no other veritable existence, whether of Matter or of Mind; there is no real individuality or personality; the "I" and the "Not-I" are essentially nowise different. We are reminded of Mr. Spencer's position, that "it is one and the same Reality which is manifested to us both subjectively and objectively." Mr. Spencer goes on to say:

> Subject and Object, as actually existing, can never be contained in *the consciousness produced by the coöperation of the two*, though they are necessarily implied by it; and the antithesis of Subject and Object, never to be transcended while consciousness lasts, renders impossible all knowledge of that Ultimate Reality in which Subject and Object are united. . . .

I do not think that a master of the higher Buddhism would dispute Mr. Spencer's doctrine of Transfigured Realism. Buddhism does not deny the actuality of phenomena as phenomena, but

[1] Edition of 1894.

denies their permanence, and the truth of the appearances which they present to our imperfect senses. Being transitory, and not what they seem, they are to be considered in the nature of illusions — impermanent manifestations of the only permanent Reality. But the Buddhist position is not agnosticism: it is astonishingly different, as we shall presently see. Mr. Spencer states that we cannot know the Reality so long as consciousness lasts — because while consciousness lasts we cannot transcend the antithesis of Object and Subject, and it is this very antithesis which makes consciousness possible. "Very true," the Buddhist metaphysician would reply; "we cannot know the sole Reality while consciousness lasts. *But destroy consciousness, and the Reality becomes cognizable.* Annihilate the illusion of Mind, and the light will come." This destruction of consciousness signifies Nirvana — the extinction of all that we call Self. Self is blindness: destroy it, and the Reality will be revealed as infinite vision and infinite peace.

We have now to ask what, according to Buddhist philosophy, is the meaning of the visible universe as phenomenon, and the nature of the consciousness that perceives. However transitory, the phenomenon makes an impression upon consciousness; and consciousness itself, though transitory, has existence; and its perceptions, however delusive, are perceptions of actual relation. Buddhism answers that both the universe and the consciousness are merely aggregates of Karma — complexities incalculable of conditions shaped by acts and thoughts through some enormous past. All substance and all conditioned mind (as distinguished from unconditioned mind) are products of acts and thoughts: by acts and thoughts the atoms of bodies have been integrated; and the affinities of those atoms — the polarities of them, as a scientist might say — represent tendencies shaped in countless vanished lives. I may quote here from a modern Japanese treatise on the subject:

> The aggregate actions of all sentient beings give birth to the varieties of mountains, rivers, countries, etc. They are caused by aggregate actions, and so are called aggregate fruits. Our present life is the reflection of past actions. Men consider these reflections as their real selves. Their eyes, noses, ears, tongues, and bodies — as well as their gardens, woods, farms, residences, servants, and maids — men imagine to be their own possessions; but, in fact, they are only results endlessly produced by innumerable actions. In tracing everything back to the ultimate limits of the past, we cannot find a beginning: hence it is said that death and birth have no beginning. Again, when seeking the ultimate limit of the future, we cannot find the end.[1]

This teaching that all things are formed by Karma — whatever is good in the universe representing the results of meritorious acts or thoughts; and whatever is evil, the results of evil acts or thoughts — has the approval of five of the great

[1] *Outlines of the Mahâyâna Philosophy*, by S. Kuroda.

sects; and we may accept it as a leading doctrine of Japanese Buddhism. . . . The cosmos is, then, an aggregate of Karma; and the mind of man is an aggregate of Karma; and the beginnings thereof are unknown, and the end cannot be imagined. There is a spiritual evolution, of which the goal is Nirvana; but we have no declaration as to a final state of universal rest, when the shaping of substance and of mind will have ceased forever. . . . Now the Synthetic Philosophy assumes a very similar position as regards the evolution of phenomena: there is no beginning to evolution, nor any conceivable end. I quote from Mr. Spencer's reply to a critic in the "North American Review":

> That "absolute commencement of organic life upon the globe," which the reviewer says I "cannot evade the admission of," I distinctly deny. The affirmation of universal evolution is in itself the negation of an absolute commencement of anything. Construed in terms of evolution, every kind of being is conceived as a product of modification wrought by insensible gradations upon a preëxisting kind of being; and this holds as fully of the supposed "commencement of organic life" as of all subsequent developments of organic life. . . . That organic matter was not produced all at once, but was reached through steps, we are well warranted in believing by the experiences of chemists.[1] . . .

Of course it should be understood that the Buddhist silence, as to a beginning and an end, concerns only the production of phenomena, not any particu-

---
[1] *Principles of Biology*, vol. I, p. 482.

lai existence of groups of phenomena. That of which no beginning or end can be predicated is simply the Eternal Becoming. And, like the older Indian philosophy from which it sprang, Buddhism teaches the alternate apparition and disparition of universes. At certain prodigious periods of time, the whole cosmos of "one hundred thousand times ten millions of worlds" vanishes away — consumed by fire or otherwise destroyed — but only to be reformed again. These periods are called "World-Cycles," and each World-Cycle is divided into four "Immensities" — but we need not here consider the details of the doctrine. It is only the fundamental idea of an evolutional rhythm that is really interesting. I need scarcely remind the reader that the alternate disintegration and reintegration of the cosmos is also a scientific conception, and a commonly accepted article of evolutional belief. I may quote, however, for other reasons, the paragraph expressing Herbert Spencer's views upon the subject:

Apparently the universally coexistent forces of attraction and repulsion, which, as we have seen, necessitate rhythm in all minor changes throughout the Universe, also necessitate rhythm in the totality of changes — produce now an immeasurable period during which the attractive forces, predominating, cause universal concentration; and then an immeasurable period during which the repulsive forces, predominating, cause diffusion — alternate eras of Evolution and Dissolution. And thus there is suggested to us the conception of a past during which there have been successive Evolutions analogous to that which is now going on; and a future during which successive other such Evolutions may go on — ever the same in principle, but never the same in concrete result.[1]

Farther on, Mr. Spencer has pointed out the vast logical consequence involved by this hypothesis:

If, as we saw reason to think, there is an alternation of Evolution and Dissolution in the totality of things — if, as we are obliged to infer from the Persistence of Force, the arrival at either limit of this vast rhythm brings about the conditions under which a counter-movement commences — if we are hence compelled to entertain the conception of Evolutions that have filled an immeasurable past, and Evolutions that will fill an immeasurable future — we can no longer contemplate the visible creation as having a definite beginning or end, or as being isolated. It becomes unified with all existence before and after; and the Force which the Universe presents falls into the same category with its Space and Time as admitting of no limitation in thought.[2]

The foregoing Buddhist positions sufficiently imply that the human consciousness is but a temporary aggregate — not an eternal entity. There is no permanent self: there is but one eternal principle in all life — the supreme Buddha. Modern Japanese call this Absolute the "Essence of Mind."

[1] *First Principles*, § 183. This paragraph, from the fourth edition, has been considerably qualified in the definitive edition of 1900.
[2] *First Principles*, § 190. Condensed and somewhat modified in the definitive edition of 1900; but, for present purposes of illustration, the text of the fourth edition has been preferred.

"The fire fed by fagots," writes one of these, "dies when the fagots have been consumed; but the essence of fire is never destroyed. . . . All things in the Universe are Mind." So stated, the position is unscientific; but as for the conclusion reached, we may remember that Mr. Wallace has stated almost exactly the same thing, and that there are not a few modern preachers of the doctrine of a "universe of mind-stuff." The hypothesis is "unthinkable." But the most serious thinker will agree with the Buddhist assertion that the relation of all phenomena to the unknowable is merely that of waves to sea. "Every feeling and thought being but transitory," says Mr. Spencer, "an entire life made up of such feelings and thoughts being but transitory — nay, the objects amid which life is passed, though less transitory, being severally in course of losing their individualities quickly or slowly — we learn that the one thing permanent is the Unknown Reality hidden under all these changing shapes." Here the English and the Buddhist philosophers are in accord; but thereafter they suddenly part company. For Buddhism is not agnosticism, but gnosticism, and professes to know the unknowable. The thinker of Mr. Spencer's school cannot make assumptions as to the nature of the sole Reality, nor as to the reason of its manifestations. He must confess himself intellectually incapable of comprehending the nature of force, matter, or motion. He feels justified in accepting the hypothesis that all known elements have been evolved from one primordial undifferentiated substance — the chemical evidence for this hypothesis being very strong. But he certainly would not call that primordial substance a substance of mind, nor attempt to explain the character of the forces that effected its integration. Again, though Mr. Spencer would probably acknowledge that we know of matter only as an aggregate of forces, and of atoms only as force-centres, or knots of force, he would not declare that an atom *is* a force-centre, and nothing else.... But we find evolutionists of the German school taking a position very similar to the Buddhist position — which implies a universal sentiency, or, more strictly speaking, a universal potential-sentiency. Haeckel and other German monists assume such a condition for all substance. They are not agnostics, therefore, but gnostics; and their gnosticism very much resembles that of the higher Buddhism.

According to Buddhism there is no reality save Buddha: all things else are but Karma. There is but one Life, one Self: human individuality and personality are but phenomenal conditions of that Self. Matter is Karma; Mind is Karma — that is to say, mind as we know it: Karma, as visibility, represents to us mass and quality; Karma, as mentality, signifies character and tendency. The primordial substance — corresponding to the "protyle" of our monists — is composed of Five Elements, which are mystically identified with Five Buddhas, all of whom are really but different modes of the One. With this idea of a primordial substance there is necessarily associated the idea of a universal sentiency. Matter is alive.

Now to the German monists also matter is alive. On the phenomena of cell-physiology, Haeckel claims to base his conviction that "even the atom is not without rudimentary form of sensation and will — or, as it is better expressed, of feeling (æsthesis), and of inclination (tropesis) — that is to say, a universal soul of the simplest kind." I may quote also from Haeckel's "Riddle of the Universe" the following paragraph expressing the monistic notion of substance as held by Vogt and others:

> The two fundamental forms of substance, ponderable matter and ether, are not dead and only moved by extrinsic force; but they are endowed with sensation and will (though, naturally, of the lowest grade); they experience an inclination for condensation, a dislike of strain; they strive after the one, and struggle against the other.

Less like a revival of the dreams of the alchemists is the very probable hypothesis of Schneider, that sentiency begins with the formation of certain combinations — that feeling is evolved from the non-feeling just as organic being has been evolved from inorganic substance. But all these monist ideas enter into surprising combination with the Buddhist teaching about matter as integrated Karma; and for that reason they are well worth citing in this relation. To Buddhist conception all matter is sentient

The Higher Buddhism

— the sentiency varying according to condition: "even rocks and stones," a Japanese Buddhist text declares, "can worship Buddha." In the German monism of Professor Haeckel's school, the particular qualities and affinities of the atom represent feeling and inclination, "a soul of the simplest kind"; in Buddhism these qualities are made by Karma — that is to say, they represent tendencies formed in previous states of existence. The hypotheses appear to be very similar. But there is one immense, all-important difference, between the Occidental and the Oriental monism. The former would attribute the qualities of the atom merely to a sort of heredity — to the persistency of tendencies developed under chance influences operating throughout an incalculable past. The latter declares the history of the atom to be purely moral! All matter, according to Buddhism, represents aggregated sentiency, making, by its inherent tendencies, toward conditions of pain or pleasure, evil or good. "Pure actions," writes the author of "Outlines of the Mahâyâna Philosophy," "bring forth the Pure Lands of all the quarters of the universe; while impure deeds produce the Impure Lands." That is to say, the matter integrated by the force of moral acts goes to the making of blissful worlds; and the matter formed by the force of immoral acts goes to the making of miserable worlds. All substance, like all mind, has its Karma; planets, like men, are shaped by the creative power of acts and thoughts; and every atom goes to its appointed place, sooner or later, according to the moral or immoral quality of the tendencies that inform it. Your good or bad thought or deed will not only affect your next rebirth, but will likewise affect in some sort the nature of worlds yet unevolved, wherein, after innumerable cycles, you may have to live again. Of course, this tremendous idea has no counterpart in modern evolutional philosophy. Mr. Spencer's position is well known; but I must quote him for the purpose of emphasizing the contrast between Buddhist and scientific thought:

> ... We have no ethics of nebular condensation, or of sidereal movement, or of planetary evolution; the conception is not relevant to inorganic matter. Nor, when we turn to organized things, do we find that it has any relation to the phenomena of plant-life; though we ascribe to plants superiorities and inferiorities, leading to successes and failures in the struggle for existence, we do not associate with them praise or blame. It is only with the rise of sentiency in the animal world that the subject-matter of ethics originates.[1]

On the contrary, it will be seen, Buddhism actually teaches what we may call, to borrow Mr. Spencer's phrase, "the ethics of nebular condensation" — though to Buddhist astronomy, the scientific meaning of the term "nebular condensation" was never known. Of course the hypothesis is beyond the power of human intelligence to prove or

[1] *Principles of Ethics*, vol. II, § 326.

to disprove. But it is interesting, for it proclaims a purely moral order of the cosmos, and attaches almost infinite consequence to the least of human acts. Had the old Buddhist metaphysicians been acquainted with the facts of modern chemistry, they might have applied their doctrine, with appalling success, to the interpretation of those facts. They might have explained the dance of atoms, the affinities of molecules, the vibrations of ether, in the most fascinating and terrifying way by their theory of Karma.... Here is a universe of suggestion — most weird suggestion — for anybody able and willing to dare the experiment of making a new religion, or at least a new and tremendous system of Alchemy, based upon the notion of a moral order in the inorganic world!

But the metaphysics of Karma in the higher Buddhism include much that is harder to understand than any alchemical hypothesis of atom-combinations. As taught by popular Buddhism, the doctrine of rebirth is simple enough — signifying no more than transmigration: you have lived millions of times in the past, and you are likely to live again millions of times in the future — all the conditions of each rebirth depending upon past conduct. The common notion is that after a certain period of bodiless sojourn in this world, the spirit is guided somehow to the place of its next incarnation. The people, of course, believe in souls. But there is nothing of all this in the higher doctrine, which denies transmigration, denies the existence of the soul, denies personality. There is no Self to be reborn; there is no transmigration — and yet there is rebirth! There is no real "I" that suffers or is glad — and yet there is new suffering to be borne or new happiness to be gained! What we call the Self — the personal consciousness — dissolves at the death of the body; but the Karma, formed during life, then brings about the integration of a new body and a new consciousness. You suffer in this existence because of acts done in a previous existence — yet the author of those acts was not identical with your present self! Are you, then, responsible for the faults of another person?

The Buddhist metaphysician would answer thus: "The form of your question is wrong, because it assumes the existence of personality — and there is no personality. There is really no such individual as the 'you' of the inquiry. The suffering is indeed the result of errors committed in some anterior existence or existences; but there is no responsibility for the acts of another person, since there is no personality. The 'I' that was and the 'I' that is represent in the chain of transitory being aggregations momentarily created by acts and thoughts; and the pain belongs to the aggregates as condition resulting from quality."

All this sounds extremely obscure: to understand the real theory we must put away the notion of personality, which is a very difficult thing to do. Successive births do not mean transmigration in the common sense of that word, but only the self-propagation of Karma: the perpetual multiplying of certain conditions by a kind of ghostly gemmation — if I may borrow a biological term. The Buddhist illustration, however, is that of flame communicated from one lamp-wick to another: a hundred lamps may thus be lighted from one flame, and the hundred flames will all be different, though the origin of all was the same. Within the hollow flame of each transitory life is enclosed a part of the only Reality; but this is not a soul that transmigrates. Nothing passes from birth to birth but Karma — character or condition.

One will naturally ask how can such a doctrine exert any moral influence whatever? If the future being shaped by my Karma is to be in nowise identical with my present self — if the future consciousness evolved by *my* Karma is to be essentially another consciousness — how can I force myself to feel anxious about the sufferings of that unborn person? "Again your question is wrong," a Buddhist would answer: "to understand the doctrine you must get rid of the notion of individuality, and think, not of persons, but of successive states of feeling and consciousness, each of which buds out of the other — a chain of existences interdependently united." . . . I may attempt another illustration. Every individual, as we understand the term, is continually changing. All the structures of the body are constantly undergoing waste and repair; and the body that you have at this hour is not, as to substance, the same body that you had ten years ago. Physically you are not the same person: yet you suffer the same pains, and feel the same pleasures, and find your powers limited by the same conditions. Whatever disintegrations and reconstructions of tissue have taken place within you, you have the same physical and mental peculiarities that you had ten years ago. Doubtless the cells of your brain have been decomposed and recomposed: yet you experience the same emotions, recall the same memories, and think the same thoughts. Everywhere the fresh substance has assumed the qualities and tendencies of the substance replaced. This persistence of condition is like Karma. The transmission of tendency remains, though the aggregate is changed. . . .

These few glimpses into the fantastic world of Buddhist metaphysics will suffice, I trust, to convince any intelligent reader that the higher Buddhism (to which belongs the much-discussed and little-comprehended doctrine of Nirvana) could never have been the religion of millions almost incapable of forming abstract ideas — the religion of a population even yet in a comparatively early stage of religious evolution. It was never understood by the people at all, nor is it ever taught to them to-day.

The Higher Buddhism

It is a religion of metaphysicians, a religion of scholars, a religion so difficult to be understood, even by persons of some philosophical training, that it might well be mistaken for a system of universal negation. Yet the reader should now be able to perceive that, because a man disbelieves in a personal God, in an immortal soul, and in any continuation of personality after death, it does not follow that we are justified in declaring him an irreligious person — especially if he happen to be an Oriental. The Japanese scholar who believes in the moral order of the universe, the ethical responsibility of the present to all the future, the immeasurable consequence of every thought and deed, the ultimate disparition of evil, and the power of attainment to conditions of infinite memory and infinite vision — cannot be termed either an atheist or a materialist, except by bigotry and ignorance. Profound as may be the difference between his religion and our own, in respect of symbols and modes of thought, the moral conclusions reached in either case are very much the same.

Selected Bibliography

Hearn, Lafcadio, *An American Miscellany*, Albert Mordell, ed., New York: 1925

Appreciations of Poetry, John Erskine, ed., New York: 1930

Barbarous Barbers, and Other Stories, Ichiro Nishisaki, ed., Tokyo: 1939

Books and Habits, from the lectures of Lafcadio Hearn, John Erskine, ed., New York: 1921

Buying Christmas Toys, and Other Essays, Ichiro Nishisaki, ed., Tokyo: 1939

Catalogue of the Lafcadio Hearn Library in the Toyama High School, Toyama: 1927

Children of the Loves, O. W. Frost, ed., Lexington, Ky.: 1957

Chita: A Memory of Last Island, New York: 1889

trans. *The Crime of Sylvestre Bonnard*, by Anatole France, London: 1921

trans. *The Crime of Sylvestre Bonnard*, by Anatole France, New York: 1890

Creole Sketches, w/illus. by the author, Charles Woodward Hutson, ed., New York: 1924

Editorials, by Lafcadio Hearn, Charles Woodward Hutson, ed., Boston and New York: 1926

Essays in European and Oriental Literature, Albert Mordell, ed., New York: 1923

Essays on American Literature, Sanki Ishikawa, ed., Tokyo: 1929

Exotics and Retrospectives, Boston: 1908

Bibliography

Fantastics, and Other Fancies, Charles Woodward Hutson, ed., Boston and New York: 1914

The Fountain of Gold, w/illus., San Francisco: 1927

Gibbeted: execution of a youthful murderer—shocking tragedy at Dayton —a broken rope and a double hanging—sickening scenes behind the scaffold-screen, Los Angeles: 1938

The Goblin Spider, w/illus., Tokyo: 1905

Gleanings in Buddha-Fields, Boston and New York: 1897

Glimpses of Unfamiliar Japan, Boston and New York: 1894

Historical Sketch Book and Guide to New Orleans and Environs, New York: 1883

A History of English Literature, Tokyo: 1927

A History of English Literature, R. Tanabe and T. Ochiai, eds., Tokyo: 1938

In Ghostly Japan, Boston: 1899

Interpretations of Literature, John Erskine, ed., New York: 1929

Japan; An Attempt at Interpretation, New York: 1904

Japan; An Attempt at Interpretation, Rutland, Vt.: 1955

Japanese Fairy Tales, New York: 1919

Japanese Fairy Tales, New York: 1948

Japanese Fairy Tales, w/color illus. by "Kay," New York: 1953

The Japanese Letters of Lafcadio Hearn, Elizabeth Bisland, ed., Boston and New York: 1910

Japanese Lyrics, Boston and New York: 1915

A Japanese Miscellany, Boston: 1901

Kimiko, and Other Chinese Sketches, Boston: 1923

Kokoro, Frankfort: 1920

Kokoro; Hints and Echoes of Japanese Inner Life, Boston: 1896

Bibliography

Kottō . . . being Japanese curios, with sundry cobwebs, w/illus. by Genjiro Yoto, New York: 1903

Kwaidan: Stories and Studies of Strange Things, Boston and New York: 1906

Lafcadio Hearn's Lectures on Tennyson, Shigetsugu Kishi, ed., Tokyo: 1941

Lands and Seas, T. Ochiai, ed., Tokyo: 1925

Leaves from the Diary of an Impressionist, Boston and New York: 1911

Lectures on Shakespeare, Iwao Inagaki, ed., Tokyo: 1928

Letters From the Raven (correspondence with Henry Watkin), Milton Bronner, ed., Boston: 1908

Letters From Tokyo, M. Otani, ed., Tokyo: 1920

Life and Literature, John Erskine, ed., New York: 1917

Literary Essays, Ichiro Nishisaki, ed., Tokyo: 1939

The New Radiance and Other Scientific Sketches, Ichiro Nishisaki, ed., Tokyo: 1939

Occidental Gleanings, w/sketches, Albert Mordell, ed., New York: 1925

Of a Mirror and a Bell

The Old Woman Who Lost Her Dumpling, w/illus., Tokyo: 19___

trans. *One of Cleopatra's Nights, and Other Fantastic Romances*, by Theophile Gautier, New York: 1915

Oriental Articles, Ichiro Nishisaki, ed., Tokyo: 1939

"*Out of the East*"; *Reveries and Studies in New Japan*, Boston and New York: 1923

The Popular Ballads, Yokohama: 1894

Pre-Raphaelite and Other Poets, John Erskine, ed., New York: 1930

The Romance of the Milky Way, O. Yamashita, ed., Tokyo: 1955

Selected Writings, Malcolm Cowley, ed., New York: 1949

Bibliography

Shadowings, Boston: 1907

trans. *The Six Greatest Novels of Anatole France*, Garden City: 1936

Sketches and Tales from the French, Albert Mordell, ed., Tokyo: 1935

Some Chinese Ghosts, Boston: 1922

Some Chinese Ghosts, New York: 1927

Some New Letters and Writings of Lafcadio Hearn, Karuko Ichikawa, Tokyo: 1925

Some Strange Literary Figures of the Eighteenth and Nineteenth Centuries, R. Ranabé, ed., Tokyo: 1927

Spirit Photography: How Intelligent People May Be Humbugged, Los Angeles: 1933

trans. *Stories from Emile Zola*, Albert Mordell, ed., Tokyo: 1935

Stray Leaves From Strange Literature, Boston: 1912

Talks To Writers, John Erskine, ed., New York: 1927

trans. *The Temptation of St. Anthony*, by Gustave Flaubert, New York: 1910

Two Years in the French West Indies, New York: 1890

The Writings of Lafcadio Hearn, New York: 1925

Youma; The Story of a West Indian Slave, New York: 1890

Bisland, Elizabeth, *The Life and Letters of Lafcadio Hearn*, Boston and New York: 1906

Boyston, Percy Holmes, *More Contemporary Americans*, Chicago: 1927

Chamberlain, Basil Hall, *Letters from Basil Chamberlain to Lafcadio Hearn*, Kazuo Koisumi, ed., Tokyo: 1935

More Letters from Basil Hall Chamberlain to Lafcadio Hearn, (and others) Kazuo Koisumi, ed., Tokyo: 1937

Frost, Orcutt William, *Young Bears*, Tokyo: 1958

Gould, George Millbry, *Concerning Lafcadio Hearn*, Philadelphia: 1908

Bibliography

Hearn, Setsu (Koizumi), *Reminiscences of Lafcadio Hearn*, Boston and New York: 1918

Kennard, Nina H., *Lafcadio Hearn*, New York: 1912

Koizumi, Kazuo, *Father and I*, Boston and New York: 1935

    Re-Echo, Nancy Jane Fellers, ed., w/illustrations and photographs, Caldwell, Idaho: 1957

Lewis, Oscar, *Hearn and His Biographers*, San Francisco: 1930

McWilliams, Vern Sesley, *Lafcadio Hearn*, Boston:

Noguchi, Yone, *Lafcadio Hearn in Japan* (w/an interview with Koizumi Setsuko), Yokohama: 1910

    Lafcadio Hearn in Japan, w/sketches, London: 1910

Penguin Book Shop, Beverly Hills, Ca. A catalogue of first editions of Lafcadio Hearn, Beverly Hills: 1933

Robert, Marcel, *Lafcadio Hearn*, Tokyo: 1950

Stevenson, Elizabeth, *Lafcadio Hearn*, New York: 1961

Targ, William, *Lafcadio Hearn: First Editions and Values*, Chicago: 1935

Temple, Jean, *Blue Ghost*, New York: 1931

Thomas, Edward, *Lafcadio Hearn*, Boston and New York: 1912

Tinker, Edward Larocque, *Lafcadio Hearn's American Days*, w/illustrations, New York: 1925